Excel 2010 Made Simple

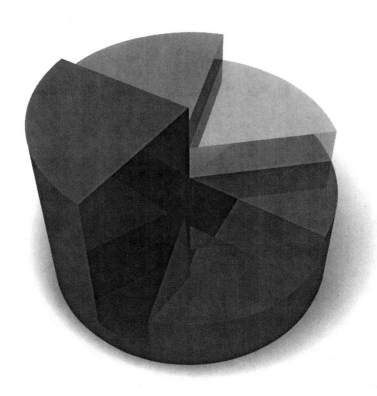

Abbott Katz

W9-AWO-799

Apress®

Excel 2010 Made Simple

ISBN-13 (pbk): 978-1-4302-3545-3

ISBN-13 (electronic): 978-1-4302-3546-0

Trademarked names, logos, and images may appear in this book. Rather than use a trademark symbol with every occurrence of a trademarked name, logo, or image we use the names, logos, and images only in an editorial fashion and to the benefit of the trademark owner, with no intention of infringement of the trademark.

The use in this publication of trade names, trademarks, service marks, and similar terms, even if they are not identified as such, is not to be taken as an expression of opinion as to whether or not they are subject to proprietary rights.

President and Publisher: Paul Manning
Lead Editor: Steve Anglin
Development Editor: Matthew Moodie
Technical Reviewer: Greg Kettell
Editorial Board: Steve Anglin, Mark Beckner, Ewan Buckingham, Gary Cornell, Jonathan Gennick, Jonathan Hassell, Michelle Lowman, James Markham, Matthew Moodie, Jeff Olson, Jeffrey Pepper, Frank Pohlmann, Douglas Pundick, Ben Renow-Clarke, Dominic Shakeshaft, Matt Wade, Tom Welsh
Coordinating Editor: Kelly Moritz
Copy Editor: Damon Larson
Compositor: MacPS, LLC
Indexer: John Collin
Artist: April Milne
Cover Designer: Anna Ishchenko

Distributed to the book trade worldwide by Springer Science+Business Media, LLC, 233 Spring Street, 6th Floor, New York, NY 10013. Phone 1-800-SPRINGER, fax (201) 348-4505, e-mail orders-ny@springer-sbm.com, or visit www.springeronline.com.

For information on translations, please e-mail rights@apress.com, or visit www.apress.com.

Apress and friends of ED books may be purchased in bulk for academic, corporate, or promotional use. eBook versions and licenses are also available for most titles. For more information, reference our Special Bulk Sales–eBook Licensing web page at www.apress.com/bulk-sales.

The information in this book is distributed on an "as is" basis, without warranty. Although every precaution has been taken in the preparation of this work, neither the author(s) nor Apress shall have any liability to any person or entity with respect to any loss or damage caused or alleged to be caused directly or indirectly by the information contained in this work.

Contents at a Glance

Contents

About the Author

 **Abbott Katz** A New Yorker living in London, Abbott Katz has introduced Excel to thousands of students in both university and corporate settings. The author of *Beginning Microsoft Excel 2010* (Apress), he has a doctorate in sociology and has contributed to numerous publications on a range of topics.

About the Technical Reviewer

 **Greg Kettell** is a professional software engineer with a diverse career that has covered everything from game programming to enterprise business applications. He has written and contributed to several books about software applications, operating systems, web design, and programming. Greg, his wife Jennifer, and their two children currently reside in upstate New York.

Acknowledgments

The Made Simple series sports two sets of authors: the ones whose names make it to the books' covers, and the ones whose labors earn their appreciations in sections such as these.

Thus, many thanks go to an international coterie of helpers, including development editor Matthew Moodie for his spot-on tweaks and knowing recommendations, coordinating editor Kelly Moritz for her redoubtable coordination of the publication process, technical editor Greg Kettell for his sage commentaries, and what is doubtless a set of literally silent partners—the able players on Apress's production team. And thanks to Dominic Shakeshaft for encouraging this project's inception. A Made Simple book isn't so simple.

An here's an additional and special thanks to my wife, Marsha, for affording me the space to ply the time that might have been otherwise spent on less literary chores. Constructing spreadsheets is one of the few things I do better than her.

Quick Start Guide

Believe it or not, you're looking at a book about one of the most widely owned—but underused—programs on the planet: Microsoft Excel, the 2010 edition. Underused? Yep, because even though millions of people around the globe apply Excel to a vast range of daily tasks, most users still don't appreciate the even wider range of things Excel can do—once they nail down its basics and begin to glimpse the huge potential that lurks behind all those cells and buttons.

What makes Excel is interesting, and even exciting, is that once you learn those basics you can start to *make things happen* onscreen. It's true—enter a number here, and something happens over there; change the values contributing to a chart, and the chart changes. Write some formulas, and you'll suddenly see something there that wasn't there before—and that something can make your work easier and more productive.

Is it worth learning about? You bet; and this Quick Start Guide will introduce you to Excel and point you to the places in this book where you can learn more about the things you have to know in order to get the most you can out of the software. So let's get started.

The Excel Worksheet: What You're Looking At

Click your way into Excel, and you'll be brought face to face with a screen that looks like Figure 1 (minus the descriptive captions, of course).

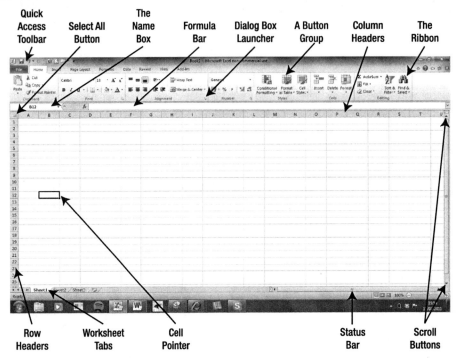

Figure 1. *The Excel worksheet*

What you're looking at is a large grid called a *worksheet*—and there's a lot more of it than you can see at one time. Don't confuse the worksheet with the *workbook*, which is the name for the whole Excel file; just as Word speaks of a *document*, Excel uses the term *workbook*. Think of a worksheet, then, as a page in the larger workbook.

The worksheet is bordered by a collection of buttons, icons, and fields that may not make all that much sense to you yet, so I'll offer a few introductory words about them and what's behind them. And don't worry, I'll explain in more detail as we move on.

- *Row headers*: These are the row numbers lining the far left of the grid. You need to know row numbers in order to determine a cell's *address*. A *cell* is the name given to all those rectangles making up the grid; each cell has an address, formed by the intersection of a row header and a column header.

- *Column headers*: These are the letters bordering the top of the grid. Cells have addresses such

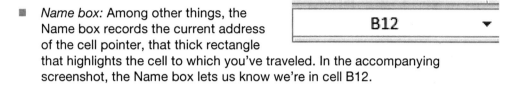

  as E34, A279, and the like (the letter always come first—e.g., there's no cell 34E, which sounds like a seat on an airplane). It's in those cells where you'll be entering your spreadsheet data.

- *Name box:* Among other things, the Name box records the current address of the cell pointer, that thick rectangle

  that highlights the cell to which you've traveled. In the accompanying screenshot, the Name box lets us know we're in cell B12.

- *Formula bar*: This white strip reveals the data you've entered in a cell (see Figure 2). If you think you can already tell that simply by looking at the actual cell, you'll soon learn that that's not always the case.

Figure 2. *The formula bar*

- *Ribbon*: This is a strip of buttons that, when clicked, carry out a wide variety of actions on the spreadsheet (see Figure 3). For example, the ribbon is responsible for formatting (i.e., changing the appearance of numbers in cells to look like, say, $45.00 instead 45, or turning any cell containing a number greater than 100 orange). Click any of the headings above the ribbon—the *command tabs*—and the contents of the ribbon changes, revealing a new set of buttons. Note that the command tabs are subdivided into Home, Insert, Page Layout, Formulas, Data, Review, View, and Add-Ins, as shown in Figure 3.

Figure 3. *The ribbon*

- *Button groups*: These are clusters of buttons that perform related tasks. Figure 3 shows the contents of the **Home** tab, which contains the button groups **Clipboard**, **Font**, **Alignment**, and so on. The arrows in the figure point to the **Alignment** and **Styles** button groups.

■ *Quick Access toolbar*: This is a set of buttons—sort of a mini-ribbon—that contains important basic commands  you're likely to use often. The advantage of the Quick Access toolbar is that it remains onscreen even if the contents of the ribbon beneath it change, and it can be customized so that you can add buttons to represent other commands you often use.

■ *Worksheet tabs*: Back to the worksheet concept, those three inserts entitled Sheet1, Sheet2, and Sheet3 tucked in 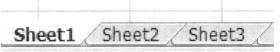 the lower left of the screen are worksheet tabs, representing the three worksheets that make up an Excel workbook for starters. Clicking any of these three will reveal another worksheet just like the others, affording you another batch of all those cells. When you start Excel, you'll be brought to Sheet1 by default. You can add many more new worksheets to the workbook if you need more space in which to store still more information.

■ *Scroll buttons*: These are four arrow-shaped buttons holding down the lower right and far right of the worksheet screen (see Figure 4). Clicking these moves the worksheet right/left and up/down on the screen. Try them and you'll see what they do.

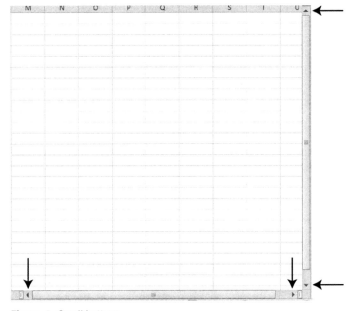

Figure 4. *Scroll buttons*

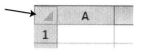

- **Select All** *button*: Clicking that rectangle wedged between the A and the 1 in the upper left of the screen will select, or highlight, all the cells in your worksheet—and why that might matter will be discussed soon.

- *Status bar*: This is the lower border of the worksheet, which contains buttons enabling you to modify ways in which the worksheet can be viewed, and which reports information about selected cells (see Figure 5). Note the mode indicator at the left of the status bar, a caption that reports the activity you're currently performing on the worksheet—Enter (for data entry), Edit, Ready, and so forth. You'll see what all that means soon.

Figure 5. *The status bar, at the bottom of the worksheet. The arrow points to the mode indicator*

- *Dialog box launchers*: These are the small arrows pinned to the lower-right corner of some of the button groups. Clicking a launcher opens a dialog box that offers command options additional to the ones shown in the group.

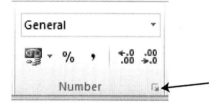

- *Cell pointer*: This is the bold rectangle that indicates your current position on the spreadsheet.

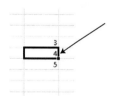

Key Tips: Accessing Buttons with the Keyboard

The standard way to access all those buttons filling Excel's ribbon is simply to click your mouse on the button you want.

NOTE: Unless otherwise stated, all mouse clicks utilize the left button.

But there's a keyboard alternative to this technique, called *key tips*. If you press the Alt key once, you'll introduce a collection of initialed minibuttons—the key tips—to the screen (see Figure 6).

Figure 6. *Note the letters that now accompany each tab.*

By typing any of the letters (or numbers, in some cases) shown, you'll be brought to the tab associated with that letter. Thus, if you press A, you'll call up the **Data** tab, as shown in Figure 7.

Figure 7. *Take a letter: Accessing the Data tab with key tips*

As shown, once you've accessed a tab, its button options can also be accessed via the key tips, some of which require tapping two keys in sequence. Thus, in Figure 7, pressing T will activate the **Filter** option (something you'll learn about in Chapter 7).

Moreover, if the button command you've selected fires up a drop-down menu, those menu commands can likewise be accessed with key tips. Thus, if you first tap H to access the **Home** tab and then press V to trigger the **Paste** button, its drop-down menu options will also be accompanied by key tips, as shown in the illustration.

NOTE: Clicking any button that features a small arrow will reveal a drop-down menu.

And each time you press the Esc key, you move back up one key tip level. That means that in the preceding screenshot, pressing Esc will close the drop-down menu and return you to all the **Home** tab key tips; pressing Esc again will take you back to the original key tips pinned to each tab, and pressing Esc still once more will turn off the key tips altogether.

Contextual Tabs

There's another set of tabs that may suddenly materialize on the screen. Called *contextual tabs*, these appear only when you've clicked certain objects, such as charts (see Chapter 6) or PivotTables (Chapter 8), and bring along tabs containing buttons specific to that object (see Figure 8).

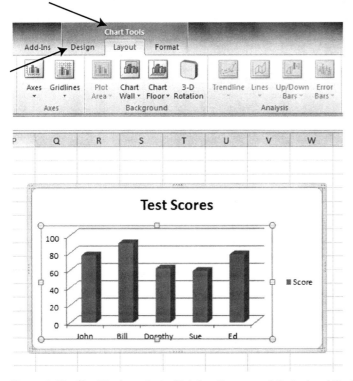

Figure 8. *The Chart Tools contextual tab (see the arrow at the top) and the Chart Tools tabs (see the lower arrow): Design, Layout, and Format*

The **Chart Tools** tab only appears when you click the chart. Click away from the chart and the **Chart Tools** contextual tab disappears, to return only when you click back on the chart. That's what makes it contextual.

A Visit Backstage

Beginning with the 2010 release of Excel, a new green tab called **File** has been added.

The **File** tab was introduced to replace the Office 2007 button, that rather ambiguous circular object that was stationed at the upper left of Excel's screen.

Click the **File** tab and you'll be brought to what's called the *Backstage*—a large behind-the-scenes area that houses commands that impact the workbook as a whole—including printing (including a print preview), saving, and sending the workbook, as well as sharing it with others (see Figure 9). It also offers numerous default settings that you can change if you want (e.g., how many worksheets a new workbook will start with). The

Backstage also lists the workbooks you've recently accessed, so that you can click any one on the list and open it again.

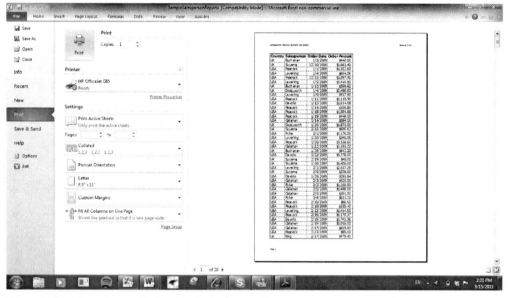

Figure 9. *A print preview as displayed in the Backstage. Note the other Backstage options in the left columns.*

> **TIP:** To exit the Backstage and return to the worksheet, press the Esc key or just click any other tab.

Customizing the Quick Access Toolbar

Now let's get back to the Quick Access toolbar, that downsized ribbon assigned to the upper left of the worksheet screen.

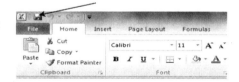

To repeat, the Quick Access toolbar stores frequently used buttons—and again, what makes the Quick Access toolbar so handy is that, unlike the larger tabs sitting beneath it, it's always there, along with its buttons, of course.

What makes the Quick Access toolbar even handier is that you can post *additional* buttons there, so they too will always remain in view and available.

There are several ways in which you can customize the Quick Access toolbar with additional buttons.

For one, you can click the small arrow at the far right of the Quick Access toolbar, revealing the menu shown in the accompanying screenshot.

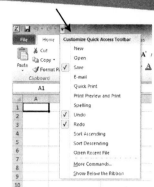

The menu offers just a small sample of all of Excel's commands, but these are among the more popular ones. Just click the commands you want to install, and buttons representing your selections will appear on the Quick Access toolbar.

You can right-click virtually any button on any Excel tab, calling up the menu shown here.

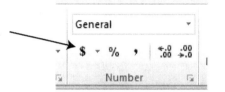

In this case the currency format button has been clicked, which gives numbers a currency-like appearance (e.g., 45.23 might be changed into $45.23).

Now that button will also show up in the Quick Access toolbar.

If you click the **File** tab to enter the Backstage, and then click **Options ➤ Quick Access Toolbar**, you'll see the dialog shown in Figure 10.

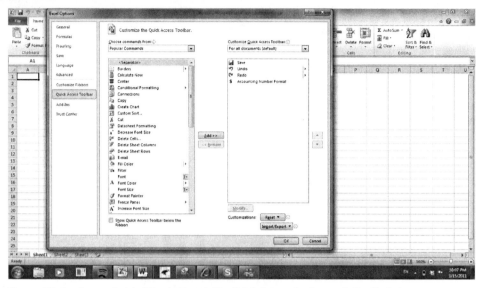

Figure 10. *Another route to adding buttons to the Quick Access toolbar—via the Backstage*

Figure 10 shows a very long list of Excel commands, any of which you can select with your mouse and then click Add in order to install it onto the Quick Access toolbar. Figure 11 shows the **Spelling...** command being selected and added it to the Quick Access toolbar, which is done by clicking the **Add** button.

Figure 11. *Adding the Spelling... button to the Quick Access toolbar*

Try it yourself. Select **Spelling...** and click **Add**, and the **Spelling...** button will be added to the right-hand **Customize Quick Access Toolbar** column, as shown in Figure 12.

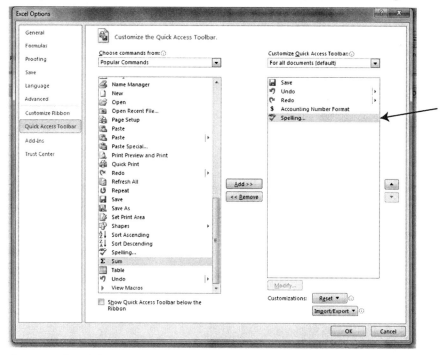

Figure 12. *There it is!*

Click **OK**, and the button will take its place in the Quick Access toolbar , as shown in the accompanying illustration.

To remove a button from the Quick Access toolbar , just right-click the button and select the first option on the resulting menu, as shown in the illustration to the right.

NOTE: By default, adding a button to the Quick Access toolbar makes that button available on the Quick Access toolbar in all your workbooks. If you want to restrict the button's appearance to the Quick Access toolbar of the current workbook only, you need to click the drop-down arrow by the Customize Quick Access field and click the name of the particular workbook (see Figure 13).

Figure 13. *Adding a button to the Quick Access toolbar for a particular workbook only*

Where to Learn More

Table1 lists the major Excel topics you'll find discussed in this book, and where to find them.

Table 1. *Major Excel Topics*

Topic	Illustration	Where to Learn More (Chapter and Section)
Navigating the worksheet		Chapter 2, "Getting Around a Worksheet"
Entering text data in cells	Apress New York London	Chapter 2, "Entering Text and Data"
Selecting (or highlighting) cells		Chapter 2, "Selecting Multiple Cells"
Getting text to fit in columns		Chapter 2, "Widening and Narrowing Columns"
Entering numerical data	2 3 4 5	Chapter 2, "Entering Numerical Data: How It's Different"
Validating data		Chapter 2, "Data Validation: Bringing Quality Control to the Worksheet"
Constructing a drop-down menu	Quincy Zachary 75,400.00 HR Marketing Sales VP	Chapter 2, "Making a List: Personalizing a Drop-Down Menu"
Making changes to data in cells		Chapter 3, "Changing Your Data"

Topic	Illustration	Where to Learn More (Chapter and Section)
Copying and moving data		Chapter 3, "Copying and Moving: Duplicating and Relocating Your Data"
Writing formulas		Chapter 4, "Customizing the Worksheet with Formulas"
Using functions		Chapter 4, "Automatic Calculations with Functions"
Copying and moving formulas	=H13+I13 =H14+I14 =H15+I15	Chapter 4, "Copying Formulas: More Than Just Duplication"
Working with relative and absolute cell references	$N6*A2	Chapter 4, "Keeping a Cell Reference Constant with Absolute Addressing"
Pasting values		Chapter 4, "Copying a Formula's Result Only"
Changing font appearances		Chapter 5, "Basic Formatting"
Changing cell alignment		Chapter 5, "Aligning (and Realigning) Your Data"
Wrapping text in its cell	This is how to use Wrap Text	Chapter 5, "Wrapping Text"

Topic	Illustration	Where to Learn More (Chapter and Section)
Merging and centering cells		Chapter 5, "Adding a Title with Merge and Center"
Inserting columns and rows		Chapter 5, "Inserting, Deleting, and Hiding Columns and Rows"
Formatting numeric data		Chapter 5, "Formatting Values: Making the Numbers Look Good"
Working with dates		Chapter 5, "Working with Dates: Dates Are Numbers Too"
Using the format painter		Chapter 5, "Copying Formats (Not Data) with the Format Painter"
Using cell styles		Chapter 5, "Applying Ready-Made Formats with Styles"
Working with conditional formatting		Chapter 5, "Conditional Formatting"
Understanding chart types		Chapter 6, "Choosing a Chart Type"

Topic	Illustration	Where to Learn More (Chapter and Section)
Constructing a chart		Chapter 6, "Creating a Column Chart"
Changing a chart		Chapter 6, "Changing a Chart"
Changing the default chart		Chapter 6, "Changing the Default Chart"
Changing chart formatting		Chapter 6, "Formatting Charts"
Adding a chart title		Chapter 6, "Adding Extra Chart Elements with the Layout Tab"
Working with sparklines		Chapter 6, "Introducing Sparklines: Mini-Charts Placed in Cells"
Sorting data		Chapter 7, "Sorting Data: Instilling Order in Your Data"
Filtering data		Chapter 7, "Finding What You Want with Filters"
Using tables		Chapter 7, "Tables: Adding User-Friendliness to Your Database"

Topic	Illustration	Where to Learn More (Chapter and Section)
Formatting and styling tables		Chapter 7, "Tables: Adding User-Friendliness to Your Database"
Removing duplicate records in a table		Chapter 7, "Finding Duplicate Records in the Table (and Removing Them)"
Learning what PivotTables can do		Chapter 8, "Looking at Some PivotTables"
Constructing a PivotTable		Chapter 8, "Creating a PivotTable"
Grouping PivotTable data		Chapter 8, "Grouping PivotTable Data: Organizing Your Time(s)"
Adding new records to the PivotTable		Chapter 8, "Refreshing the PivotTable: Changing the Data"
Learning how to use the Slicer		Chapter 8, "Viewing which Records Are Filtered: Using the Slicer"
Formatting a PivotTable		Chapter 8, "Formatting the PivotTable"

Topic	Illustration	Where to Learn More (Chapter and Section)
Devising a PivotChart		Chapter 8, "Creating Charts from PivotTables Using PivotCharts"
Adding and moving new worksheets		Chapter 9, "Adding and Moving New Worksheets"
Hiding and unhiding worksheets		Chapter 9, "Hiding Sheets"
Grouping sheets	Book3 [Group]	Chapter 9, "Grouping Sheets: Changing Multiple Sheets at the Same Time"
Writing formulas with cells in different worksheets		Chapter 9, "Referring to Cells in Other Worksheets: Using Them in Formulas"
Displaying or hiding gridlines, headings, and formulas		Chapter 9, "Using the View Context Tab to Show and Hide Basic Screen Elements"
Freezing screen panes		Chapter 9, "Keeping Important Data in View with the Freeze Panes Option"
Protecting worksheets and workbooks		Chapter 9, "Protecting the Worksheet and the Workbook"
Printing the entire worksheet		Chapter 10, "Printing the Entire Worksheet"
Printing a selected range of the worksheet		Chapter 10, "Printing a Selection"

Topic	Illustration	Where to Learn More (Chapter and Section)
Working with the Print Backstage		Chapter 10, "Surveying Printing Options: The Print Backstage"
Setting the print area		Chapter 10, "Setting the Print Area"
Imposing a page break		Chapter 10, "Working with Page Breaks"
Working with page break previews		Chapter 10, "Previewing the Page Break: Getting a Bird's-Eye View of the Printout"
Working with headers and footers		Chapter 10, "Adding Headers and Footers"
Recording and editing basic macros		Chapter 11

Excel Keyboard Equivalents

Because there are so many things you can do with Excel, it naturally needs to offer its users a long list of commands—and along with them, a long list of keyboard equivalents.

Needless to say, you may never have to use some of these, but they're available, and as your knowledge of Excel expands you may want to explore more of them. Table 2 lists a lengthy assortment of keyboard equivalents that employ the Ctrl key. While you may not yet understand what some of them do, by the time your reach the end of this book they should make a lot more sense.

Table 2. *Ctrl Key Shortcuts*

Ctrl Key Combination	What It Does
Ctrl+Shift+)	Unhides any hidden columns within the selection.
Ctrl+Shift+(	Unhides any hidden rows within the selection.
Ctrl+Shift+~	Applies the General number format.
Ctrl+Shift+$	Applies the Currency format with two decimal places (negative numbers in parentheses).
Ctrl+Shift+%	Applies the Percentage format with no decimal places.
Ctrl+Shift+!	Applies the Number format with two decimal places, a thousands separator, and a minus sign (–) for negative values.
Ctrl+Shift+:	Enters the current time; that is, the actual time as data, not a formula result.
Ctrl+Shift+"	Copies the value from the cell above the active cell into the cell or the formula bar. That is, if you click in a blank cell, this shortcut will copy any value in the cell immediately above it. If that value is the result of a formula, this shortcut will paste only that value, not the formula.
Ctrl+;	Enters the current date as data, not a formula result.
Ctrl+`	Alternates between displaying cell values and displaying formulas in the worksheet. That is, this shortcut will display a cell formula on the screen instead of its value. Tap the shortcut a second time and the value will return. This option is available for the workbook via **File ➤ Advanced ➤ Show formulas in cells instead of their calculated results**.
Ctrl+'	Copies the formula from the cell above the active cell into selected cells or the formula bar. The copied formula cell references change as per relative cell references. You need to select the source cell along with the destination cells at the same time.
Ctrl+1	Displays the **Format Cells** dialog box.
Ctrl+5	Applies or removes a strikethrough effect through characters populating cells.
Ctrl+9	Hides the selected rows.
Ctrl+0	Hides the selected columns.

Ctrl Key Combination	What It Does
Ctrl+A	Selects the entire worksheet. If the worksheet contains data, Ctrl+A selects the current region—that is, an area of cells populated by data (e.g., a table)—if you click in that region. Pressing Ctrl+A a second time selects the entire worksheet. If you click in a blank area of the worksheet, Ctrl+A will initially select the entire worksheet.
Ctrl+B	Applies or removes bold formatting with alternating taps.
Ctrl+C	Copies the selected cells.
Ctrl+D	Uses the Fill Down command to copy the contents and format of the topmost cell of a selected range into the cells immediately below.
Ctrl+F	Displays the **Find and Replace** dialog box, with the **Find** tab selected. This works similarly to the Find and Replace option in Word. This dialog is also available via the **Find & Select** option in the **Editing** button group on the **Home** tab.
Ctrl+Shift+F	Opens the **Format Cells** dialog box with the **Font** tab selected.
Ctrl+G	Displays the **Go To** dialog box (as does F5).
Ctrl+H	Displays the **Find and Replace** dialog box, with the **Replace** tab selected.
Ctrl+I	Applies or removes italic formatting with alternating taps.
Ctrl+L	Displays the **Create Table** dialog box (equivalent to Ctrl+T).
Ctrl+N	Creates a new, blank workbook.
Ctrl+O	Displays the **Open** dialog box to open or find a file.
Ctrl+P	Displays the **Print** tab in Microsoft Office Backstage view.
Ctrl+R	Uses the Fill Right command to copy the contents and format of the leftmost cell of a selected range into the cells to the right.
Ctrl+S	Saves the active file with its current file name, location, and file format.
Ctrl+T	Displays the **Create Table** dialog box.
Ctrl+U	Applies or removes underlining with alternating taps.
Ctrl+V	Performs the classic Paste command. Pressing Ctrl+V inserts the contents of the Clipboard at the insertion point and replaces any selection. This option is available only after you have cut or copied text, cell contents, or an object.

Ctrl Key Combination	What It Does
Ctrl+Alt+V	Displays the **Paste Special** dialog box, enabling you to paste only the *results* of a copied formula, by clicking the **Values** option in the dialog box. If, for example, a formula in cell A17 states =SUM(A2:A13) and yields 3224, **Paste Special** will return only the value 3224 in the destination cell. It will not copy the formula. This option is also available via the **Paste** button on the **Home** tab and on the **Paste** shortcut menu.
Ctrl+W	Closes the selected workbook window.
Ctrl+X	Cuts the selected cells
Ctrl+Y	Performs a redo; that is, it undoes the last command you've undone via Undo. But it also repeats any last command or action, if possible.
CTR+Z	Uses the Undo command to reverse the last action or delete the last entry you typed. Successive presses of Ctrl+Z continue to undo the immediately previous command.

The shortcuts shown in Table 3 work with the function keys (the "F" keys stationed in the upper row of your keyboard).

Table 3. *Function Key Shortcuts*

Function Key	What It Does
F1	Displays the Excel Help task pane.
	Ctrl+F1 displays or hides the ribbon.
	Alt+F1 creates a chart of the data in a current range in which you've clicked, on the worksheet containing the data.
	Alt+Shift+F1 inserts a new worksheet.
F2	Edits the active cell and positions the insertion point at the end of the cell contents. It also moves the insertion point into the formula bar when the capability to edit in a cell is turned off. This keystroke draws a temporary border around the cells that contribute to any formula in the cell you're editing. Thus, tapping F2 while in a cell containing =AVERAGE(A6:A10) will trace a border around cells A6:A10. It provides an easy way to identity cell relationships.
	Shift+F2 adds or edits a cell comment.
	Ctrl+F2 displays the print preview area on the **Print** tab in the Backstage view (as does Ctrl+P).
F3	Displays the **Paste Name** dialog box. This option is only available if there are range names in the workbook.
	Shift+F3 displays the **Insert Function** dialog box.

Function Key	What It Does
F4	Repeats the last command or action, if possible.
	Ctrl+F4 closes the selected workbook window, as does Ctrl+W.
	Alt+F4 closes Excel. As usual, you'll will be prompted to save your changes should you not have already done so.
F5	Displays the Go To dialog box.
	Ctrl+F5 restores the window size of the selected workbook window.
F6	Switches between the worksheet, ribbon, task pane, and zoom controls. In a worksheet that has been split, F6 includes the split panes when switching between panes and the ribbon area. (You can split a worksheet via View ➤ Manage This Window ➤ Freeze Panes ➤ Split Window.)
	Shift+F6 switches between the worksheet, zoom controls, task pane, and ribbon.
	Ctrl+F6 switches to the next workbook window when more than one workbook window is open.
F7	Displays the Spelling dialog box to check spelling in the active worksheet or selected range.
F8	Turns Extend mode on or off. In Extend mode, "Extended Selection" appears in the status line, and the arrow keys extend the selection. Extend mode allows you to select consecutive cells with the keyboard arrow keys without requiring you to hold down the Shift key. Tapping F8 a second time toggles this command off.
	Shift+F8 enables you to add a nonadjacent cell or range to a selection of cells by using the arrow keys. That is, after having selected one range, tapping this shortcut lets you click elsewhere and drag or key-select another range, even as the original range remains selected.
	Alt+F8 displays the Macro dialog box, for creating, running, editing, or deleting a macro.
F9	Calculates all worksheets in all open workbooks. You'll rarely use this one nowadays. You might, however, if your workbook features thousands of formulas. When you enter new data, Excel recalculates every formula whose result has changed since the last calculation. On a slow computer, that process can be rather time-consuming. If this is the case, you can click Formulas ➤ Calculation ➤ Calculation Options ➤ Manual, which prevents Excel from recalculating formulas when you enter new data. F9 will then calculate the worksheet when pressed. The Calculate Now button in the Calculation button group calculates the workbook in which you've clicked.
	Shift+F9 calculates the active worksheet.
	Ctrl+Alt+F9 calculates all worksheets in all open workbooks, regardless of whether they have changed since the last calculation.
	Ctrl+F9 minimizes a workbook window to an icon.

Function Key	What It Does
F10	Turns key tips on the ribbon on or off. Pressing Alt does the same thing.
	Shift+F10 displays the shortcut menu for a selected item.
	Ctrl+F10 maximizes or restores the selected workbook window; it's equivalent to clicking the lower tier of maximize/minimize buttons in the upper right of your screen.
F11	Creates a chart of the data in the current range in a *separate* chart sheet.
	Shift+F11 inserts a new worksheet.
F12	Displays the Save As dialog box.

Table 4 shows a collection of other shortcut keys.

Table 4. *Additional Shortcut Keys*

Shortcut Key	What It Does
Arrow keys	Moves one cell up, down, left, or right in a worksheet.
	Ctrl+arrow key moves to the edge of the current data region in a worksheet (a data region is a range of cells that contains data and that is bounded by empty cells or datasheet borders).
	Shift+arrow key extends the selection of cells by one cell.
	Ctrl+Shift+arrow key extends the selection of cells to the last nonblank cell in the same column or row as the active cell; or if the next cell is blank, it extends the selection to the next nonblank cell.
	Left arrow or right arrow selects the tab to the left or right when the ribbon is selected via the Alt Key. When a submenu is open or selected, these arrow keys switch between the main menu and the submenu. When a ribbon tab is selected, these keys navigate the tab buttons.
	Down arrow or up arrow selects the next or previous command when a menu or submenu is open.
	In a dialog box, arrow keys move between options in an open drop-down list, or between options in a group of options.
	Down arrow or Alt+down arrow opens a selected drop-down list.
Backspace	Deletes one character to the left in the formula bar.
	In cell-editing mode, it deletes the character to the left of the insertion point (as in Word).
Delete	Removes the cell contents (data and formulas) from selected cells without affecting cell formats or comments.
	In cell-editing mode, it deletes the character to the right of the insertion point (as in Word).

Shortcut Key	What It Does
End	Turns on what's called *End mode*. In End mode, you can then press an arrow key to move to the next nonblank cell in the same column or row as the active cell. If the cells are blank, pressing End followed by an arrow key moves the cell pointer to the very last cell in the row or column—that is, row 1048576 or column XFD. End also selects the last command on the menu when a menu or submenu is visible. Ctrl+End moves to the last cell on a worksheet—that is, the lowest used row of the rightmost used column. However, see the additional discussion about this in Chapter 2. If the cursor is in the formula bar, Ctrl+End moves the cursor to the end of the text. Ctrl+Shift+End extends the selection of cells to the last used cell on the worksheet (lower-right corner). If the cursor is in the formula bar, Ctrl+Shift+End selects all text in the formula bar from the cursor position to the end—this does not affect the height of the formula bar.
Enter	Completes a cell entry from the cell or the formula bar, and selects the cell below it (by default). In a data form, it moves to the first field in the next record. It also opens a selected menu (press F10 to activate the menu bar) or performs the action for a selected command. In a dialog box, it performs the action for the default command button in the dialog box (the button with the bold outline, often the **OK** button). Alt+Enter starts a new line in the same cell—a kind of a manual text wrap. Ctrl+Enter fills the selected cell range with the current entry. Shift+Enter completes a cell entry and selects the cell immediately above.
Esc	Cancels an entry in the cell or formula bar. It also closes an open menu or submenu, dialog box, or message window. It also closes full screen mode when this mode has been applied, and returns to normal screen mode to display the ribbon and status bar again.
Home	Moves to the beginning of a row in a worksheet. Moves to the cell in the upper-left corner of the window when Scroll Lock is turned on. Selects the first command on the menu when a menu or submenu is visible. Ctrl+Home moves to the beginning of a worksheet. Ctrl+Shift+Home extends the selection of cells to the beginning of the worksheet.

Shortcut Key	What It Does
Page Down	Moves one screen down in a worksheet.
	Alt+Page Down moves one screen to the right in a worksheet.
	Ctrl+Page Down moves to the next sheet in a workbook.
	Ctrl+Shift+Page Down selects the current and next sheet in a workbook.
Page Up	Moves one screen up in a worksheet.
	Alt+Page Up moves one screen to the left in a worksheet.
	Ctrl+Page Up moves to the immediately previous sheet in a workbook.
Spacebar	In a dialog box, performs the action for the selected button, or selects or clears a check box.
	Ctrl+spacebar selects an entire column in a worksheet.
	Shift+spacebar selects an entire row in a worksheet.
	Ctrl+Shift+spacebar selects the entire worksheet, behaving as Ctrl+A.

Chapter 1

Introducing Excel 2010

Most people don't quite appreciate it, but lurking in the inner recesses of their hard drives in the Microsoft Office suite is a mighty, flexible—and often dormant—tool for working with information in countless ways: Microsoft Excel.

Of course, people know it's in there somewhere, but even in an age in which computer savvy is increasingly widespread, computer users often just don't realize exactly what they have in their PCs, and how a deeper understanding of Excel can make the work they need to do easier, both on the job and at home.

When I speak to people about Excel, they marvel at the programming wisdom that enables it to do what it does (or rather what it *can* do). But the next step—actually applying Excel productively to a task, or applying a technique that can do a job more deftly than it's being done currently—is often something else again.

This book is here to help. Excel 2010 is the latest version of that best-selling application, and while there's always more to learn about it, we want to introduce you here to the important basics that will let you do actual work.

The Advantages of Learning More

Ask someone how well they know Microsoft Word, and they're likely to reply with the "I know what I need to know" answer. That is, their expertise extends to the limits of the jobs they need to do—writing correspondence, batching up a mail merge, working with styles, and so on. And that's fine. But Excel is different, because learning about its capabilities, even when you *don't* think you need to know them, can be a valuable thing. Once you discover something new about Excel, you may begin to appreciate how you *can* use it—and now. And with your additional knowledge you'll start to glimpse the nearly limitless range of things you can do with it.

It's one thing, for example, to be able to total your company's monthly or annual receipts, and you might be able to carry out that task without a spreadsheet, after all. But what if you needed to know how much each salesperson earned? Again, you might be able to get away with that job without any aid from Excel, but things will start to get messy if you go it alone. But if you need to know how much each salesperson earned *each month*, as in Figure 1–1, well, that's a job for Excel.

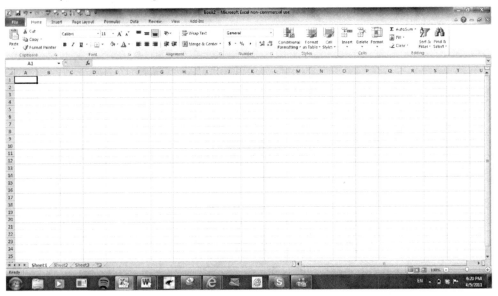

Figure 1–1. *Try that one with a calculator!*

And it's worth learning how to do it.

Spreadsheets Defined

But we haven't quite answered the question of what a spreadsheet is. So here goes. A spreadsheet is a program that emulates, but far surpasses, those vast, green, lined ledgers on which accountants and bookkeepers used to enter columns and rows of numbers. Because spreadsheets work electronically, of course, they can do a great many more things with their data than any ledger could do with its handwritten entries. And the spreadsheet "ledger" is far vaster than the hard copy version (see Figure 1–2).

Figure 1–2. *A spreadsheet (in actuality, just part of one)*

In fact, this figure shows only a very small fraction of the whole ledger.

A calculator also works electronically, but here too a spreadsheet has got it beat, and by a mile. Enter a number into the slender calculator readout and all you'll be able to see is one number. Add a number to it and the second will replace the first on the screen — that's it.

But add a series of numbers on a spreadsheet—each one stored in a rectangular space called a *cell*—and they all remain visible on the screen, as in Figure 1–3.

	4
	5
	8
	32
	45
	7
Total	101

Figure 1–3. *The sum total of a column of numbers: What you see is what you get on a spreadsheet*

And you can add millions of numbers in one go, all of which are available on the screen for your review and inspection (after all, there might be a couple of data entry mistakes among those millions). And that's just for starters; with spreadsheets you can also change the ways the numbers (and text) look—that is, you can format them, you can perform all sorts of mathematical operations on them, and you can capture numerical information in chart form, too (see Figure 1–4).

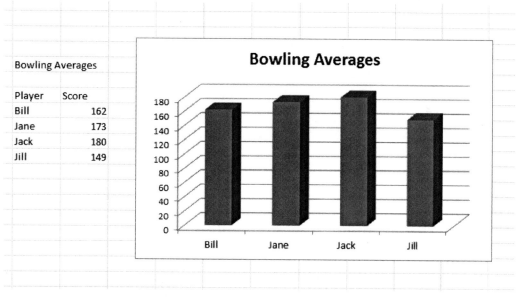

Figure 1–4. *A chart in Excel*

Once you learn the basics of charting, you can turn out the type of chart shown in the figure in about 10 seconds.

Excel Can Be Fun

"Excel can be fun" may sound like a nerdy thing to say, but once you start to get the hang of it, Excel *can* be a rather entertaining application, in addition to simply being a tool for enhancing your work routine. There's a kind of interactive, video game quality to the way Excel does its thing—enter a number in one cell, and watch another cell change, even if that cell is many rows away. Enter a value and watch the cell in which you've typed it automatically turn a different color (there's a reason for that, of course—to be discussed in Chapter 5). Change one of the bowling averages from Figure 1–4 and the chart will change—again, automatically. And it's all happening under your direction. (Unfortunately, the video game analogy doesn't go much farther than this, though—no machine guns, aliens, or Formula 1 racetracks here.)

Summary

Let's face it; there are lots of intelligent people out there who can think of an awful lot of things they'd rather do than concoct a spreadsheet—not out of lack of interest, but because it's hard to hold a mouse in your hand when you have cold feet. It's important not to let self-intimidation get in the way of acquiring basic (and even more advanced) spreadsheet skills, and there isn't much reason why you can't do so.

It's also important to note that if you have experience with pre-2007 releases of Excel only, you'll have to acquaint yourself with a different interface—that is, a revised arrangement of the buttons and commands on the screen. So, with the learning, there may be a bit of unlearning, too. But speaking from experience, it's all doable.

While of course you'll need to experiment and practice with it a bit, remember that there are millions of people worldwide who use Excel, and not one of them was born knowing how. And all of them have more to learn.

So let's start learning!

Chapter 2

Getting Around the Worksheet and Data Entry

The Journey Starts Here

Whether you use a map, a satnav, a web-drawn itinerary, or do the retro thing instead and question an actual human being, any trip begins with knowing where you're going, knowing how to get there, and then deciding what to do once you've pulled into your destination. Your travels across an Excel worksheet aren't much different. You need to know where you want to go and how to track that destination down; and once you're there, you need to know how to fill that destination with the data that'll make the worksheet do what you want it to. It's a **work**sheet after all, and we're going to start doing that essential work now.

Looking Around

The grid in Excel is a good deal larger than what you're viewing on screen, and that's putting it mildly. In fact, every Excel 2010 worksheet contains 1,048,576 rows, probably way more than you'll ever need, and probably more than your computer could handle anyway were all those rows to be filled with data. And each workbook is outfitted with 16,384 columns, raising an obvious address question: if the 26th column is called Z, then what does Excel call number 27? The answer: AA, followed by AB, etc. And when Excel runs out of double-letter combinations—at column ZZ, it adds a third letter, yielding AAA, and so on—all the way down to column XFD. Thus, ABC123 is a perfectly legal cell address.

Getting Around a Worksheet

Now in order to enter data in any cell you have get there first, by maneuvering the cell pointer into the desired address. Excel gives you many ways of getting there. Here are some of the standard ways:

You can utilize these navigational techniques with the keyboard:

- The Enter key—pressing Enter moves the pointer down one row.

- The Arrow keys—pressing any of these moves the pointer in the appropriate direction. That means the down arrow really does the same thing as Enter when you're navigating to the next cell– it takes you down one row.

- Tab—moves the pointer one column to the right.

- Shift-Tab—moves the pointer one column to the left. (But the Backspace key won't work here!)

- PgDn/PgUp—when pressed moves the pointer down or up **one screen's** worth of rows. Keep in mind that because you can change the height of rows, the number of rows you travel with these command may vary.

- Alt-PgDn/Alt-PgUp—A less-well-known pair of keyboard combinations. Pressing Alt-PgDn advances the pointer ahead one screen's worth of **columns**. Pressing Alt-PgUp takes the pointer **back** one screen's worth of columns. Again, because you can modify the width of columns, the distance you'll travel could vary.

- Ctrl-Home—a surprisingly useful combination. Ctrl-Home takes you to cell A1—the first cell in the worksheet. It's good to know about when you've travelled a long way across the worksheet, and you need to get back to the sheet's beginning.

NOTE: Holding any keyboard navigational key(s) down, and keeping it down, will move the cell pointer rapidly in the desired direction. Thus if you hold the Enter key down, you'll scoot swiftly down the rows of the column in which you find yourself.

ANOTHER NOTE: As we've already noted, clicking the scroll buttons moves the worksheet across, or up or down, the screen. But the scroll buttons *don't* move the cell pointer. For example—if the cell pointer has been positioned in cell A12 and you then click the right scroll button, you'll start to see columns well to the right of the A column—but the cell pointer will *remain* in A12. Scroll buttons *don't* move the cell pointer to a new cell—rather, they just shift the rows and columns you see across the screen.

Consider this scenario, then: You're in cell B22 and you want to make your way to cell Z18. You can click the right scroll button until the Z column appears on screen. Then just click on Z18 (the column letter doesn't have to be upper case, by the way). Try it!

Of course you can get to your cell destination with the mouse, by simply clicking it onto the cell to which you want to go (note that unless otherwise indicated, all mouse clicks call upon the left button).

You can also use the Name Box to visit a cell. Just click into the box, type your cell destination, and press Enter. Voila—you're there.

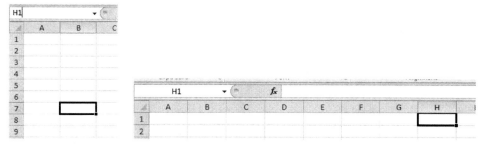

Figure 2–1. *Note the cell pointer in cell B7. Typing H1 in the Name box in pressing Enter takes you to....cell H1.*

The Name Box is a cool way to travel long distances in the worksheet with precision -so if you need to get to cell XY38451, and fast, just type it in the Name Box and press Enter. Now want to get back where you came? Press Ctrl-Home, and you're returned to cell A1.

This table summarizes the techniques we've described:

Table 2–1. *Navigational techniques summarized*

Technique	Type of Movement
Enter key	Moves one row down
Shift-Enter	Moves one cell up
Tab	Moves one cell to the right
Shift-Tab	Moves one cell to the left
Arrow keys	Moves one cell in desired direction
Page-Down/Up	Moves one screen's worth of rows up or down
Alt-Page Down/Up	Moves one screen's worth of columns right or left
Ctrl-Home	Always moves to cell A1
Name Box	Moves to cell whose address you've typed in box after
Mouse	Enables user to click into any cell
Scroll buttons/bars	Moves to a new area of the worksheet; but does not directly select any cell

Remember that when you travel to any cell the current location of the cell pointer is always recorded in the Name Box.

Selecting Multiple Cells

In the course of your spreadsheet activity you may decide that you need to highlight, or **select**, more than one cell at a time. Why? There are several reasons you may want to do this, including these:

- You want to format the data in a group of cells all at the same time. For example: You want a group of numbers—perhaps a very large group—to display that currency format we spoke about earlier. By selecting all those cells simultaneously you can introduce the currency format to all of them, rather than having to change each cell individually. (See Chapter 4.)

- You may want to copy, or move, or delete, a group of cells at the same time. (See later this chapter.)

- You may want to print some, but not all the cells, in a worksheet. To carry this out, you'd first need to select just the cells you want to print. (See Chapter 8.)

- You may want to subject a group of cells to a mathematical operation—say, add the numbers in certain cells. (See Chapter 3.)

Selecting multiple cells, then, is your way of informing Excel exactly which cells you want to modify or work with.

There are several related ways in which you can select cells, and they're all pretty easy. The standard way is simply to click in the first cell you want to select, hold down the left button, and **drag** with your mouse across, or down, the other cells. The technique is very similar to the way you'd select a group of words in Word.

Thus if I wanted to select cells A6 through A19 I'd

1. Click cell A6.

2. Hold the left mouse button down.

3. Drag to cell A19.

4. Release the mouse.

Carry out this sequence, and again, your screen should look like this:

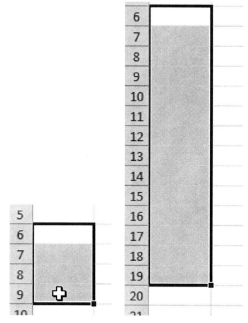

Figure 2–2. *Selecting cells. Start by dragging (left screenshot) and when you've selected them all, release the mouse (right screenshot).*

Note that the cell pointer—the thick black border—has expanded to include all the selected cells, which have turned temporarily blue (with the exception of A6, the first cell we've selected. (Why A6 hasn't changed color will be discussed a bit later in more detail, but the blank cell represents the cell in which the data will go when you start to type. It's the blue color that tells you that these are the cells you've selected. Now you can go ahead and reformat the cells, or copy or print them (of course you'd want to put data in them first!)

Now of course you're eventually going to have to turn off the selection area in order to go ahead and do something else. To stop the selection process and banish the blue from your screen, just click your mouse, or press any arrow key.

Selecting Cells Down and Across the Worksheet

And when we select cells, we're not restricted to cells in one column. Once we've started to select we can keep that left mouse button down and drag to the right (or left, if we have room in that direction, or even up) as well, and select cells in additional columns:

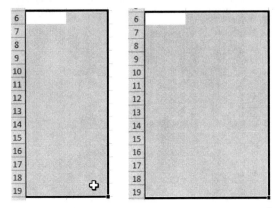

Figure 2–3. *Selecting rows and columns, as we start to drag to the right*

Selecting Cells with the Keyboard

You can also select cells with the keyboard. Click in the first cell you want to select, release the mouse, and then

1. Hold down the Shift key.

2. Leaving the Shift key down, tap any of the arrow keys in the direction of the cells you want to select.

3. You can change arrow keys as you proceed, so that you can select cells to the right of the start cell by tapping the right arrow key, and then begin to select cells downward by tapping the down arrow key.

Selecting *All* the Cells

Now back to that Select All button:

	A	
1		
2		

Figure 2–4. *Remember—it's to the left of the A column heading, and above row heading 1.*

Remember that clicking Select All highlights all the worksheet cells at the same time—all 1.7 billion or so of them. You'd turn to Select All, then, if you wanted reformat all those cells uniformly—say to implement the same font change in all of them. (Note: clicking Ctrl-A will also normally select all worksheet cells. (There's an exception to this rule, though: if you click anywhere in a group of consecutive cells that contain data—called a range, a topic which is coming next—Ctrl-A will select *only* those cells.)

Figure 2–5. *Complete coverage: what the worksheet looks like when you've selected all its cells*

As we just indicated, a group of adjoining cells of the kind we've illustrated above is called a **range**, a key spreadsheet concept. Knowing how to identify ranges in formulas—something we're going to learn about soon—will enable you to work with large numbers of cells at the same time: to add the numbers entered in those cells, calculate their average, find the smallest number among them, and to carry out a nearly unlimited number of other tasks.

Still One More Selection Technique—The Name Box

And while we're at it, here's another cool way to select a range. You can click in the Name Box and type a range reference, something like

Figure 2–6. *Entering range coordinates in the Name Box*

Now what does that mean? It means we want to select all the cells from A12 *though* C23 (including A12 and C23). That's what the colon does—and if you press Enter next, all those cells will be selected.

Entering Text and Data

Data entry in Excel is as easy as it is important. Just select the cell you need, and type the entry—although that doesn't quite finish the process. When you type in Word, all you do, after all, is...type. But data entry in Excel requires an additional, but simple step. You need to confirm what you've entered with an additional command—almost always a navigational keystroke or mouse click.

Let's illustrate. The typical way to enter data is to select a cell, type whatever you want, and press the Enter key—and that's it.

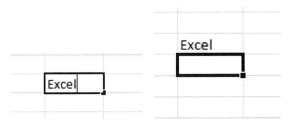

Figure 2–7. *Note the cursor alongside the letter I in the first shot. That indicates that you're still "in" the cell. When you press Enter, the cell pointer travels down one row.*

Pressing Enter does two things:

1. It "installs" whatever you've typed in the cell

2. It bumps the cell pointer down one row, as Enter normally does— nothing new there (as you'll see, there's an exception to this rule—when you select a range and then enter data into its cells).

> **Note**: If you're in the process of entering data in a cell and decide you don't want to continue, pressing the ESC key will cancel what you're doing and leave the original cell contents intact.

That's the way it works—type your data in the cell, and press Enter—OR an arrow key, OR PgDn or PgUp, OR click the mouse into another cell. Typing data into a cell and following it up with say, a tap of the right arrow key, also does two things: it installs the data, and then in this case delivers the cell pointer one column to the right. Completing the data entry with a mouse click instead will simply land the cell pointer into the cell in which you've clicked—after the data has been installed in the original cell. I told you it was easy. The idea is that the pointer moves in the desired direction after carrying out the data entry.

There's also another way to carry out the data entry process. Select your cell, type away, and instead of executing one of the standard navigational moves we've described above click the gray check mark alongside the formula bar:

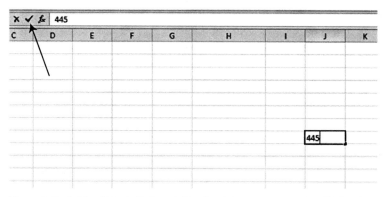

Figure 2–8. *Getting ticked off: Completing the data entry process by clicking the gray tick*

This click-the-tick approach will also finish off the data entry as with all the other techniques, but this time—and unlike the other methods listed above- will leave the cell pointer in the **same** cell. Note also the X to the left of the tick; click it instead and the 445 you've started to type above will be canceled

Aligning Your Data—Where It Appears in the Cell

Now let's look at a little more closely at the data you'll enter and how they appear in cells. When you type a textual entry the results appear **left-aligned**—that is, starting at a cell's left edge—by default, and that's simply because our Roman alphabet proceeds from left to right. But type a number—or what Excel calls a **value**, and it will position itself by default—that is, for starters—at the cell's right edge, because our number system is Arabic, extending right to left:

Excel

56

Figure 2–9. *Choosing sides: Text aligned left, numbers right*

Text data entry differs in some important ways from its numeric cousin. For one thing, if you type a lengthy phrase in a cell—and you can actually type over 32,000 characters in a cell—Excel will allow the excess text to spill into adjoining columns:

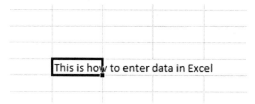

This is how to enter data in Excel

Figure 2–10. *Crossing the line: a text phrase advancing into other cells*

Just type away and let the text do its thing, bearing in mind that, appearances to the contrary, all the text you see in the above screen shot inhabits just one cell—the cell in which you started to type. That's all perfectly legal. But crossing cell boundaries can cause a problem.

Let's say the text we see above has been inscribed in cell B6. If we go ahead and type an entry in cell C6—the cell to its immediate right, we see something like this:

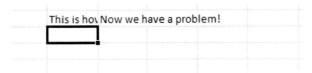

Figure 2–11. *Now you see it, now you don't: The case of the missing text.*

What happened? What happened is that the new phrase in C6 is simply claiming its own turf, so to speak. C6 was empty, after all, and all we did was enter a bit of text there—obscuring, but *not deleting,* that part of the text in B6 that had overstepped its bound.

And how do I know that none of the text in B6 has been deleted? I can verify that fact by clicking on B6 and looking at the Formula Bar. You'll see

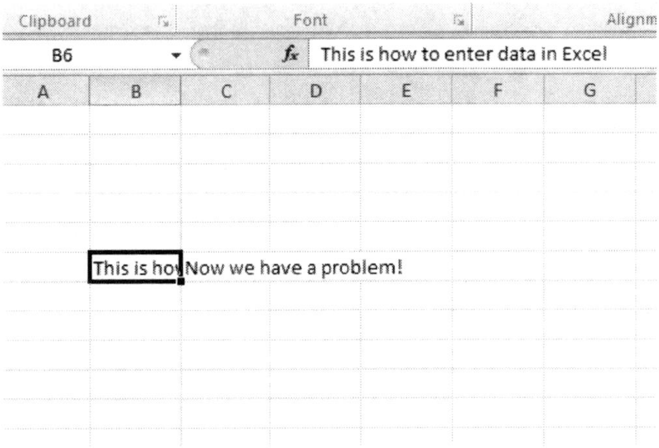

Figure 2–12. *All there: the text in B6, revealed in the Formula Bar*

Now we can begin to understand how the Formula Bar reveals the data you've entered in a cell. By that I meant that a glance at the actual cell doesn't always tell you what's really going on inside of it, and we'll see more evidence of this when we starting looking at formulas. Here we see that because of the data in C6, some of the phrase in B6 isn't visible—at least not on the worksheet itself. And if you were to go ahead and print the worksheet in its current state, the text in B6 would remain eclipsed as you see it above. But the Formula Bar reassures us that that it's all still there just the same.

Widening and Narrowing Columns

But that explanation still leaves us with the problem: we can't see the whole phrase in B6—and we want to. It's a classic spreadsheet dilemma—and the way to resolve it is to widen the column containing the "missing" text, revealing it completely on the worksheet.

There are several ways in which to widen Excel columns, and we'll explore what are probably the two most popular:

- Altering a column manually
- Using the auto-fit feature

Altering a column manually

Let's try the first method to widen a column:

1. Position the mouse over the *right* border of the column you want to widen—in this case column B—and click (don't release the mouse). You'll see:

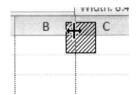

Figure 2–13. *The first step toward widening a column. Note the double-arrowed cursor.*

2. Now drag the column boundary toward the right. You'll see the B column expand, revealing more of the text in B6 as you drag. When you've exposed all of the text, release the mouse.

That was easy, wasn't it? Just click on the right column boundary (it *must* be the right), and drag to widen. Just keep in mind that you need to click on the column boundary, and *not* on row 1 of the worksheet in order to carry out this task.

If you want you can *narrow* a column, too, by dragging to the *left*, in the same way.

Now that's pretty neat, but the process is slightly hit-or-miss and trial-and-error—because if you've written a very lengthy text phrase in a cell, you may have to try the click-and-drag repeatedly until you've widened the column to precisely the dimension you want. And that takes us to Method 2—the auto-fit.

Using the Auto-fit Feature

Let's try an auto-fit:

1. As with the Method 1, glide the mouse atop the right column boundary, until you see the double-arrowed cursor.

2. Double-click the mouse. The column should be widened to reveal all of the contents of the cell.

Got that? Again, it's called auto-fit, and we see that double-clicking any column's right boundary resizes the column until all the data in that column is revealed. And that also means that if you've entered data into *many* cells in the B column and many of them exhibit obscured text, a double-click will widen the column to reveal them all. In other words, the auto-fit resizes the column to the width of the *widest* data entry in the column.

You can execute an auto-fit on several columns at the same time. That means that if several columns suffer from the obscured-text-syndrome at the same time, you can widen them all in one shot. Here's how: Let's say that columns A through D all have data in some of their cells which are hidden by data in the adjoining columns, something like this:

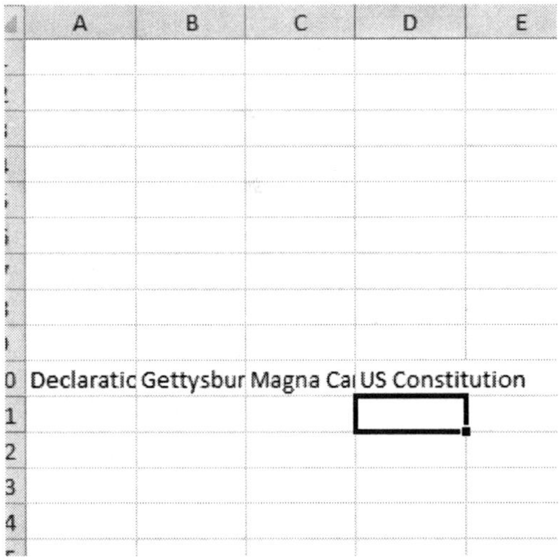

Figure 2–14. *But the words get in the way…four columns' worth of obscured text.*

3. Click atop the first column *heading* you want to auto-fit (in this case, A)— and not its boundary, this time—keep the left button down, and drag across the headings of the adjoining columns you want to auto-fit:

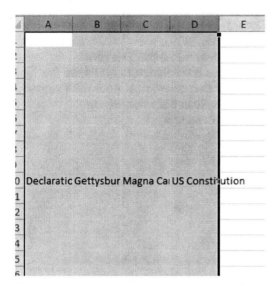

Figure 2–15. *Selecting the columns by their headings*

4. Double-click *any* one of the column boundaries selected—and all the columns will be auto fit:

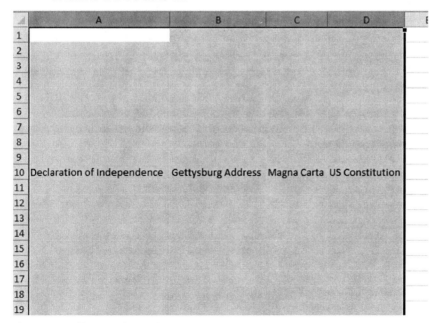

Figure 2–16. *Fit to be tried!*

5. Then click anywhere on the worksheet to turn off the blue selection color.

Pretty handy. Just remember that this multi-column auto-fit won't engineer identical widths for each column, because each width is tied to the widest entry in each column.

Entering Numerical Data—How it's Different

Now let's say a few words about entering values—that is, numbers. The basic techniques are identical for text entry: select a cell, type the value, and conclude the process with a navigational keystroke, mouse click, or that green tick. And don't worry about commas, decimal points, and currency symbols. Those are formatting embellishments that don't change the actual value you've entered.

NOTE: See Chapter 5 for working with commas, decimal points, and currency symbols.

2356.78	$2,356.78	2357

Figure 2–17. *Some ways in which you can format values. Note the rounded off value in the third case.*

So far so good. But there's a quirk about values you'll want to know about early on: Excel *won't* allow a large value to barge across into the neighboring column. That is, if you type 1000000000—however that value is translated into English—Excel simply will prevent it from trespassing into the column next door. So what does Excel do instead?

It does one of several things, depending on what's gone on in the worksheet before you entered the value.

By default, Excel carries out a kid of automatic auto fit on a lengthy value—that is, it will automatically expand the column to display the value in its entirety, without you having to double-click the column boundary.

But if you had already *narrowed* that column before you entered the value, Excel assumes you had a good reason for having done so, and leaves the column width alone. So instead, it does one of two things:

Displays the value in scientific notation, so it looks something like Figure 2–18. While you probably haven't seen a value expressed that way since high school, it does represent a more compact way of displaying the value in a narrowed column.

1000000000	1E+09

Figure 2–18. *Remember these? A long value in scientific notation. The two values are identical.*

But if the column is *very* narrow, such that it can't even accommodate the scientific notation, Excel displays the data as shown in Figure 2–19. Called pound signs in the US and hash marks in the UK, they tell the user that the column is simply too narrow to display anything else. Pound signs *don't* suggest you've made a mistake—what

1000000000	####

Figure 2–19. *There's a value in there somewhere, and it's the same as the one you can see.*

they always mean, rather, is that a value's in there (never text), and you just can't see it. All you need to do here is to widen the column—but truth to be told, you can leave it as is, if you want to only use it in formulas and the like.

Entering Data into a Selected Range

Now let's get back to a data entry issue I pointed to earlier, but didn't discuss. You'll recall that when you select a range of cells, the first cell in the group remains white—that is, it doesn't turn blue:

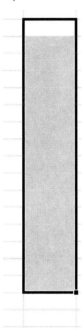

Figure 2–20. *Drawing a blank: the first cell in the selected range won't change color.*

Time to explain why. The first cell in a selected range maintains its original white appearance to let you know that when you start typing, the *data will enter that cell*. Moreover, if you conclude that data entry by pressing the Enter key, the range remains selected—and the *next* cell turns white:

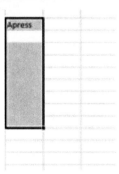

Figure 2–21. *Type now and the data will once again enter the white cell.*

You get the idea. Each tap of the Enter key turns the next cell white, designating the cell into which you'll be entering data.

But you may have a question about this sequence of events, because we don't appear to be learning anything new here. After all, pressing Enter *always* takes you down one row — so what's really different here? Good question.

The answer can be gleaned by considering this range selection, in this case L9:M18 (just to get you accustomed to range references):

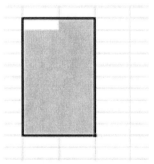

Figure 2–22. *A two-columned range selection*

Here's the point. If you enter data in each cell and press Enter, you'll once again bump down the column, for example:

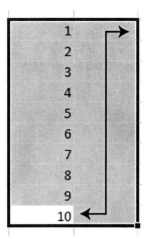

Figure 2–23. *Right now you're in cell L18.*

Now if you type a number and press Enter, you *won't* descend down a row; rather, you'll shoot up to cell M18—the first cell in the second selected column:

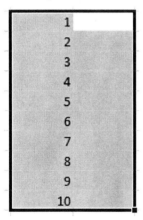

Figure 2–24. *Staying in range*

That's what it's about. Press the Enter key after you enter each item in a selected range and the white cell stays within the range bounds, rather than simply plunging down the column as it normally does. And again, after you've entered all the data in the range, click anywhere onscreen; the blue disappears, and the range is de-selected.

Using Auto Fill to Speed Up Data Entry

By now you may have taken notice of the small rectangle holding down the lower right corner of the cell pointer. It's called the fill handle:

Figure 2–25. *There it is.*

Why is the fill handle so named? It's because, among other things, you can fill a range with a collection of sequenced data—but what does that mean?

Copying a Value with Auto Fill

First, if you enter just *one* value or text item in a cell and drag on that cell's fill handle, you'll *copy* that item to as many cells as you drag. Thus if I enter 2 in a cell, click back into that cell and drag on the fill handle down its column, I'll copy the 2 into as many cells as I want:

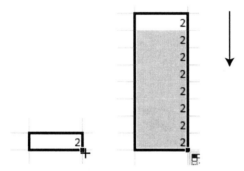

Figure 2–26. *One way to use the fill handle: to copy a value*

Auto Filling a Numeric Sequence

To see what I mean:

1. Type the values 1 and 2 anywhere in a column in adjacent rows.

2. Then select those two cells and release your mouse—an important step in an auto fill, which is what we're about to do:

Figure 2–27. *Having your fill—selecting the cells*

3. Then glide the mouse directly over the fill handle. You'll see a slender black cross:

Figure 2–28. *A new kind of cursor*

4. When you see it, click on it, and drag it down the column for as many rows as you wish. You should see:

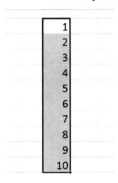

Figure 2–29. *Value-added: auto fill at work*

Pretty cool, no? What we did is start with just two values, which established a fill interval—in this case an interval of 1 (the 2 minus the 1). That tells Excel that every subsequent value will receive an increment of…1.

But you can really stipulate any increment you want. Start by entering say, the values 2 and 5 instead, and you'll auto fill 8, 11, 14, 17, etc. Enter 1 and 2.78 and you'll wind up with additional values of 4.56, 6.34, 8.12, etc.—that is, values pumped by 1.78.

Remember that to execute this kind of auto fill you need to enter the two starting values, select them and *then* release your mouse, without dragging. Only then do you return to the selection and start dragging.

Using Auto Fill with Text

But there's more. Enter the word Tuesday in any cell. Return to the cell, grab onto the fill handle, and start dragging to the right (as opposed to down the column. You can always drag the fill handle vertically or horizontally). You'll see:

| Tuesday | Wednesd; | Thursday | Friday | Saturday | Sunday |

Figure 2–30. *Those were the days.*

You see what's happened, and it isn't magic. Excel supplies the user with four built-in auto fill sequences—

- Days of the week
- Three-lettered abbreviations of days of the week (e.g. Tue, Wed)
- Months of the year
- Three-lettered abbreviations of months of the year (e.g., Jul, Aug).

And you can start any of these sequences at any point—that is, you needn't start with January, for example; and when you run out of months or days the sequence starts over again. Start with July, and when you reach the 13th cell in the sequence you get July again.

> **NOTE:** For appearance's sake you may need to tinker with the column widths, because each day consists of different word lengths—look at Wednesday in the above screen shot, for example.

Using the Auto Fill Option Button

When you drag the fill button and complete a filled list, you'll notice a button neighboring the fill handle, entitled Auto Fill options. If you had dragged a list featuring values spaced two apart by starting with the numbers 1 and 3, you see:

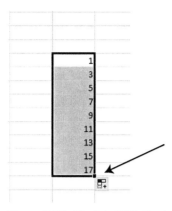

Figure 2-31. *The Auto Fill Option button*

Click it and you'll see these options:

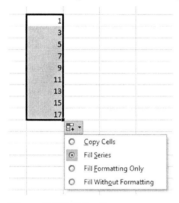

Figure 2-32. *Fill options*

The default selection, **Fill Series**, really identifies what you've just done. If I click **Copy Cells**, a curiously retroactive thing happens—the initial values, 1 and 3, are simply copied down the range:

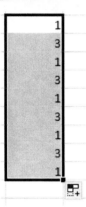

Figure 2–33. *The Copy Cells option*

The **Fill Formatting** option only copies the *formatting* associated with the original cells you've copied. Thus if the values 1 and 3 had exhibited a yellow background (we'll see how to do that in Chapter 5: "Formatting Your Data") selecting **Fill Formatting** will result in this:

Figure 2–34. *Fill Formatting—here, the values aren't filling down the range; only the formatting in the source cells carries over to the selected cells.*

The last option, **Fill Without Formatting**, executes the fill, but *doesn't* copy the formatting along with it:

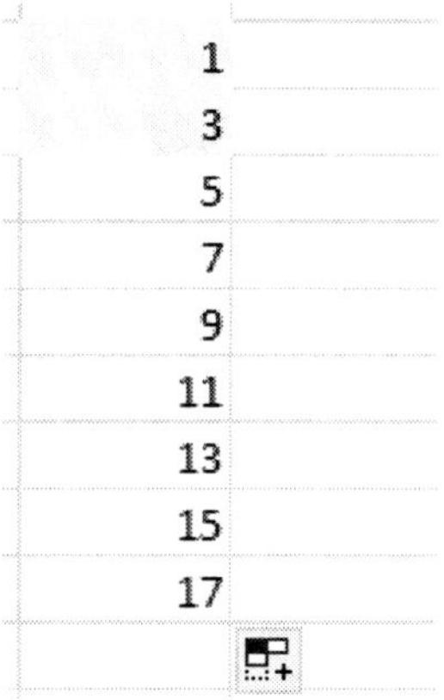

```
    1
    3
    5
    7
    9
   11
   13
   15
   17
```

Figure 2–35. *Fill Without Formatting—only the numerical sequence is carried out, without bringing the formatting along for the ride.*

Customizing Auto Fill Lists

Want more? You can also customize an auto fill list, say of friends or clients. That means that if you type one of the names in your customized list and drag it with your mouse, all the other names in the list will appear—just like the built-in days of the week list.

To devise a customized auto fill list:

1.   Click the **File tab** ➤ **Options** ➤ **Advanced** ➤ **Edit Custom Lists...** button:

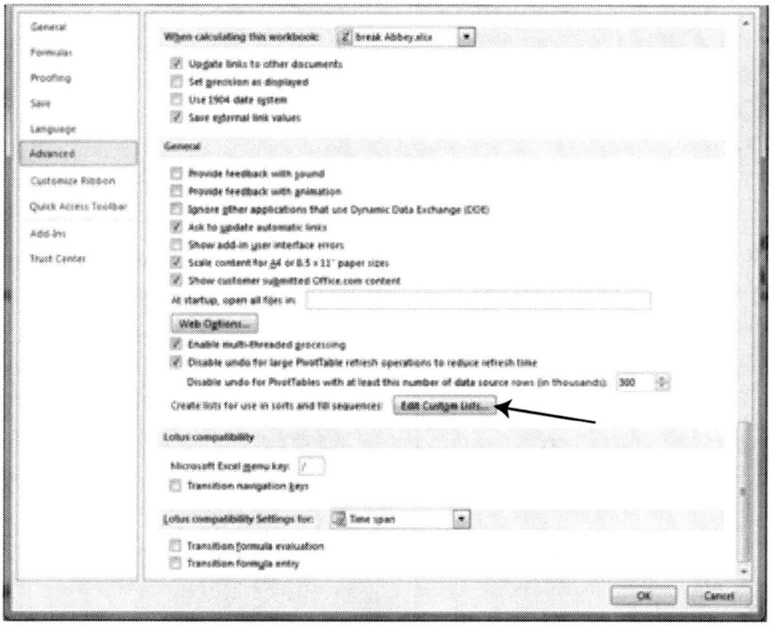

Figure 2–36. *The Edit Custom Lists button*

2.   You'll see the following. Note the four built-in lists we discussed earlier.
To start composing your own, just type the names in the List entries
area, and press Enter after each entry:

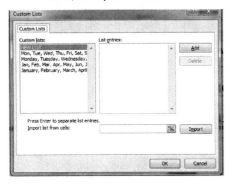

Figure 2–37. *The Custom Lists dialog box*

3.   When you're done, click the Add button. You'll see:

Figure 2–38. *Your own custom list*

4.   Click OK.

Now when you enter any one of those names in a cell (again, it doesn't have to be the
first in the list) and drag it with the fill handle, all the other names will appear across a
row or down a column, depending on the direction in which you drag, of course. Your
friends—and maybe even your boss—will be impressed.

Data Validation: Bringing Quality Control to the Worksheet

It isn't exciting, but data entry is at the heart of every worksheet. The most ingenious,
jaw-droppingly-brilliant melange of formulas and charts won't be worth a pixel if the
information it works with is suspect, and Excel recognizes that critical point by providing

its users with a series of data entry-control, or validation, options that help reduce the likelihood that bad data will compromise your results.

Here's a simple example: Suppose you need to enter the names of states in a range by their two-character abbreviation, the way the post office codes them. You could devise a data validation rule that restricts any data entry in a range of cells to exactly two characters—meaning that if you were to accidentally type CAL instead of CA, you'd be prevented from doing so.

You see the point. By engineering a data validation rule requiring two, and only two, characters in the designated cells your chance of inadvertently making a data entry mistake is narrowed. Of course, our rule wouldn't stop you from erroneously entering NY when you really wanted to type CA, because both have two characters, but it's a start.

So let's try to set up that two-character data validation rule to see how it works.

1. Select any cell and click the Data tab ➤ Data Validation button in the Data Tools button group. This sounds strange, but click either the upper half of the button or click the lower half or the small arrow and then click Data Validation. Quirky, but that's how this, and some other Excel buttons, work.

2. Now click the drop-down arrow by Allow in the Data Validation dialog. You'll see:

Figure 2–39. *Granting permission: The Data Validation Allow menu lets you decide what sort of data to allow in the selected cells.*

3. Click Text length and then "equal to" after you click the drop-down arrow by Data. You'll now see:

Figure 2–40 *Character test—specifying a two-character data entry requirement.*

NOTE: Clicking the button at the right end of the Length field will temporarily collapse, or shrink, the dialog box when you click it. Collapsing will allow you to see more of the worksheet. Just click the button a second time and the dialog box will return to its original size:

Figure 2–41. *Selected short subject: collapsing the dialog box, an option you'll see in many dialog boxes.*

4. Remember—we want to restrict the data in the selected cell to entries of exactly two characters, so just type 2 in the Length field and click OK.

5. Then try to type CAL in your selected cell and press Enter. You should see:

Figure 2–42. *Oops—we've typed one character too many.*

6. Because we've violated the data validation rule we established—by attempting to enter *three*-characters—Excel reminds us we can't do it. Either click Retry or Cancel and give it another go, this time restricting the input to two characters. This time, it'll work.

Just keep in mind that by clicking on "equal to" in the Data field we do mean exactly two characters. Entering one character in the cell will also provoke an error prompt. Had we wanted to specify a maximum two characters we could have selected the "less than" data option and typed 3, or "less than or equal to" and typed 2.

But note that Data Validation rules work with a kind of grandfather clause. If you've already entered CAL in a cell in which you *then* institute a two-character limit, Excel will let the current entry stand. Just don't try typing ARI in the cell *now*, though.

> **NOTE:** Establishing a text length data validation rule also affects the data entry of *values*. Thus the rule we've devised would also allow you to type 34, but not 3 or 344.

Once you understand how that example works you can try out some of other data validation options, such as between or greater than; these should now be pretty easy to work out.

And if you want to remove a data valuation rule, just select the relevant cells and click Data Validation ➤ Clear All ➤ OK.

> **NOTE:** If you want to *change* a data validation rule for a range of cells, just click one of the cells click Data Validation, make the change, and tick the "Apply these changes to all other cells with the same settings" check box. All the cells affected by the original rule will take on the rule change.

Making a List—Personalizing a Drop-Down Menu

One of the cooler data validation options is the ability to let you construct your own drop-down menu, from which you can choose from your own list of data. Thus instead of having to type Department names for each employee in our little database, you could batch up something that looks like this, and just click:

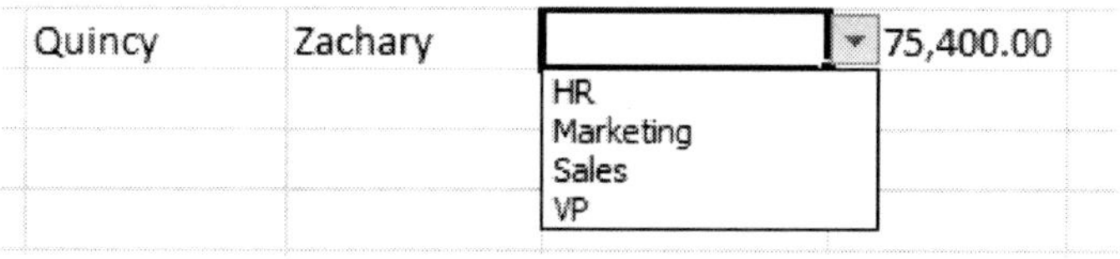

Quincy	Zachary		75,400.00
		HR	
		Marketing	
		Sales	
		VP	

Figure 2–43. *Fast-track data entry: Drop-down personalized menu*

It's easy to devise, too:

1. Enter the items that will populate the menu in consecutive cells. For example, in cells A2:A5 you could enter HR, Marketing, Sales, VP.

HR
Marketing
Sales
VP

Figure 2–44. *These names will populate the drop-down data entry menu.*

2. Select the range of cells where you want to use the drop-down menu (this is a different range from the one containing the options). That is, you want to select the cells in which the menu will actually appear when you click in any of its cells. In the figure below we'd select the cells in the Department column (you'll see this collection of data again in Chapter 7), but you can really select any column of cells to illustrate the point.

First Name ▼	Last Name ▼	Department ▼	Salary ▼	Raise ▼
Don	Albert	Sales	▼ 31,458.00	$33,030.90
Nora	Barnacle	Sales	$ 33,000.00	$34,650.00
Walter	Barton	HR	$ 25,000.00	$26,250.00
Brenda	Dawkins	VP	$ 72,000.00	$75,600.00
Alan	Dreiser	HR	$ 29,563.00	$31,041.15
Mary	Edwards	HR	$ 28,500.00	$29,925.00
Inez	Greer	Sales	$ 31,000.00	$32,550.00
Ted	Harris	Marketing	$ 30,000.00	$31,500.00
Greg	Heinz	HR	$ 42,568.00	$44,696.40
Donna	Lee	HR	$ 27,600.00	$28,980.00
Carl	Nunez	Marketing	$ 48,100.00	$50,505.00
Ned	Paulson	Sales	$ 40,000.00	$42,000.00
Bill	Rodgers	Sales	$ 32,000.00	$33,600.00
Kate	Vinson	VP	$ 72,451.00	$76,073.55
Quincy	Zachary	VP	$ 75,400.00	$79,170.00

Figure 2–45. *These cells will exhibit the drop-down menu.*

3. Click Data Validation. Select List in the Allow field.

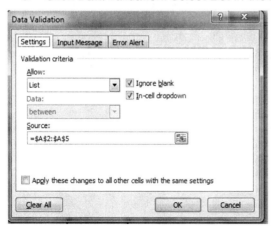

Figure 2–46. *Here's where you select the data that will appear in the drop-down menu.*

4. Click in the Source field, and select the range containing the drop-down menu items—in our case =$A$2:$A$5, or whatever range you're using. Note the dollar signs appear automatically when you select the range, because the drop-down menu will likely appear in a whole range of cells—and Excel doesn't want the drop-down source range for each of the cells to change as a result of relative cell addressing (see Chapter 4), i.e., A2:A5, A3:A6, A4:A7. Also remember that if you *name* the source range—to say Dept—all you need do is type =Dept in the Source field, and that's it.

5. Click OK.

6. The drop-down menu should be ready to go in the selected cells. Just click the drop-down arrow in each cell.

If you change any of the data whose entries appear in the drop-down—say VP to Vice-President—that new phrase will appear in all subsequent data entry using the drop-down menu. But existing records displaying VP won't be changed.

> **NOTE:** Instead of entering the *range* which contains the drop-down items in Source, you can also enter the actual drop-down items *directly in* the Source field instead, by typing HR, Marketing, etc., each separated by a comma. With this technique there are no dollar-sign issues.

Explaining Data Validation Errors with Error Alerts

Once you've subjected a range to a data validation rule you may want to provide the user with some information about what the rule does. We've already seen that Excel does that by default, by broadcasting the "The value you entered is not valid" message we saw in Figure 2–42. But you can customize that message via the Data Validation Error Alert feature, so that the user is told exactly what sort of data is and is not permitted in the cell. Thus you can compose a prompt that declares: "You must enter two characters in this cell"—and you can also provide an Error Alert that warns the user that the cell entry is wrong, but the cell will accept it anyway if the user wants to go ahead anyway.

There are three sorts of Error Alerts:

- Stop—Excel's default, which blocks entries that violate the data validation rule

- Warning—This notifies the user that the data entry violates the rule, but allows her either to try again or to override the rule

- Information—This one sounds like the others, but it just tells the user the data entry violates the rule—and goes ahead and accepts it

Let's see how to customize a data validation prompt:

1. Select the range of cells to which you've assigned the Data Validation rule.

2. Click Data Validation and click the Error Alert tab.

3. Select the Error Alert type you want to apply from the Style drop-down menu.

4. Type a Title and customized message. For example—if you select the Warning type, you could entitle the message Character Limit, and write: Only two characters permitted in this cell.

5. Click OK.

Once that's done, enter CAL—that is, three characters, and press Enter; you'll see

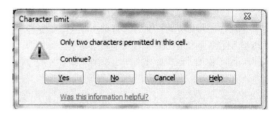

Figure 2–47. *Don't say we didn't warn you: A Warning Error Alert. The user will still be allowed to enter three characters anyway.*

Note the Continue? prompt, which is supplied by Excel.

Adding Data Entry Instructions with Input Messages

We've seen that Error Alerts tell the user if they've violated a data validation, and what they've done wrong. Input messages tell the user what sort of data is permitted in cells *before* the data is entered.

To demonstrate how this works:

1. Select that same range of cells with which you've been working.

2. Click Data Validation ➤
Input Message. You'll see:

Figure 2–48. *Delivering the message: The Input Message dialog box.*

3. Type Two-character limit in the Title field and "You must enter exactly two characters in this cell" in the Input Message field, and click OK.

4. Click in any cell in the selected range; you'll see:

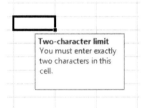

Figure 2–49. *Proactive prompt: an input message*

The idea is to pre-empt possible data entry mistakes, by letting the user know in advance what's allowed in the cells.

Summary

We've covered lots of ground in this chapter—literally. We've learned how to travel the length and breadth of the spreadsheet and how to introduce data into cells, once we've parked ourselves inside the ones we want, and we've learned how to fend off potential data enty miscues with an array of data validation techniques.

Knowing how to get around the worksheet, select its cells, and post data to them rank among the most essential Excel skills—and as you've seen, they're pretty easy. But sometimes you need to change what you've already done, and in the next chapter we'll see how to go about editing the contents of cells. It's pretty easy, too.

Chapter **3**

Editing Data

Once you've gotten the principles of data entry nailed down, you'll need to learn about the ways in which you can modify, or edit, the information you've posted to their cells. I'm going to introduce those editing techniques now, because, as someone once said, "Change is good" (when you need to make a change). And when you're working with Excel, it's easy too.

Changing Your Data

Needless to say, there will be times when you'll need to make changes to at least some of the data you've posted to your worksheet. For example, you may have made an error or two, or a data update may be in order. Excel makes editing easy, too, and as usual, presents you with a couple of options.

First and most simply, you can edit the contents of a cell by simply typing over what's already there. If you've entered the number 7 and discover you needed a 77 instead, just select the cell and type 77. Excel overwrites the original number.

However, if you've entered a lengthy expression that contains one small error into a cell, retyping all the contents of the cell for the sake of one correction doesn't seem terribly efficient. For example, say you typed "Now is the time for all good *mean*," but you meant *men*. Again, you could retype the whole phrase, but there are less troublesome ways to get what you want. Here's a more efficient tack:

1. Select the cell.

2. Click in the formula bar, right next to the *a* you want to remove, as shown in Figure 3–1.

V15	▼	⊙	✗	✓	*fx*	Now is the time for all good me|an

◢	G	H	I	J	K	L	M	N	O	P	
1											

Figure 3–1. *Nobody's perfect—I didn't mean "mean." Note that this correction is being made to the phrase in cell V15.*

3. Remember the formula bar—that strip in the upper reaches of your screen that affords you a view of exactly what you entered in the cell. Among other things, the formula bar gives you a place to very easily edit a cell. Here you can click precisely at the place in the phrase you want to change. and do some basic word processing. If you click to the left of the *a*, press the Delete key once and the letter will disappear. If you click to its right, press Backspace instead.

4. When you've finished your edits, press Enter or click the green check mark, and the edit is completed. Simple!

You can also add text to the cell in much the same way:

1. Click in the formula bar at the appropriate point in the text and just type. As with Word, the text will push the adjoining words aside.

2. Then press Enter or click the green check.

You can also edit data in a cell by deploying an ancient spreadsheet keystroke: the F2 key. Here, instead of clicking inside the formula bar, click the cell and press F2. The cursor will be placed at the end of text, as shown in Figure 3–2.

Now is the time for all good mean|

Figure 3–2. *Using the F2 key to get inside the cell*

Once the cursor is in the cell, you can press the left arrow key to make your way back to that surplus *a*. Once you're there, just backspace or delete, and then press Enter, and the deed is done.

Note as well that when you start to edit cells, the mode indicator lurking in the lower left of the status bar changes, as shown in Figure 3–3.

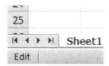

Figure 3–3. *The Edit mode indicator turns on when you begin the cell-editing process.*

Undoing an Edit

There's yet another way to revise the contents of your cells, though you might not think of it as an editing command—it's the Undo button, stored in the Quick Access toolbar (shown in Figure 3–4).

Figure 3–4. *The Undo button*

By clicking that button (or utilizing its keyboard equivalent, Ctrl+Z), you can nullify the command you've just executed (note that a small number of commands can't be undone, such as adding a new worksheet to the workbook). Moreover, if you click Undo repeatedly, each previous command will be repealed in succession. And if you click the small drop-down to the right of Undo, a history of the commands you've carried out this session will be shown on the screen, something like Figure 3–5.

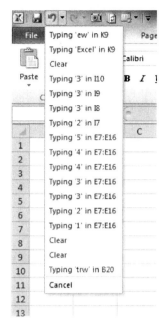

Figure 3–5. *Long memory: The Undo drop-down menu*

Drag your mouse through those commands you want to undo, as shown in Figure 3–6. Click your mouse, and those selections will be undone.

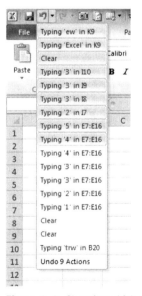

Figure 3–6. *Choosing which commands to undo*

NOTE: You can't skip over commands in the Undo history, undoing just some of them out of sequence. You can only undo consecutive commands.

Undoing What You've Just Undone with the Redo Button

There's a flip side to the Undo command, too: Redo, represented by that right-curling arrow just to the right of Undo, as shown in Figure 3–7.

Figure 3–7. *Having second thoughts? Undo the undos with Redo.*

When clicked (keyboard equivalent: Ctrl+Y), Redo can undo your undos, if that's not too discombobulating. That is, if you execute an undo and instantly regret it, then click Redo and that undo will be forgotten. And as with Undo, Redo also sports its own history via a drop-down menu (revealed by clicking the little arrow to the right of the Redo button), recording the commands you've undone. It works the same way as the Undo drop-down.

Deleting Cell Contents

Of course, the most dramatic way to edit a cell is to delete its contents—and if that's what you want to do, just select the cell and press the Delete key. But bear in mind that if you want to delete a *group* of cells, select them by using one of the methods already described in Chapter 2, and *then* press Delete, as shown in Figure 3–8.

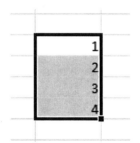

Figure 3–8. *First select the range of cells, and then press Delete.*

Copying and Moving: Duplicating and Relocating Your Data

There will be times—probably many times—when you'll want to make a copy of a range of data. The basic means for doing so are pretty basic and easy, and resemble the ways you'd carry out the process in Word. At other times you'll want to move a range—an equally easy process that also goes under the storied name of cut-and-paste.

Copying Data

As usual, Excel presents the user with several ways in which to copy data, but we'll start with the textbook approach. To copy, do the following:

1. Select the range you wish to copy.

2. Click Home tab, and choose Copy from the Clipboard button group (see Figure 3–9).

Figure 3–9. *The Copy button*

3. Your range will be surrounded by what are called *marching ants* (really), those animated dashes trooping around the range (see Figure 3–10).

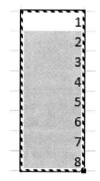

Figure 3–10. *On the march: The ants are part of the copy process.*

4. Click in the *first* cell of the destination range—that is, the area in the worksheet to which you want to paste the copied data (see Figure 3–11).

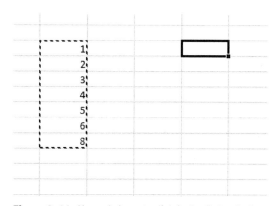

Figure 3–11. *You only have to click in the first cell of the destination range.*

5. Click Home, and then click Paste in the Clipboard button group (see Figure 3–12).

Figure 3–12. *The Paste button*

You're done (see Figure 3–13). The keyboard equivalents for copy and paste, by the way, are Ctrl+C and Ctrl+V, respectively.

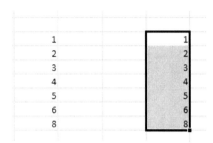

Figure 3–13. *The destination range receives all the copied cells.*

To summarize, the copying process asks you to select what it is you want to copy, and then to indicate where the copy is going to be pasted on the worksheet. Note that when you paste, you need only click in the first cell of the destination range, because Excel is smart enough to know that if you're copying 12 cells, you're going to paste 12, too (see Figure 3–14). And note there's another keyboard equivalent to Paste available in this context—pressing the Enter key.

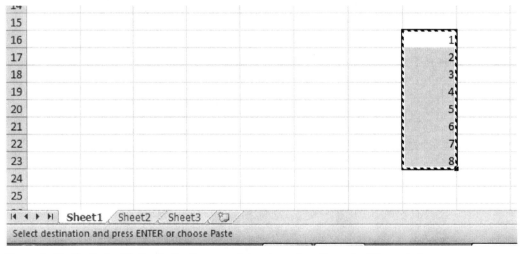

Figure 3–14. *The first cell in the destination range determines where the rest will be pasted.*

Moving Data

Moving data isn't much different from copying and pasting it. Select the range, but this time click Home ➤ Cut (see Figure 3–15). The keyboard equivalent for cut is Ctrl+X.

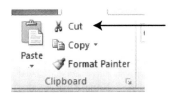

Figure 3–15. The Cut button

Note that, curiously, clicking Cut *doesn't* cause the range to disappear from the screen immediately; the data stays there until you click in the first cell in the destination range and then click Paste (or press Ctrl+V). Only then does it get uprooted from its original position and move to its new range.

> **NOTE:** Deleting data is not an equivalent to cutting it. When you press the Delete key, the data you've erased cannot be pasted elsewhere on the worksheet—it's gone. Pasting is possible only when you *cut* the data first.

The Clipboard: The Storage Area for Copied and Cut Data

By now, you may have taken note of the button image characterizing the Paste command: a clipboard, in the Clipboard button group (see Figure 3–16).

Figure 3–16. The Paste button

The image alludes to an area in Excel's brain, naturally enough called the Clipboard, in which data that you've copied and/or cut is stored until you decide to paste it. The Clipboard can warehouse up to 24 *different* copied or cut items, all of which can be pasted to your worksheet when you wish. To see what I mean, let's try it out.

1. On a blank worksheet, type the text shown in Figure 3–17 (i.e., the text in cells C9:C12 and the values in cell I11:I13.

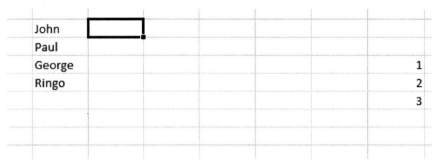

Figure 3–17. *The Fab Four and three values*

2. Then click the dialog box launcher in the Clipboard button group. That's the small arrow by the Clipboard title, as shown in Figure 3–18.

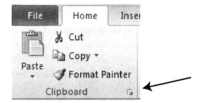

Figure 3–18. *The Clipboard dialog box launcher*

3. The Clipboard dialog box will appear, as shown in Figure 3–19. Select the text in cells C9:C12.

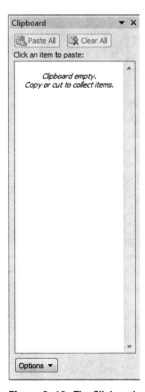

Figure 3–19. *The Clipboard area*

4. Click Copy, and the text shown in Figure 3–20 will appear in the Clipboard area.

Figure 3–20. *Your copied text, stored and ready to paste*

5. Then immediately select the values in cells I11:I13, and copy them as well. The Clipboard should now displays what's shown in Figure 3–21.

Figure 3–21. *Your choice: You can paste either—or both!*

The Clipboard now records two entries, either one of which can be pasted by simply clicking in a destination cell and then clicking the Clipboard item you need.

Note as well that by clicking Clear All you can empty the Clipboard, and by clicking the X in the Clipboard's upper-right corner you stop it from being displayed.

Summary

Once you build up your data entry and editing chops, you'll want to start learning about the ways you can *do* something with the data—that is, writing formulas and using other means for gleaning something new from the information you've posted to the workbook. Entering test scores is one thing; but calculating a test *average*—ah, that's what Excel's about. Just turn the page.

Chapter 4

Number Crunching 101: Functions, Formulas, and Ranges

What makes Excel so powerful, and maybe even exciting, is its ability to bring something to the worksheet that wasn't there before. Taking a column of sales figures and finding their average or determining the highest score on a test—automatically—is really what Excel is about. If all you're doing is entering names and values on the worksheet without *doing* something to that information, you're probably using the wrong application—sort of a souped-up Word, only with cells instead of paragraphs. Learning how to compose your own Excel formulas and use Excel's built-in calculations, called *functions*, allow you to use some of Excel's real potential.

And you'll see that formulas tie into ranges—because your formulas often work with many cells at the same time (e.g., for computing sums, averages, and many other mathematical operations).

Of course, this is a mighty big subject, and learning all the things Excel can do in this area would require a book a whole lot larger—and more expensive—than you'd be prepared to pay for. What we're going to do here introduce the essentials—the things you have to know in order to get your money's worth—both from this book and from Excel.

Automatic Calculations with Functions

We'll start with functions and see how to carry out all sorts of calculations on your data.

Adding a Column of Numbers

So let's cut to the chase. Say you need to add that column of numbers—the classic Excel task.

1. In cells H3:H7, enter the values shown in Figure 4–1.

    45
    67
    81
    23
    51

Figure 4–1. *It will all add up: The numbers we want to add.*

NOTE: Don't get the wrong idea—the actual values we've entered don't particularly matter, and more importantly the *number* of values populating in the column doesn't really matter either. The procedure for adding 50,000 values in a column works the same way as adding just 5.

2. Next, click in cell H8, click the **Home** tab, and choose **AutoSum** from the **Editing** button group (see Figure 4–2).

Figure 4–2. *The Editing button group*

You should now see what's shown in Figure 4–3.

Figure 4–3. *In summation: We're about to add all those numbers.*

Let's take note of what we're looking at. Clicking the **AutoSum** button in H8 installs the expression shown in Figure 4–3. This expression uses Excel's built-in SUM function:

`=SUM(H3:H7)`

And what is that expression telling us? It's telling us that Excel plans to add all the values in the range H3:H7. Press Enter and you'll see the result, 267, in cell H8. Voila!

This expression is called a *formula* (you can tell a formula because it starts with an equal sign (=), and this formula displays the result of the SUM function. You can read the formula as "The contents of this cell equal the result of the SUM function." In the "Customizing the Worksheet with Formulas" section later in this chapter, I will teach you how to write formulas from scratch. For now we are going to use the built-in functions, which make writing formulas quick and easy (and it's the functions that we really care about, because they do the hard work for us).

> **NOTE:** If you *double-click* the **AutoSum** button, it will display its result immediately in its cell, without stopping to reveal its formula as in Figure 4–3.

Now type **71** in cell H4, replacing the original 67. Cell H8 will now show 271. This demonstrates what's perhaps the single greatest contribution of spreadsheets to Western civilization: automatic recalculation. Once a formula has been placed on a worksheet, any change in the values used in the formula will immediately change the formula's result. There's no need to rewrite the formula—it delivers the new result automatically. Just change the contributing values, and the answer changes.

Returning to our example, we see that it works because SUM is programmed to add all the values in the cells directly above it (or to its left, if you're adding values in a row); that is, it adds the cells that actually *contain* a value. And that means that if we had encountered this range shown in Figure 4–4 in H3:H7 instead, and had clicked **AutoSum** again in H8, we'd have seen the result shown in Figure 4–5.

45
67
23
51

Figure 4–4. *Something's missing: Adding (or trying to add) the values in this range*

Figure 4–5. *Same range, different result: Excel adds the cells containing values, until it encounters a cell that's either blank or contains text.*

What Excel does here is incorporate each cell directly above H8 into its formula, until it lands upon a cell that's vacant—in this case, H5. Thus, Excel here would plan to add only the values in H6 and H7.

This is interesting, but it presents us with a problem—what do we do if we still want to add all the values in the range H3:H7?

Selecting the Range You Need

To remedy this, instead of pressing Enter as in the previous example—which produced the result 267—this time click and drag H3 through H7, as shown in Figure 4–6. Now the expression in H8 should read as follows =SUM(H3:H7), just as it did in our original case. Then press Enter.

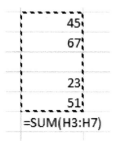

Figure 4–6. *Selecting the entire range you want*

What you should learn from this second case—the case of the missing value in cell H5—is that the user can always override Excel's decision about which cells are going to be added with SUM. When you click **AutoSum**, Excel first displays the range it's about to add, as per the screenshots; and if you approve, just press Enter. But if you want to add the cells in a different range—which can be anywhere in the worksheet—not just in the same column—then click and drag across that range, and only then press Enter (see Figure 4–7).

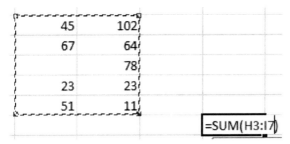

=SUM(H3:I7)

Figure 4–7. *Note that SUM is being calculated in a different column here, and that the range to be summed spans two columns.*

> **NOTE:** Another AutoSum button is available on the **Formulas** tab in the **Function Library** button group, and it works in precisely the same way.

Now here's another question: what does AutoSum do when you place it in a cell that's *both* at the bottom of a column and to the right of a row of data, as in Figure 4–8?

Figure 4–8. *Placing the cursor at the bottom right of the data*

In this case, AutoSum adds the values in the *column*, on the assumption that people more typically add values in the vertical direction.

Viewing and Editing Your Formula: Back to the Formula Bar

We've already talked about the formula bar—that long white strip bordering the upper rim of the worksheet, used for recording the contents of the cell in which you've clicked. Now you're going to see what the formula bar is really about. Click in cell H8 and direct your attention to the formula bar. You'll see what's shown in Figure 4–9.

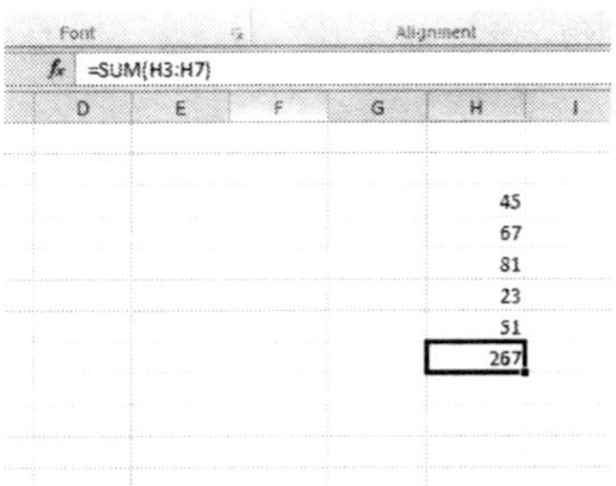

Figure 4–9. *Compare and contrast: Look at H8 and its contents in the formula bar.*

Quite a contrast! The value 267—the result of the SUM we carried out—appears in H8, and of course that's what we want to see on the screen. But the formula bar displays the *formula* in H8 that gave rise to that 267. That's an important difference, because it lets you—or someone else—know that we didn't merely type the value 267 in cell H8; rather we performed a mathematical operation that brought about that total, and the formula bar verifies that claim. So if you *really* want to know what's going on in a cell, click in it and look to the formula bar.

> **NOTE:** Clicking the **Formulas** tab and then **Formula Auditing ➤ Show Formulas** displays *formulas* in the cells in which they've been written, instead of the formula *results* you normally see. To get back to the results, just click **Show Formula** again. This option is a useful way to see all the formulas you've written, if you need to edit them.

And the formula bar provides an easy place in which you can edit the formula, too. For example, as in Figure 4–10, you can edit the range in the formula bar to add the cells in the range H3:I7 instead. Just click in the bar containing a formula, make the changes you need, and press Enter or click the Enter check mark alongside the formula bar.

Figure 4–10. *Editing the formula*

In a nutshell, that's how to use AutoSum, a fast way to execute probably the most important mathematical operation you'll need to perform in a worksheet. But Excel has many more functions in its bag of tricks (including some additional ones that appear when you click the arrow alongside **AutoSum**), which calculate all sorts of things, most of which you probably won't need to know. It's not likely, for example, that you'll ever have to calculate the inverse matrix for a matrix stored in an array—whatever that might mean. But while you and I might not be concerned about that kind of capability, there are people out there who are, and there's probably a function in there that does just what they're looking for.

However, the more functions you know, the better, and there are at least a few that you *should* know about. If you click the drop-down arrow alongside **AutoSum** you'll see the list shown in Figure 4–11.

Figure 4–11. *Additional popular functions*

These work in an identical manner to AutoSum itself; that is, you can click in a cell directly beneath a range of values if you want Excel to automatically use that range, and then click any of the functions shown in the figure. Let's look at each one in turn. Table 4–1 summarizes them.

Table 4–1. *Additional Functions You Can Access Directly by Clicking the AutoSum Button*

Name	What It Does
Average	Calculates the average of a range of values; ignores cells containing text
Count Numbers	*Counts* the number of cells in a range containing values
Max	Calculates the highest value in a range of values
Min	Calculates the smallest value in range of values

NOTE: The functions described in Table 4–1 ignore any blank cells they encounter in the designated range. That means, for example, that AVERAGE won't treat a blank cell as if it were equal to zero.

Calculating an Average

So, let's see how to calculate an average, with the blank-cell rule from before in mind. Now, if you were to click **Average**, you'd get the AVERAGE function in cell H8, and you'd see what's shown in Figure 4–12.

Figure 4–12. *Just your AVERAGE Excel function*

Press Enter and you'll see 56.6 in cell H8.

> **NOTE:** Don't worry yet about decimal points and how to round them off; that's covered in Chapter 5.

And as with SUM, you can always drag your mouse across an alternative range if you don't like the one that Excel suggests. And there's no reason why you can't drag across several columns as well as down many rows. This expression is perfectly legal, then:

=AVERAGE(A12:C32)

Displaying Values Based on a Certain Condition

Again, there are a couple of hundred other functions out there for you to explore, but we're going to illustrate just one more. It's called IF, and it carries out an action in a cell provided another cell meets a certain condition (or conditions) that you establish.

What does that mean? Consider this simple scenario: you're a teacher who's given an exam with a passing grade of 65. You want to be able to list your class scores on a worksheet and automatically determine at a glance which students have passed.

In cell I12, enter the grade 66. OK, we know the grade is a pass, but we could be assessing dozens, or even hundreds, of scores at the same time, where the pass/fail evidence in every student's case wouldn't be quite so clear, because you might miss a score as you visually scan a long column of scores.

Click in cell J12 and type =I. I know that's a rather cryptic thing to write, but we're stopping there because you'll notice that something is already happening on the screen, as shown in Figure 4–13.

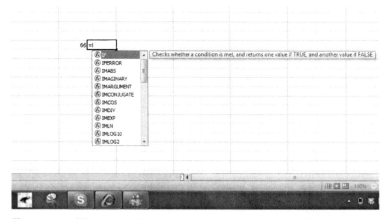

Figure 4–13. *What starts to happen when you begin to enter the IF function (or any function)*

What's happening is that Excel already knows you've started to write a function. It knows because you've begun the expression by typing the = sign plus a letter (in this case *I*). This has triggered what's called the *Formula AutoComplete*, that drop-down menu that lists function names, narrowing down the selection as you continue to type letters. Since IF happens to be the first function starting with the letter *I*, the blue highlight you see in the screenshot lands on it. Then press Tab (not Enter), and you'll see what's shown in Figure 4–14.

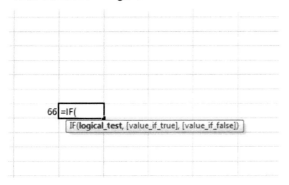

Figure 4–14. *The caption identifies the elements of the function.*

The Formula AutoComplete is trying to tell you the kinds of things that make up the IF statement—things like logical tests. But for now we're going to just type. Inside that open parentheses type the following, and then press Enter:

```
I12>=65,"Pass","Fail")
```

You should see the word *Pass* in cell J12, as shown in Figure 4–15. We've done it. The student has passed the exam—and again, while we knew that already, we've let the cell make that decision, not us.

Figure 4–15. *A passing grade—barely*

Now type 60 in cell I12; the word *Fail* will now appear in cell J12.

Now I'll explain what we've written. The IF statement in its entirety reads as follows:

```
=IF(I12>=65,"Pass","Fail")
```

- I12>=65 is called a *logical test*, which is the condition that the value in cell I12 is asked to meet; that is, is the test score equal to or greater than 65? If it is, then what? Well, then the word *Pass* appears in cell J12—the cell in which we've placed this function.

- *Pass*—or "Pass", as it has been written, is called the *value if true* (see the caption in Figure 4–14), which is the result that will appear in J12 if the condition is met. Since in our first case, in which the student scored 66, the condition is indeed met, *Pass* appears in the cell.

- In our second try, in which the student scored 60, the word *Fail* appears instead. This is because the score hasn't met the condition (the logical test), and failure to meet that condition triggers the *value if false* (see Figure 4–14.—in this case, the word *Fail*.

Got all that? If not, with a bit of playing around with the expression (e.g., you could edit it to enter a different passing score), it will start making more sense. As usual, practice is the hidden ingredient.

Revisiting Function Structure

Now I'll offer a few general observations about how to use functions:

- You must write an equal sign (=) before you can use the function (functions can only appear in formulas).

- The equal sign is always followed by the function's name (e.g., SUM or AVERAGE).

- A parenthesis always comes next in the expression, and the function always concludes with a closed parenthesis, like so: =AVERAGE(A23:A72)

- The kind of information you enter *between* the parentheses varies, from ranges to logical tests.

NOTE: You can also always type the function if you wish, instead of clicking button options.

Locating Functions in the Function Library

As already stated, Excel has hundreds of functions that do all kinds of things. When I was first exposed to functions sometime during the last century, I was mystified why anyone would actually want to use these curiously named things, and they seemed bewilderingly obscure. But as I began to learn more about spreadsheets, I began to appreciate the many uses to which functions can be put, and the more you know about them, the more you'll be able to do in Excel.

All of Excel's functions are stored in a collection of buttons in the **Function Library** button group on the **Formulas** tab, as shown in Figure 4–16.

Figure 4–16. *Good reading: The Function Library*

Table 4–2 briefly summarizes the types of functions contained in each group.

Table 4–2. *Function Types*

Group Name	Kind of Function
AutoSum	Contains the same function list you'll see when you click the AutoSum button on the Home tab.
Recently Used	Lists the last ten functions you've used.
Financial	Lets you perform many kinds of financial calculations, including interest projections and investment yields.
Logical	Includes IF and other functions that help you decide between alternatives (e.g., AND and OR). For example, the statement =IF(OR(A2>=65,A3>=65),"Pass","Fail") means that if *either* score in cell A2 or A3 equals 65 or higher, then the student passes.
Text	Contains functions that let you learn information about cells containing text. For example, =RIGHT(D12,2) will yield an answer of AB in a cell containing the text XYZ-AB, by identifying the two rightmost characters in the cell.
Date & Time	Lets you work with chronological data. For example, the function NOW(), which has nothing between its parentheses, will tell you the precise time when you enter new data in the spreadsheet, and will update whenever you enter new data.
Lookup & Reference	Lets you find particular data in a range, among other tasks. The VLOOKUP function, for example, can look up a person's income in a table and tell her how much tax she owes.
Math & Trig	Contains many mathematical and trigonometric functions, including SUM.
More Functions	Contains a host of additional functions, including ones that perform statistical and engineering tasks.

By clicking the arrow at the bottom of each button, you'll be able to view a list of all the functions assigned to that group; hovering your arrow over any name yields a brief description of what that function does. Figure 4–17 shows what you'll see if you rest your mouse over IF, stored in the Logical group.

Figure 4–17. *Excel describes the function when you scroll over it.*

If you go ahead and click IF, you'll be brought to a dialog box that prompts you to fill in the blanks—blanks consisting of precisely the parts of the function between the parentheses shown in Figure 4–18.

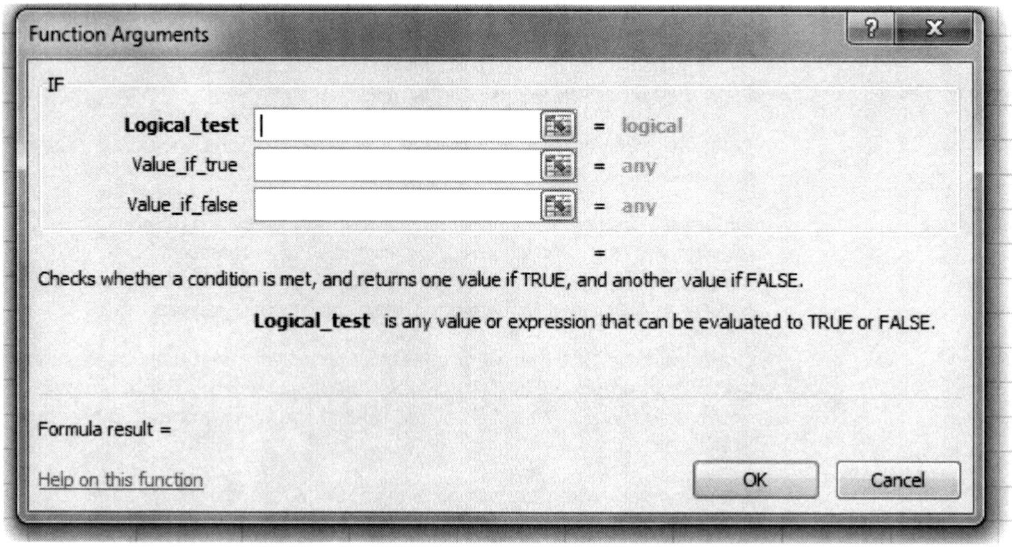

Figure 4–18. *Look familiar? The dialog box prompts you to enter data in the three IF elements between the parentheses. In our test example, "Pass" is Value_if-True, and "Fail" is Value_if_False.*

Thus, if you look back to that exercise, you would type **I12>=65** in the Logical_test field, and and then supply the value_if_true and value_if false consequences, e.g., "Pass" or "Fail" (note that these between-the-parentheses elements are called *arguments*), and when they're all filled, you'd click OK. And as you click in each of the fields, a small explanation what the field does appears in the dialog box. If you click the **Help on this function** link in the lower left of the dialog box, you will be delivered a lengthier discussion of how the function works and is written. Just remember that each function will ask you to fill in a different set of blanks, depending on what it does.

Customizing the Worksheet with Formulas

While functions are an integral part of the spreadsheet process, there may be times when you need to do something more specific to your data, something that a built-in function can't anticipate. For example—what if you wanted to give every student a bonus of three points after a challenging exam? Or what if you needed to calculate the local sales tax on a series of purchases? Excel can't supply a function to carry out just those intentions, and so you may have to write a formula—or a series of formulas—which do the work you need done.

Formulas can be very simple, or can get very complicated. They can incorporate Excel functions, or they can exist in a stand-alone capacity. Here we're going to explore the essentials of formula writing, so you can get going and do real work with them.

Writing a Basic Formula

Formulas always begin with the equal sign. They follow with cell references, actual values, and one or more mathematical operators. OK—what does that all mean?

Let's see. Here's an example of a very simple formula:

=6+8

And here's another one:

=D3/R9

In the first case, we're adding 6 and 8—pretty obvious, but just remember to include that equal sign. Leave it out, and all you'll see in the cell is 6+8.

In the second case, we're *dividing* the contents of cell D3 by the contents of cell R9. Change the contents in either or both cells, and the result automatically recalculates, as usual. You can simply type that formula or click the respective cells—that is, type =, click cell D3, type the division sign (/), click cell R9, and press Enter (Figure 4–19):

Figure 4–19. *Note that the two cells referenced by the formula are surrounded by borders as you write it.*

Table 4–3 shows how Excel represents mathematical operators.

Table 4–3. *Excel Operators*

Operator	What It Does
+	Addition
-	Subtraction
/	Division
*	Multiplication
^	Exponentiation (4^2 means 4 squared, or 16)

And by the way, it's perfectly fine to combine functions with your own formula elements in the same expression; and as you grow more experienced, you'll probably be doing that sort of thing often. For example—you could write

=SUM(A12:A68)/7

This formula would add all the values in cells A12:A68, and divide that result by 7.

You could also write

`=7/SUM(A12:A68)`

This would divide 7 by the sum of all the values in cells A12:A68.

And that's just for starters. When you begin to see and appreciate how these various parts can interact, you'll be making a leap in your Excel understanding.

> **NOTE:** Remember, formulas are subject to automatic recalculation, so any change in the values contributing to the formula will immediately change the formula's result.

Working Out the Order of Operations in a Formula

Once you start writing formulas, you need to keep something else in mind—something you may not have thought about since high school. Ask yourself, what result does this formula deliver?

`=32+4/3`

Hmmm. You could be adding 32 and 4 and then dividing that result by 3, yielding 12—or are you starting with 32 and simply adding 4/3 to it?

That sort of ambiguity leads us to Excel's order of operations—a priority listing of which sort of mathematical operation is carried out first when a formula encounters the kind of mixed message just shown. Here's the listing, arrayed in order of priority (don't worry, I'll explain):

1. Parentheses

2. Exponentiation

3. Multiplication

4. Division

5. Addition/subtraction

Consider this formula:

`=(54+6)*3-2`

Here, Excel takes the two values between the parentheses, 54 and 6, and adds them, yielding 60. It then multiplies that result by 3, and *then* subtracts 2 from 180, winding up with 178. Finally, 60 times 3 equals 180, and 180 minus 2 yields 178. The order of operations is confirmed:

1. Treat the values within parentheses as a unit.

2. Then give priority to multiplication, and then to subtraction.

What Excel *won't* do, then, is take the 60 and multiply it by 3 – 2, yielding 60. Play around with some of your own examples and the order of operations will become clearer.

Copying Formulas: More Than Just Duplication

I've already discussed how to copy data and formats through the format painter. But copying formulas introduces something new, something important. Let's see what that means.

1. Enter the test data shown in Figure 4–20 in a blank spreadsheet, starting at cell J7.

Student	Score
John	77
Bill	91
Dorothy	62
Sue	59
Ed	78

Figure 4–20. *Tough test*

2. Save the file under the name Student Scores.

3. Now let's say that, because the scores are on the low side (these could be scores relative to a test score maximum of say, 120, but it doesn't much matter), the teacher decides to award a five-point bonus—and as a result, needs to write a formula that will impart that bonus to all the students. Enter the word **Bonus** to serve as a heading in cell L7, and in L8, write

   =K8+5

That little formula delivers a score of 82 to John, boosting his original 77. The question is how to award the same bonus to all the students, along with the implied question of what would happen if the class consisted of 100 students instead of just the five in our example.

The one thing the teacher *won't* do is write the formula for each student—that's way too inconvenient. The alternative is to *copy* the original formula down the L column, but we need to describe how that works.

There are several ways to copy a formula; we'll look at two of them. The first is very similar to the technique discussed in Chapter 2.

The Classic Copy-and-Paste Method

1. Click the cell you want to copy—in this case L8.

2. Click the **Copy** button via **Home ➤ Clipboard ➤ Copy** sequence.

3. Select the destination cells—in this case L9:L12.

4. Click the **Paste** button (in the **Clipboard** button group) or press Enter. You should see what's shown in Figure 4–21.

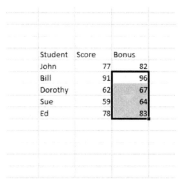

Student	Score	Bonus
John	77	82
Bill	91	96
Dorothy	62	67
Sue	59	64
Ed	78	83

Figure 4–21. *Teacher with a heart: There's that five-point bonus.*

Note that we obviously *haven't* copied John's grade to the other students—we've copied his *formula*; and when you copy a formula, Excel changes the cell references in the destination cells to reflect their distance from the source cell. That means that since our source formula reads

=K8+5

Bill's formula is going to read

=K9+5

because his data sits one row beneath John's. That one row down brings about a one-row change in his formula—from K8 to K9. And since Ed's grade-bonus formula is positioned in cell L12, it reads

=K12+5

to reflect its distance in rows—four rows, to be exact—from John's source formula.

This property of copied cell references—the fact that they record their degree of distance from the original source cell—is called *relative cell addressing* (or referencing), because the copied cells change their addresses *relative* to the source cell—the one that's being copied.

And that also means that if you were to copy a source formula horizontally (i.e., across a series of *columns*, not down a series of rows as per our example), relative cell addressing would change the *column* element of the cell address—its letter. Thus, if you copy =K8+5 one column to the right, the destination cell will read

=L8+5

Relative cell addressing is one of those Excel features you have to know, because copying formulas to destination cells is an extremely common part of the spreadsheet construction process. Relative cell addressing requires that you write just one formula in one cell—all you need to do next is copy that one formula to all the other cells with which you're working. Thus, if our hypothetical class consisted of 100—or even 1,000—students, you'd still need only construct one formula, which you'd then copy to all the other cells.

Next I'll discuss the second way in which to copy a formula. First, delete cells L9:L12, because we're trying out copy method number two. Then do the following:

1. Click back in the source cell, L8.

2. Click the fill handle—that small square holding down the lower-right corner of the cell pointer (see Figure 4–22).

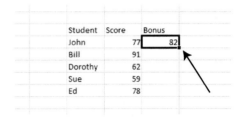

Student	Score	Bonus
John	77	82
Bill	91	
Dorothy	62	
Sue	59	
Ed	78	

Figure 4–22. *The fill handle revisited*

3. Click the fill handle and drag it through cell L12.

Different technique, same result. And there's a cool, very useful variation on that technique you'll want to know about. If you click L8 and *double-click* the fill handle instead of dragging it, the source formula will be copied to all the cells through L12, too. This double-click method works when consecutive cells to the *immediate* left or right of the formula column have values in them. Thus, if K10 had been blank in our case, this technique would have copied the formula only through L9.

> **NOTE:** When I introduced copying in Chapter 2, I stated that you only have to click *one* destination cell when you copy multiple source cells, because Excel knows that all the source cells have to be pasted. But here, because you're only copying *one* cell to multiple cells, you need to go ahead and select all those cells to which you're copying.

Moving Formulas: An Important Difference

You can move formulas with the techniques described in Chapter 2:

1. Select the formula-bearing cells you want to move.

2. Click the **Cut** command.

3. Click in the first destination cell.

4. Click **Paste**.

But when you're moving formulas, you're moving cell references, and here's where the difference lies. When you move a formula, the cell references in the formula *don't change.* That's because Excel assumes you want that formula to continue to refer to the *same* cells, even though it's being relocated.

Thus, if you write

=A2+C2

in cell D2 and move it somewhere—anywhere—else, Excel will think that you still want the formula to add cells A2 and C2 (see Figure 4–23).

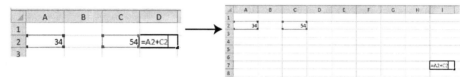

Figure 4–23. *Moving the formula won't change its cell references. Notice it's fjrst been posted in cell D2, and in the second screenshot has been moved to I7 without an change in its cell references.*

On the other hand, say you leave your formula in place in cell D2 but move the number in A2 instead, to cell B6. The formula will now state

=B6+C2

That is, it *will* reflect the new destination of the *values that contribute to a formula.*

The bottom line is this: if you move a formula, or any of the cells that contribute to the formula instead, Excel assumes either way that you won't want to change the *result* of the formula—and so it makes the adjustments necessary to see to it that the result is unchanged by any changes in cell addresses.

Keeping a Cell Reference Constant with Absolute Addressing

As stated, understanding relative cell addressing is one of those must-know features that Excel depends on in order to, well, make it Excel. But there's an additional aspect to copying formulas that's just about as important.

Let's say our teacher isn't yet sure how large that grade bonus should be, and wants to try out different point awards to see how they affect the test grades. In cell N7, the teacher enters the number 4 instead, and rewrites the original formula in cell L8 to read

=K8+N7

As you see, we've removed the number 5 and replaced it with a cell reference—cell N7, which currently contains the value 4. Thus, John's bonus score right now stands at 81, as shown in Figure 4–24.

Figure 4–24. *John's bonus-awarding formula*

The advantage of using the cell reference is that if the teacher decides to change the grade bonus, all she needs to do is type that new bonus in cell N7 and John's grade will change automatically. The next step, then, is to copy this new formula to all the other students down the L column, as before, using any of the methods described previously. But this time something is going to go wrong.

When you go ahead with our formula copy, you'll see the content of Figure 4–25.

Student	Score	Bonus		4
John	77	81		
Bill	91	91		
Dorothy	62	62		
Sue	59	59		
Ed	78	78		

Figure 4–25. Not much of a bonus! Note the 4 points in cell N7.

What went wrong is that it appears that only John received the bonus. Why hasn't anyone else received it?

Absolute Addressing: When We *Don't* Want It to Work

Here's the answer. If you look at cell L9—the cell containing Bill's "bonus" grade (all you have to do is click L9 and look at the formula bar)—you'll see the following:

=K9+N8

Well, that's supposed to happen, because of the relative cell addressing feature introduced previously. But what value is in cell N9? Nothing; cell N9 is blank. And 91 plus nothing is 91. Bill's score is unchanged.

And if you look at Dorothy's cell, L10, you'll see

=K10+N9

Same problem. Both cell references have changed as we would expect, but again, there's nothing in cell N10—and so on for all the other students. Only John's bonus has kicked in. It's all because here we want all the students' formulas to refer to cell N8, the cell in which the bonus is stored. But because copied formulas exhibit relative cell addressing, they *change* their references relative to their distance from the source cell. What to do?

Introducing an Absolute Cell Address

What we do is edit the original source formula in cell L8—the cell containing John's bonus—to read

=K8+N$7

Note the obvious change: the addition of a dollar sign to the left of the 7, which identifies the row in the cell reference of N7. The dollar sign doesn't represent a currency format; rather, it freezes the 6 so that when you copy this formula down the L column, the cell reference N7 won't change.

To see what that means, delete the bonus data in the L column and enter

=K8+N$7

in John's bonus score cell of L8. Copy that formula down the column again. You should see the data shown in Figure 4–26.

Student	Score	Bonus		4
John	77	81		
Bill	91	95		
Dorothy	62	66		
Sue	59	63		
Ed	78	82		

Figure 4–26. *That's more like it!*

Save the workbook. At last, the bonus has been applied to all the students, because *all* the bonus cell formulas now reveal the N$7 reference, which won't change, even if you were to copy it down 1,000 rows. Check any bonus cell out to see what I mean.

And by the same token, if the test scores had been entered this way—that is, horizontally (with the data beginning in cell J9), you'd see the results shown in Figure 4–27.

J	K	L	M	N	O
				4	
Student	John	Bill	Dorothy	Sue	Ed
Score	77	91	62	59	78
Bonus	81	95	66	63	82

Figure 4–27. *The grades organized horizontally, starting at cell KJ9. Note John's formula in the formula bar.*

John's bonus formula would now read

=$N7+K11

See why? Here, the dollar sign has been inserted to the left of the N, that part of the cell reference that indicates the cell's *column* letter. And we need to freeze the column letter here because John's formula has to be copied *across* a set of columns—and without the dollar sign, Bill's bonus formula would read

=O7+L11

And there's nothing in cell O7.

In fact, you can freeze both parts of a cell reference (e.g., $N$7). Copying this reference in either direction—down a column or across a row—won't change the reference at all. This is good to know if you need to refer to that cell in a variety of locations in the worksheet.

It's true that newcomers to Excel sometimes find the subject of relative and absolute cell addressing a bit daunting at first, so don't be discouraged if you're feeling the same. Just bear in mind that you need that dollar sign *only* when formulas in different cells have to refer to the same cell over and over again—as with our last example, in which all the test scores need to refer to the same bonus-point cell—N7. Again, the advantage here is that if you need to change the bonus, you need only change the value in N7, rather than having to edit every student's formula. You could even recolor N7 to remind users that it's the only cell they need to change (recoloring will be discussed in Chapter 5).

Copying a Formula's Result Only

There may be times when you need to save a value on a worksheet that's been generated by a formula. For example—suppose you needed to record those student test scores with their bonuses to a different area of the worksheet for future reference. Well, that causes a bit of a problem—because the bonus-adjusted scores were brought about by a series of *formulas*. John's bonus-score cell (in the Student Scores workbook) doesn't really say 81—it says =K8+N7, and if we copy that expression to another cell, both the K8 and the N7 are going to change, due to relative cell addressing—and we won't see 81 in the destination cell as a result.

One way out of this problem is to copy the test scores as usual, but to paste them into destination cells using the Paste Values option, which pastes *only the results of formulas, not the formulas the themselves.* Let's try it out, and the concept will become clearer.

1. First, open the Student Scores workbook if you haven't done so already.

2. Then select and copy cells L8:L12, which contain the bonus grades.

3. Then click in cell P8, which will serve as the first of the destination cells to which we want to paste the scores (Figure 4–28).

Student	Score	Bonus		4		
John	77	81				
Bill	91	95				
Dorothy	62	66				
Sue	59	63				
Ed	78	82				

Figure 4–28. *A different kind of copy and paste*

4. Then, instead of clicking the standard **Paste** command in the **Clipboard** button group, click the down arrow beneath **Paste**. You'll see what's shown in Figure 4–29.

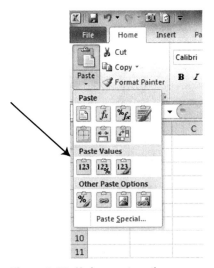

Figure 4–29. *Various paste options*

5. Click **Paste Values** (the first button in the **Paste Values** group). The bonus test scores will appear in cells P8:P12 in addition to their original location—and they will appear as *values*, as if you had simply typed them There are no formulas in the destination range, and that means simply that the values in those cells won't be changed by data entry anywhere else in the workbook. They've been fixed.

> **NOTE:** Notice the two other **Paste Values** buttons in Figure 4–29. The middle button, **Values and Number Formatting**, will paste cell values plus any special formatting brought to those values (e.g., currency formatting). The right button, **Values and Source Formatting**, pastes the cell values along with *any* new formatting imparted to those cells (e.g., a different font or color). Again, we'll discuss formatting in Chapter 5.

Clarifying Cell References by Naming a Range

I've already introduced the pivotal concept of ranges, and you've already worked with quite a few of them besides. But there are a few additional aspects of ranges that are useful to know about.

For one thing, ranges can be named. That is, instead of working with a set of cell references such as C23:C42 and using that reference in a formula, you can substitute a name for it and use the name in the formula. For example, if this range contained test scores, you could name the range Scores—and instead of writing

`=MAX(C23:C42)`

you could write

`=MAX(Scores)`

Naming a range helps you and other people who view your worksheet to better understand exactly what sort of data has contributed to the range. Scores is a lot more revealing than C23:C42—and probably easier to write, too. And there are other advantages to naming a range, which we'll discuss here too.

Naming a range is easy, although as usual, Excel grants us several ways in which to carry out this task.

Naming a Range in the Name Box

The simplest technique is to name a range with the **Name** box:

1. Select the range you want to name.

2. Then click in the **Name** box—that field in the upper left of your worksheet—type your name, and press Enter. (see Figure 4–30)

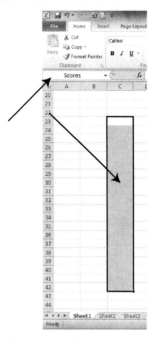

Figure 4–30. *Cells C23:C42, now named Scores*

Try this with the preceding cells. It makes no difference whether the cells in a named range are empty or populated with data. Either way, you can name it. And if you click the drop-drown arrow to the right of the **Name** box, you'll see a list of all the range names you've added to the worksheet, as shown in Figure 4–31.

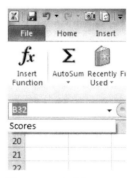

Figure 4–31. *Where range names are listed—one of several places*

Click any range name in that drop-down list, and Excel will select, or highlight, that range. It's a handy way to remind you exactly where a named range is located, and to navigate to it too.

> **NOTE:** A range name can consist of several words, but those words must be joined by an underscore. Thus, Test Scores is an illegal range name; TestScores or Test_Scores are acceptable, though.

Again, once a range is named you can apply it to a formula—and Excel helps you with that process, through the Formula AutoComplete feature discussed earlier. If, for example, you wanted to calculate the average of the Scores range, you'd do the following:

1. Begin by typing **=AVERAGE** (or really, **=A**, after which Formula AutoComplete will take you to functions starting with the letter *A*).

2. After you've gotten as far as **=AVERAGE(**, start to type the range name **Scores**. You'll see what's shown in Figure 4–32.

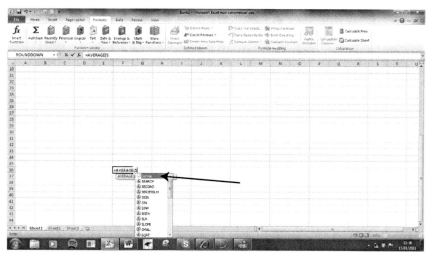

Figure 4–32. *Keeping scores: Note the Scores range listed.*

3. Formula AutoComplete is at it again, this time supplying you with the name of a *range*, instead of its usual functions. Now press the Tab key to select Scores, type the closed parenthesis to complete the expression, and press Enter.

You can also define a range name with the Define Name option, available through the **Formulas** tab ➤ **Defined Names** button group ➤ **Define Name**. Click the button and you'll see the dialog in Figure 4–33.

Figure 4–33. *The New Name dialog box*

Here you can type the range name, and even add a descriptive comment about the range if you like. The **Refers to:** field lets you type the range coordinates (e.g., C23:C42) without having to actually select those cells first, unlike the first technique.

NOTE: The =Sheet1! prefix identifies the sheet in which the range was drawn.

Scope refers to the worksheets in the workbook in which you can use the range. By default, the scope of a range is defined as Workbook, and that means that you can use the range name in any of the worksheets that make up the book—so even if you've devised Scores on Sheet1, you'll be able to write the following in Sheet2 as well:

=AVERAGE(Scores)

But if you confine the scope of Scores to Sheet1, you'll only be able to use Scores in formulas in Sheet1 (see Figure 4–34).

Figure 4–34. *You can't get there from here: don't try using Score in Sheet2 now.*

But why would you want to bother imposing such a restriction? Because you might be working with different sets of test scores on different worksheets, and you might want to use the range name Scores on each sheet—to represent *only* that sheet's scores. True, that's not a likely scenario, but Excel makes the option available.

Naming Ranges from the Data in Your Worksheet

Now let's look at yet a third way to construct range names, an approach that lets you derive the names from data you've already entered on the worksheet.

1. On a blank workbook, enter grades shown in Figure 4–35 in cells I9:L13.

Student	Soc.	Poli. Sci.	Phil.
Walt	75	60	88
Sally	82	80	78
Brian	61	93	68
Ann	77	71	82

Figure 4–35. *Title search: They're soon to become range names.*

2. Save the workbook as Test Scores. Now select all the cells in that range and click **Formulas ➤ Defined Names ➤ Create from Selection.** You'll see what's shown in Figure 4–36.

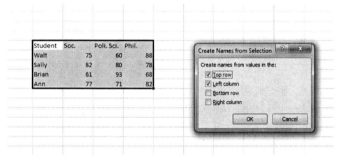

Figure 4–36. *Range finder: Excel suggests range names culled from the titles in your data.*

3. Click **OK.** Nothing will seem to have happened on the screen, but if you click the down arrow by the **Name** box, you'll see what's happened (see Figure 4–37).

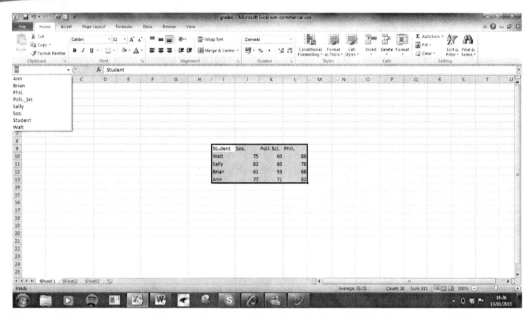

Figure 4–37. *Range names, batched up directly from the data—the titles in the left column and the top row*

True to the **Create Names from Selection** dialog box, Excel has composed range names from the data in the left column and top row, by assuming that those areas are likely to contain header information that you could use as range names. That means that you can now write a formula like this:

=AVERAGE(Walt)

> **NOTE:** These ranges *don't* include the cells in which the range names themselves appear. Thus, the range called Walt spans J10:L10, not I10:J10. Note as well that even though the subject heading Poli. Sci. consists of two words, Excel calls its range Poli._Sci..

Naming A Range Containing One Cell: Why Bother?

Now here's an important tip. You can assign a range name to exactly one cell—but why would you want to? Because when you copy a formula with a range name, that range is treated as an absolute reference—that is, the cells the range refers to *don't* change relative to their movement from the source cell that's being copied.

Thus, if we look back at our bonus-grade example, we could have named the bonus cell N7 Bonus. Our original source formula in L8 (John's score) would then have read

=K8+Bonus

And if we had then copied *that* expression down the column, all the other students' bonuses would have been correctly figured right away—without the need for those dollar signs. And that's because the range name Bonus would always mean N7—no matter where it's copied.

The Name Manager: Where They're All Ar-ranged

If your worksheet has many named ranges—and take it from me, it can—you'll find them all listed and inventoried in the **Name Manager**. You get there by clicking the **Formulas** tab, and choosing **Name Manager** from the **Defined Names** button group. Continuing with the preceding example, the **Name Manager** will look like Figure 4–38.

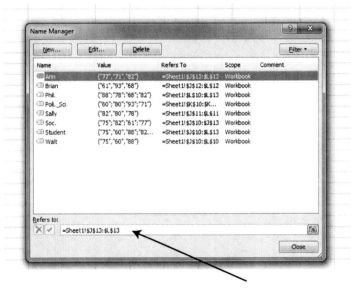

Figure 4–38. *The Name Manger. Note the range coordinates indicated for the range Ann, which has been selected.*

All the workbook range names are cataloged (along with names of any tables, which we haven't discussed yet; that's coming up in Chapter 7). You can edit the cell coordinates of any range by clicking its name in the list and typing new cell references in the **Refers to:** area. And by clicking the **Edit...** button, you'll be brought to a dialog box in which you can change the name of an existing range (see Figure 4–39).

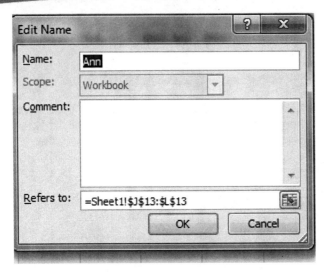

Figure 4–39. *Misspelled it? Call the range Anne instead.*

And by clicking the **New…** button you'll be brought to the same **New Name** dialog box shown earlier when you clicked the **Define Name** button—so that's still one more way to initiate a new range name.

There's one more feature of the **Name Manager** you may want to know about: its ability to let you delete range names. Click the **Delete** button (or press the Delete key on your keyboard) on any range name in the list and you'll spark a prompt that asks if you're sure you want to go ahead. Click **OK** and the name will disappear. But don't worry—the *data* in the range remains in its cells—you've only deleted the range name.

Summary

Call it number crunching or whatever you please—but however you characterize it, knowing how to write formulas and deploy Excel functions takes you to the heart of the spreadsheet enterprise. The more you know about Excel's capabilities, the more you'll be able to do with your spreadsheets, and while acquiring that knowledge takes a bit of practice, the investment should pay off. Once you get the hang of it, you'll come to realize there isn't much you can't do with Excel.

Next you'll see how to make all those numbers look good by learning about Excel's many formatting features. Just turn the page, and you'll see how to give your data a makeover.

Chapter 5

For Appearance's Sake: Formatting Your Data

Now that you've gotten a handle on some of the ways you can make all that data work for you, through Excel's functions and your own self-devised formulas, you'll want to go on and think about how all those results should *look*—because you're likely to have to show your work to someone else, and you know what they say about first impressions. Excel makes a huge assortment of formatting options available to its users, and we're going to take a look at some of these important, easy-to-apply options now.

What Formatting Does (and Doesn't Do)

The first thing you need to bear in mind about formatting in Excel is that when you dab at its palette of possibilities you're not "doing" anything to the data. That is, when you reformat a value, you merely change the way it looks; you don't modify the value itself. Thus, whether 72 looks like Figure 5–1 or 5–2, it's still equal to 36 × 2.

72

Figure 5–1. *Either way…A number using one type of formatting*

72.00

Figure 5–2. *The same number with different formatting applied*

Reformatting works to change the appearance of your data, and that's all. That 72 is still usable in formulas and the like, no matter how it looks, and that's a point you'll want to remember as we proceed.

Basic Formatting

Most of Excel's formatting options have been assigned to the **Home** tab, where they're easily accessible. Start with the **Font** button group (shown in Figure 5–3), each of whose buttons introduce a formatting change when clicked.

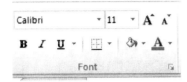

Figure 5–3. *The Font button group*

Many of the buttons here may look familiar to you if you've used Microsoft Word, and they do similar, though not identical, things here. Note the default Calibri 11-point font, the same one that starts you off in Word. Points are units of typographic measurement—units of height, to be exact—of which there are 72 per inch. Thus, 12-point text is one-sixth of an inch in height, for example.

Changing the Font

The basic principle behind making formatting changes is known as *select-then-do*; that is, you select a cell or cells (or even *some* of the text in a cell if that's what you want to change), and then execute the change. Thus, to change the fonts in a range of cells

1. Just select the range.

2. Click the down arrow beside the font field (where it currently says "Calibri" in Figure 5–3). This will present the **Font** drop-down menu, as shown in Figure 5–4.

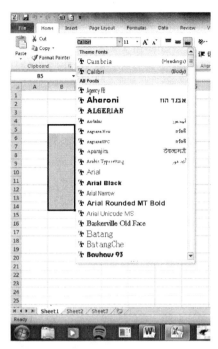

Figure 5–4. *The Font drop-down menu*

3. Just click the font you want, and you've made the change (you can reveal more fonts by clicking the arrows at the right side of the font window and scrolling down the font list).

NOTE: When you scroll down the **Font** drop-down menu in search of a new font, simply hovering your mouse over a new font will change the selected cells to that font in preview mode, letting you know what the cells will look like if you actually click that font. The same previewing feature works with many other formatting options, too, such as font size, and fill and font color; but not others, such as the bold, italics, or bordering-cells options.

Notice that Figure 5–4 shows a range that seems to contain nothing in it. It's true—the range is blank, but that's not a problem. That's because you can format a range prospectively, even before it contains any data. When you actually type the data, it will take on the changes you've brought about. Note also when you make a formatting change on a designated range, the range remains selected in case you want to make additional changes there.

Changing the Font Size

In much the same way, you can change the font size of the data. Just select your range and click the down arrow alongside the font size field (currently showing the default 11 points), and click the desired size.

> **NOTE:** Remember that if you want all the cells in the worksheet to acquire the same new font size, you can click the **Select All** button. Once all the worksheet cells are selected, enter the new size. If you want to change the font for all the cells in a particular row, click its row header; all the cells will be selected. To do the same to a column, click its heading.

Note, on the other hand, that the **Font** drop-down menu lists 11-, 12-, and 14-point sizes, but not 13. That's not a matter of superstition; rather, it's because Excel simply lists commonly used font sizes. If you really want your range to display 13- or 17-point-sized data, you can do the following:

1. Click in the font size field.

2. Type the size you want, as shown in Figure 5–5.

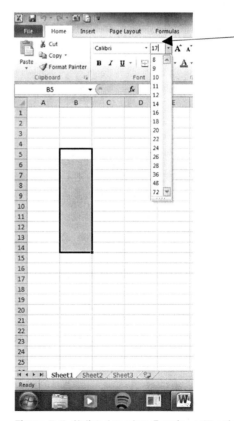

Figure 5–5. *Unlisted number: Entering a 17-point font*

3. Then press Enter to finalize the change.

> **NOTE:** When data is enlarged with a new font size, the row heights of the affected data automatically increase if necessary to make room for the upgrade. Excel will not allow data to barge vertically into a cell above it, even though it does allow text to move horizontally into a cell to its right.

Now what about those two *A*s stationed to the right of the font fields? They're called Increase Font Size and Decrease Font Size, respectively (see Figure 5–6).

A˄ A˅

Figure 5–6. *A pair of quick ways to increase or decrease font size*

Click the larger **A** on a range of cells, and the data there will receive a font size boost up to the next available interval in the font size window. That means that if the current size in a cell or cells is 12 points, clicking the large **A** will pump the size up to 14, which is the next higher size recorded in the drop-down menu. If you click the smaller **A**, those same 12-point cells with be downsized to 11 points, the next lower interval listed.

Using Bold, Italics, and Underline

Now let's turn to the B, I, and U buttons (see Figure 5–7).

Figure 5–7. *B, I, and U (bold, italics, and underline)*

These buttons represent bold, italics, and underline, respectively—and again, to format data with any or all of these effects, select the cells in question and just click the appropriate button(s). These three buttons behave as *toggles*, meaning that by clicking them in succession you turn their formatting effects on and off. Click the B button once, and the cells you've selected turn boldface; click it again, and the bold effect disappears.

Note, by the way, that the U button is accompanied by a drop-down arrow. Click it, and this little menu makes its way onscreen, as shown in Figure 5–8.

Figure 5–8. *Between the (under)lines*

Note the first of the two menu options is nothing but the default underline—what you'd normally get if you just clicked the U straight away. So why do you need it? Because if you click the **Double Underline** option, you'll indeed draw double underlines beneath data in the selected cells. Additionally, the **Double Underline** button will then appear in the **Font** button group, *replacing* the standard **Underline**, at least until you exit Excel completely or reuse the single underline (see Figure 5–9).

Figure 5–9. *Seeing double*

Determining a Cell's Formatting

You can learn a lot about the formatting of a particular cell by simply clicking in it and then scanning the information conveyed about it in the **Font** button group. So, if cell C12 is currently underlined and boldfaced, and features a Bauhaus 93, 12-point font, click C12 and you'll see this information in the **Font** button group, as shown in Figure 5–10.

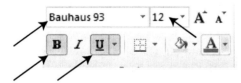

Figure 5–10. *What's happening in cell C12. The data there is boldfaced and underlined, and exhibits the Bauhaus 93 12-point font.*

Notice that the B and U buttons are illuminated, telling us that those effects are activated in C12; and we're also told about the Bauhaus 93 12-point font.

Adding a Border

To the right of the **U** button you'll find the **Borders** button, which doesn't format cell data as such, but rather lets you inscribe lines around some or all the four borders of cells (see Figure 5–11).

Figure 5–11. *Borderline call: The Borders drop-down menu*

Again, the technique for drawing borders is the same as for other kinds of formatting:

1. Select the cells.

2. Click the **Borders** button, and select the border option of your choice from the drop-down menu.

Play around with these and you'll see how they work; particularly the **All Borders** and **Outside Borders** selections, which you may decide to use often.

All Borders draws borders around *all* the selected cells. This option can be particularly useful for emphasizing a particular group of cells (see Figure 5–12).

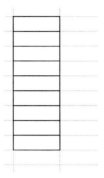

Figure 5–12. *We've got you covered: The All Borders option surrounds all the selected cells' borders with lines.*

Outside Borders limns a border around the perimeter of a range of cells, not individual cell borders. It's effective for singling out a range of cells for emphasis (see Figure 5–13.

Figure 5–13. *The Outside Borders option*

You'll want to know about the **No Border** option, too, which removes borders around selected cells if you decide they're no longer needed:

1. Just select cells exhibiting the borders.

2. Click **No Border**, and the borders will vanish.

If you're wondering why you couldn't simply click the **Undo** button to achieve the same result, you could—maybe. Remember that Undo works in sequence, and if you decide you want to remove some cell borders well after you've drawn them, you'll have to undo all the commands you've executed in between, too.

NOTE: You can change the color of the borders by clicking the **Line Color** option on the Borders drop-down menu. You can also modify the texture and appearance of the line with the **Line Style** option, also available on that menu (see Figure 5–14).

Figure 5–14. *The Line Color and Line Style options*

Adding Color to Your Cells

That leaves us with two remaining buttons in the **Font** button group: the **Fill Color** and **Font Color** buttons. **Fill Color**, as represented by the pail icon, has nothing to do with the fill handle discussed earlier; rather, it fills the selected cells with a color you choose from a drop-down menu (see Figure 5–15).

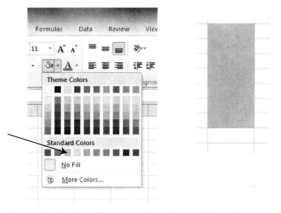

Figure 5–15. *Click the arrow alongside the Fill button to produce this drop-down menu and result.*

Use this option when you want to impart emphasis to selected cells. Note that the color you see right beneath the pail icon (the color underlining the pail) is the current fill default color—the color that will appear in the selected cells if you click the **Fill Color** button instead of its drop-down arrow. And if you want to turn off the current fill color tinting any cell(s), just select the cells in question and click the **No Fill** option.

> **NOTE:** If you're artistically inclined, you can devise subtler shadings with the **More Colors...** option, which when clicked lets you modulate color values and produce exactly the hue you want.

The **Font Color** button, represented by the **A**, changes the color of the data in the selected cells. It too sports a drop-down menu exhibiting the same color options displayed in the **Fill Color** menu, as shown in Figure 5–16.

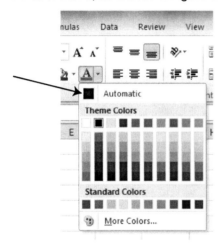

Figure 5–16. *The Font Color drop-down menu. The Automatic option represents the default font color, black.*

Just select your cells and click away.

> **NOTE:** The **Automatic** option, when clicked, returns the cells' font color to the operative default color, black.

Adding Extra Formatting

Finally, note that the **Font** button group has one of those dialog launcher arrows—that little indicator squirreled in the lower right of the group (see Figure 5–17).

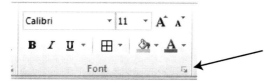

Figure 5–17. *There's that dialog box launcher again.*

Click it and you'll bring up what's called the **Format Cells** dialog box (shown in Figure 5–18).

Figure 5–18. *The Format Cells dialog box. Note the various tabs.*

Note the various font-formatting options here, most of which you've already seen in button form in the button group. There are, however, a few additional possibilities here—namely in the **Effects** area, where you can draw a strikethrough line through data. Figure 5–19 shows an example.

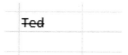

Figure 5–19. *The strikethrough effect*

NOTE: The **Format Cells** dialog box consists of numerous tabs, each one housing a different variety of formatting possibilities. This same dialog box appears again when you click the dialog box launcher in the **Alignment** and **Number** button groups, but these groups highlight a different tab in **Format Cells**.

Aligning (and Realigning) Your Data

The group to the immediate right of the **Font** button group is called the **Alignment** group. It's shown in Figure 5–20.

Figure 5–20. *The Alignment button group*

Its buttons don't quite change the appearance of data; rather, they *reposition* data in its respective cells. Recall that numeric data, or values, appear by default at the right edge of cells, while text data is positioned, or aligned, at the left. The **Alignment** buttons allow you to relocate the data to different positions, called *orientations*—both horizontal and even vertical—in cells.

Changing Horizontal Alignment

The trio of buttons in the lower left of the group (see Figure 5–21) controls the horizontal placement of data (you'll see these in Word, too).

Figure 5–21. *The horizontal alignment buttons*

What they do is pretty self-evident. Here's a quick exercise involving text alignment:

1. Click the far left button, **Align Text Left**, after you've selected a range of cells, and their contents will be shifted to the cells' left edges (of course, if you're working with text data, that's where they'll be anyway).

2. Click the next button along, called **Center**, and the data will zip to the center of its cells.

3. Click the third of the three, **Align Text Right**, to shunt the data to the right edge.

Thus, if you've entered values, the buttons will bring about the kinds of results shown in Figure 5–22.

	34
34	
	34

Figure 5–22. *Right, left, and centered values*

Keep in mind that many people like to center values down a column, enjoying the symmetrical effect that centered data brings. But you may want to think about that decision, because if your data contains values of different lengths you can wind up with something like what's shown in Figure 5–23.

45
4
673
32
5467
1
36

Figure 5–23. *Out of whack: What centered values can look like*

You see the problem—but it's your call.

Changing Vertical Alignment

The next set of buttons, **Top**, **Middle**, and **Bottom Align** do something more exotic (see Figure 5–24).

Figure 5–24. *The vertical alignment buttons*

They let you align data vertically, enabling you realize the kind of effect shown in Figure 5–25.

Figure 5–25. *The sky's the limit with the Top Align button*

Now, in order to make that happen, you need to learn how to heighten a row. We've already talked about widening a column; row heightening works in a similar way:

1. Move your mouse above the *lower* boundary of the row you want to heighten (see Figure 5–26).

Figure 5–26. *Placing the cursor here with let you heighten row 15.*

2. Click and drag the boundary down until the row achieves the desired height. Release the mouse.

3. You can heighten multiple rows at the same time by dragging atop adjoining row headers (see Figure 5–27).

Figure 5–27. *Heightening several rows simultaneously*

4. Then drag *any* one of the selected row boundaries to the desired height and release the mouse. All the rows will acquire the same new height.

5. Click anywhere to turn off the blue selection color.

6. If you've dragged too far you can also execute a *row autofit* by double-clicking a row's lower boundary.

Once you've completed that task, all you need to do is select your data and click one of the **Vertical Align** buttons to bring about the effect you want. Of course, **Bottom Align** is Excel's default—data will automatically position itself on the bottom of a row unless you decide to make a change.

Changing Data Orientation

The next alignment button, called **Orientation**, will let you do something even more unusual: incline data at an angle. Click its drop-down arrow, and you'll see the options shown in Figure 5–28.

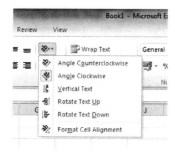

Figure 5–28. *Everybody's got an angle: The Orientation drop-down menu*

These options are pretty cool, but need to be used judiciously, as they reposition the data at severe angles. Select a cell and try the various orientations. You'll get some pretty striking results, which can work with both text and values. Just make sure that your audience will be happy to see a value that looks like Figure 5–29, for example.

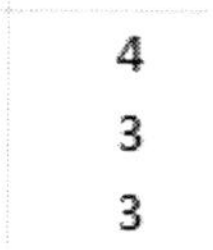

4

3

3

Figure 5–29. *That number—433—can still be used in formulas.*

That's 433, and appearances to the contrary, that value is lodged in only one cell. All you need do to achieve this effect is select the cell(s), and select the **Vertical Text** option (shown previously in Figure 5–28).

The last drop-down option, **Format Cell Alignment**, will deliver you to the same **Format Cells** dialog box shown earlier—only this time the **Alignment** tab is pushed to the foreground, as shown in Figure 5–30.

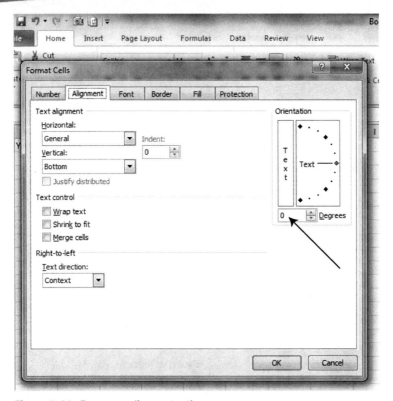

Figure 5–30. *Even more alignment options*

Among other things, you'll see an **Orientation** area at its right edge. If you type in a number in its **Degrees** field, the data in cells you've selected cells will be pitched at just that angle (note the arrow in Figure 5–31). Also, if you click cells containing angled text and type **0** in the **Degrees** box, the data will be restored to its original, unangled appearance.

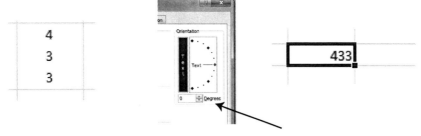

Figure 5–31. *Select the cells you want to restore, type 0 degrees in the Degree field (you have to actively type 0 even if it's already displayed), and click OK.*

Indenting Data

The next two buttons are titled **Decrease Indent** and **Increase Indent**, respectively, and all they do is push data in their cells slightly to the left or right by small increments, much in the way that the indent option works in Word. Each click advances or pulls back the data a bit more in their cells. Between you and me, I don't recall ever having used these buttons in an actual worksheet—but they're there (see Figure 5–32).

Figure 5–32. *The Indent buttons*

Wrapping Text

The next button, **Wrap Text**, is a good deal more useful. Clicking **Wrap Text** is the option of choice when you enter text in a cell that extends beyond its current column width and you don't want to widen the column. We've seen this problem before, of course, but **Wrap Text** proposes a different solution:

7. Enter the phrase shown in Figure 5–33 in cell B19.

Figure 5–33. *Getting carried away: Too much text*

8. Click back in cell B19 and click **Wrap Text**. You'll see what's shown in Figure 5–34.

Figure 5–34. *Back where it all belongs*

Wrap Text treats the current column width as a fixed margin and heightens the row instead, in order to confine the text within that margin. **Wrap Text** is thus an option you'll turn to if you need to maintain a column's width as it presently stands.

Adding a Title with Merge and Center

The final alignment option, **Merge and Center**, provides a set of suboptions in its drop-down menu, as shown in Figure 5–35.

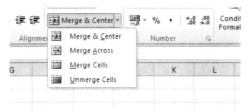

Figure 5–35. *Merge and Center: Getting cells together*

Merge and Center was devised to solve an old spreadsheet problem. Say you have a worksheet that currently looks like Figure 5–36.

Figure 5–36. *Want that title to be centered among the month names? Stay tuned.*

What if you want the Yearly Sales Totals title to be centered across the 12 months? Here's how to do it:

1. Say the month names you see in the screenshot span the range A2:L2 (remember, you can enter these names using the fill handle), and that the title Yearly Sales Totals appears in cell A1. Select cells A1:L1—that is, the range directly above all the months, in the row containing the phrase Yearly Sales Totals.

2. Now click the **Merge and Center** button directly (no need to activate the drop-down menu), and you'll see what's shown in Figure 5–37.

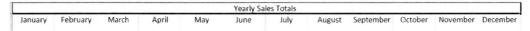

Figure 5–37. *Middle ground: The title is precisely centered above the months.*

Merge and Center does two things:

- It combines, or merges, all the selected cells into one megacell.
- It then centers the text across it.

This option spares you the challenge of figuring out exactly where to find the center point above the months.

NOTE: Merge and Center only works if the data you want to center is in the leftmost cell of the range you want to merge, and if the other cells in the range are empty. If any of these cells also contain data, their contents will be deleted.

You're far less likely to use the other two active merge options—Merge Across and Merge Cells.

- Merge Across lets you select a range consisting of several rows and columns, and turns *each* individual row into a single cell (see Figure 5–38).

Figure 5–38. *Note the merge effect: Tuesday and July now each occupy a large, merged cell.*

- Merge Cells lets you turn any range (which can include both rows and/or columns) into *one* supercell.

But as with **Merge and Center**, these only work properly when data is positioned in the leftmost cell of the selected range (these commands will work with completely empty ranges, however).

Finally, the awkwardly named **Unmerge Cells** option restores any merged cells back to their original state. Select the merged megacell, click **Unmerge Cells**, and all the original cells will reappear (see Figure 5–39).

Figure 5–39. *Now Tuesday is back in its original cell, and all the cells that had been merged with it are back, too.*

Inserting, Deleting, and Hiding Columns and Rows

Merging cells hints at some other important ways in which you can modify the structure of the worksheet itself, in addition to the data that the worksheet contains. There may be times when you need to insert or delete a row or column in the worksheet. Say you've constructed a list of employees along with identifying column headings, as in Figure 5–40.

	A	B	C	D	E	F
1	Last Name	First Name	Address	Telephone Number	Dept.	Hire Date

Figure 5–40. *The headings for an employee directory. Note the columns have been autofit.*

It then occurs to you that you've inadvertently omitted a Salary field, which you want sandwiched between Telephone Number and Dept. You'll need to insert a column.

Inserting a Column or Row

As usual, there are several ways in which to do this. Here's one:

1. To insert a column, right-click anywhere on the column heading to the immediate *right* of where you want the *new* column to be inserted. In the example in Figure 5–41, you'd right click the E column heading, because you want Salary to be installed to the left of Dept.

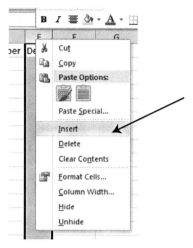

Figure 5–41. *After right-clicking the E heading, click the Insert option.*

2. Click Insert, and the new column will appear, as shown in Figure 5–42.

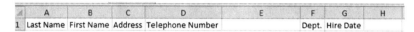

Figure 5–42. *Now you can type "Salary."*

A different method allows you to insert a column by clicking *anywhere* in the column to the right of where you want the new one inserted:

3. Click a cell in the column to the right of where you want to insert the column.

4. Then click the **Home** tab, and choose **Insert ➤ Insert Sheet Columns** from the **Cells** button group, as in Figure 5–43.

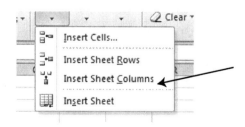

Figure 5–43. *An alternative way to insert a column. Note the Insert Sheet Rows option, too.*

You'll get the same result—the new column.

To insert rows, the procedures are nearly identical:

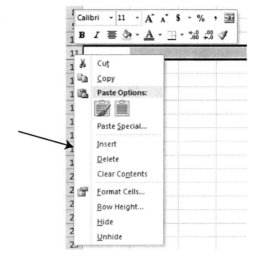

5. Here, the first method requires you to right-click anywhere in the *row* directly *beneath* where you want the new one to appear. Thus, if you want to insert a new row between rows 10 and 11, you right-click row 11, as in Figure 5–44.

6. Then just click Insert.

Figure 5–44. *Just click Insert, and the new row will appear above the current row.*

To apply the second method to rows, do the following:

1. Click anywhere in the row directly *beneath* where you want the row to appear.

2. Click the **Home** tab, and click **Insert ➤ Insert Sheet Rows** from the **Cells** button group.

Inserting Multiple Columns or Rows

If you need to insert several columns or rows at the same time, you first need to select as many column or row headings as correspond to the number you want to insert. Thus, if you want to insert three columns, select the three column headings to the right of where you want the new ones to appear by simply dragging your mouse across the headings (not the worksheet cells), as in Figure 5–45.

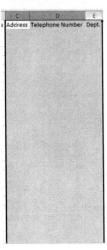

Figure 5–45. *Here, columns C through E have been selected; thus, the three new columns will appear to the right of column C.*

You can then utilize either of the two insert methods just described (i.e., clicking **Insert** or **Insert Sheet Columns**). For rows, select multiple rows directly beneath where you want the new rows to appear.

What Inserting Does to Formulas

Inserting columns and rows may or may not impact existing formulas on the spreadsheet. If cell D12 contains

=AVERAGE(A12:C12)

and you insert a column to the left of column D, the expression won't be rewritten. It will continue to read =AVERAGE(A12:C12), even though it now finds itself in cell E12. Excel tries to maintain the original formula relationships in the face of row and column movement. And that means that if you were to move all the values in cells A12:C12 to A5:C5 instead, you'd see

=AVERAGE(A5:C5)

Again, that's because Excel assumes you still want to compute the average of those numbers, even though they've be moved.

Deleting Columns and Rows

The general approach to carrying out column or row deletions is, again, to select the columns or rows you want to delete using the selection techniques just described. Again, you can call upon either of the two insert methods, but this time of course you'll click Delete (see Figure 5–46).

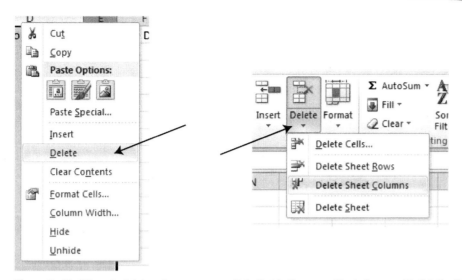

Figure 5–46. *Where to delete columns or rows. Note that in the second technique you'll click the Delete button alongside the Insert button.*

Just keep in mind that if you're deleting cells whose data contributes to a formula, that formula will suddenly have nothing to work with—and instead of a result, you'll be left with an error message in the cell.

Hiding Rows and Columns

It's not unusual for Excel users to want to hide selected columns or rows—not so much in order to maintain the secrecy of the data, but to improve the appearance of a spreadsheet; perhaps columns with complex formulas don't need to be seen, or perhaps you'll want to hide those formulas so that you won't accidentally overwrite them; but if you do hide them, remember that all the data posted there remains active, and any cell references to them remain in force, too.

Again, there are two standard techniques for hiding. Here's the first:

3. Right-click the column or row heading you want to hide.

4. Click **Hide** in the resulting context menu (again, you can drag across multiple headings), as in Figure 5–47.

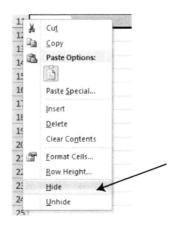

Figure 5–47. *Where to hide columns or rows*

Your worksheet will then exhibit a gap where the hide was executed, as shown in Figure 5–48.

Figure 5–48. *Row 11 isn't there, but its data is still usable.*

The second technique for hiding columns and/or rows is as follows:

5. Select what you want to hide.

6. Click the **Home** tab, and then choose **Format ➤ Hide & Unhide ➤ Hide Rows** or **Hide Columns** from the **Cells** button group (see Figure 5–49).

Figure 5–49. *An alternative way to hide columns or rows*

NOTE: The second technique lets you select columns/rows to be hidden either by clicking on column or row headings or clicking anywhere in the column(s) or row(s) you want to hide.

Unhiding Columns and Rows

Unhide is one of those awkward Excel verbs, but that's the description for bringing back hidden columns or rows. Now, because the hidden areas can't be clicked directly—they're hidden, after all—you need to select columns or rows on either side of the hidden elements. Thus, if column K were hidden, you'd drag across headings J and L, as in Figure 5–50.

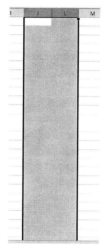

Figure 5–50. *Trying to get back column K*

Then right-click anywhere in that blue selection area and click **Unhide** (see Figure 5–51).

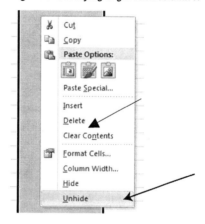

Figure 5–51. *Just click Unhide, and K will reappear.*

Alternatively, click the **Home** tab, and choose **Format ➤ Hide & Unhide ➤ Unhide Rows** or **Unhide Columns** from the **Cells** button group.

NOTE: If you've hidden the A column, there will be no column to its left that you can select. Thus, you need to click the **Select All** button to the left of A, which selects the entire workbook. Then right-click anywhere and click **Unhide** on the context menu.

Inserting and Deleting Cells

You can also insert and delete selected cells, not just entire rows and columns—a possibility that isn't quite as obvious. If you click in cell A12 and carry out the Insert Cells command, for example, you'll push A12 down a row—but you won't push down row 12 in its entirety. Only the A column will be affected by the command. Any data in cell B12 will remain there, for example.

To insert or delete cells, select in the cell or cells with which you're working and either right-click the selected area and click Insert..., or click the Home tab and select the Insert ➤ Insert Cells... option from the Cells button group (see Figure 5–52).

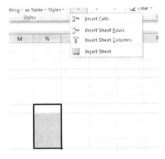

Figure 5–52. *Here, cells N8:N12 have been selected.*

You'll see the dialog shown in Figure 5–53. If you click OK on the Shift cells down option, cells N8:N12 will be bumped down five rows—equal to the number of rows in N8 through N12. But no cells in other columns in the worksheet will be affected.

Figure 5–53. *The Insert cells dialog box*

To delete selected cells, select the cells you wish to delete and either right-click the selection and click Delete... or click Delete Cells... in the Cells button group (see Figure 5–54).

Figure 5–54. *Where to begin deleting selected cells*

Either way, you'll see the dialog shown in Figure 5–55. Just click the desired choice. Note that in the screenshot selection the cells' deletion would move the cells currently in O8:O12 one column to the left, so that *they* become N8:N12. You may have to think about this one—or better yet, experiment on a worksheet.

Figure 5–55. *The Delete cells dialog box*

NOTE: Deleting cells does exactly that—the command deletes entire cells, not just the contents of the cells.

Formatting Values: Making the Numbers Look Good

Most of the work you'll do with Excel will likely be numbers-based, and many of the formatting options you need to know about impact numerical data only. Excel's **Number** button group (see Figure 5–56) contains a raft of ways to represent values that will make your data more meaningful.

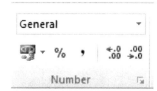

Figure 5–56. *The Number button group*

NOTE: Unlike the B, I, and U font format buttons, the first three buttons in the **Number** button group (**Accounting Number Format**, **Percent Style**, and **Comma Style**) are *not* toggles—that is, clicking any of these twice does not alternately turn their effects on and then off. We'll get to some ways you can remove them soon.

Turning Values into Currency

When you need to format numerical data so that it appears in currency form—dollars, pounds, euros, or just about any other denomination you can think of—just go to what's called the **Accounting Number Format** option, represented by the button shown in Figure 5–57.

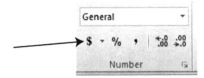

Figure 5–57. *Where to turn values into currency formats; note the dollar sign.*

Just select the cells you want and click that button. The values should take on the currency format of your country (that country-specific setting should have been established by your computer's control panel before you purchased or when you first configured your PC), and exhibit these default characteristics:

- The indigenous currency symbol

- A comma for any value exceeding 999

- Two decimal points to signify cents, pence, or whatever the case may be

Click the **Accounting Number Format** button on cells containing the values 4523, 75, and 2, and you'll see what's shown in Figure 5–58.

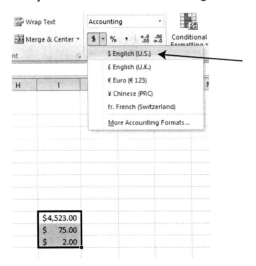

Figure 5–58. *Cashing in: Where to initiate the Accounting Number Format*

Looking for additional currency symbols? Click the down arrow alongside the button and you'll see what's shown in Figure 5–59.

Figure 5–59. *Currency exchange: Additional currency symbols*

And here we need to issue a reminder. Substituting a $ for a £ in a value does not alter the numerical value of the data you've originally entered. In strictly mathematical terms, $4,523.00 is equal to £4,523.00; Excel won't calculate any currency exchange rates or anything of the sort. The currency symbol is just an embellishment of the number you wrote (as is the comma and the two decimal points). These are all format changes, and to repeat the declaration I issued at the outset of the chapter, formatting only changes the way a number looks.

If you need additional proof, do the following:

1. Enter 4523 in any cell.

2. Dress it up in a currency format.

3. Click back in the cell and direct your attention to the formula bar.

While your cell will display $4,523.00, the formula bar will reveal 4523.

And if you need still more symbols—if you're trading in Latvian lats or Bulgarian levs or any of a host of other international currencies, click the **More Accounting Formats...** option, shown previously, and you'll be brought to the dialog shown in Figure 5–60.

Figure 5–60. *Scrolling for dollars . . . and other currencies*

Scroll that ample list, and select your currency. Then click OK.

> **NOTE:** The **Currency** format option in Figure 5–60 is distinguished from the **Accounting** format option by the way it positions the currency symbol. In the accounting format, the symbol is always lined up in the same place. With currency, the symbol is always placed right alongside the value. In Figure 5–61, the first column of values exhibits the accounting format, and the second shows the currency format.

$ 345.00	$345.00
$ 6.00	$6.00
$ 32.00	$32.00

Figure 5–61. *Symbolic gestures: Accounting and Currency formats*

Working with Percentages

The next number button, **Percent Style**, is represented by—surprise—the percent symbol (see Figure 5–62).

%

Figure 5–62. *The Percent Style button*

Percent Style represents a number as a percentage, and as a result can be a bit tricky. Again, you just select the desired cell(s) and click the **Percent Style** button. Thus, the number 0.34 would appear as follows:

34%

That's easy enough, but keep in mind that the number 1 expressed in percentage terms is 100%, not 1%. If you're expecting that result, you'll have to enter **.01** in the cell before you click **Percent Style**.

> **NOTE:** If you actually *type* the percent symbol alongside a value instead of clicking **Percent Style**, you *can* type **1%** and it will mean 1%, and will appear that way in the formula bar.

Punctuating Values

The **Comma Style** button actually does two things to the values you select:

- It adds a comma to any value exceeding 999.
- It posts two decimal points.

Thus, click the button on a cell containing 56802, and you'll get 56,802.00.

Formatting Decimal Points

The final two buttons on the lower tier of the **Number** button group are **Increase Decimal** and **Decrease Decimal**, important options that require a bit of introduction. As its name suggests, **Increase Decimal** adds a decimal point to a value with each click. In the case of a whole number, say 74, clicking **Increase Decimal** point results in

74.0

in which no real additional value is expressed. But if you had written the formula =4/7 instead, you'd originally see

0.571429

However, click **Increase Decimal** here, and you'll see

0.5714286

This adds a degree of additional precision to this repeating decimal.

> **NOTE:** The number of decimal places you'll initially see depends on the current width of the cell, the current font size, and the nature of the fraction you're working with (e.g., 1/2 vs. 1/3. The former will appear by default as 0.5).

On the other hand, if you *narrow* the column in which the preceding number appears, Excel will reduce its number of decimals so that you can continue to see the number. But it will also round the decimal off. Narrow the column here and you'll see

0.57143

Narrow it some more and you'll see

0.5714

and so on.

By the same token, type 4.67 in a cell followed by **Decrease Decimal** and you'll see

4.7

Click **Decrease Decimal** again and you'll see

5.0

But mathematically, that value is still really worth 4.67. Multiply it by 2 in a formula and the answer will come to 9.34, not 10. Again, we're only *formatting* the value, not changing its actual quantity.

Working with Dates: Dates Are Numbers Too

Enter the expression 3/4 in a cell and you may be in for a surprise. You know that 3/4 can't qualify as an actual fraction, because you've written it without the equal sign. So maybe it's just a bit of text, you may surmise. But it isn't; Excel will treat is as a date.

Depending on where in the world you live, that expression will be treated as either March 4 or April 3—but either way, it's a date. That's because Excel has decided that 3/4 and expressions like it will be regarded by default as a date, and assumes the date occurs during the current year—because people often like to write dates that way.

Treating 3/4 as a date is one instance of what's called Excel's *general* format, the default worksheet setting. The general format tries to understand what you have in mind when you enter data in a cell—*before* you've carried out any of the formatting changes discussed previously. Thus, Excel makes an educated guess about that 3/4, assigning it the status of a date unless and until you tell it otherwise.

But what you really need to know about dates is that they're numbers. In fact, March 4, 2011 is actually 40606—but what in the world does that mean? It means this: each date is assigned a sequenced number denoting the total days separating that date from January 1, 1900. Thus, March 4, 2011 arrived 40606 days after the baseline January 1, 1900—and that's a very good thing to know, because now you can determine the number of days between any two dates.

Here's an example:

1. Enter 3/4 in cell A2.

2. Then enter 1/15 in A3.

3. In cell A4, write **=A2-A3**, and you answer will be 48.

The 48 represents the number of days between January 15, 2011 and March 4, 2011, a result made possible because the later date has that numerical value of 40606, and the January date is really 40558. And 40606 − 40558 = 48.

Excel is well stocked with additional ways to format dates:

1. Click that January 15 entry in cell A3.

2. Then click what's called the **Number Format** drop-down menu (see Figure 5–63). This menu shows you what A3—which again is really 40193— would look like as per some of Excel's other formatting options.

3. Click the second **Date** option on the menu, and A3 will then display 1/15/11, replacing the current 1/15.

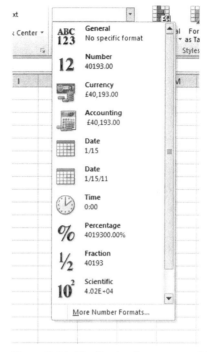

Figure 5–63. *The Number Format menu: Different guises for the same value*

4. If you click the **More Number Formats...** options at the bottom of the menu, you'll be returned to the trusty **Format Cells** dialog box, this time with the **Date** option already selected (see Figure 5–64).

Figure 5–64. *Dates on the menu: Date options in the Format Cells dialog box*

5. Choose whichever option you like, and then click OK. They're all different guises for the same number. And note that when you click any of the formatting possibilities, you'll see a preview of what the date is going to look like if you click OK, as in Figure 5–65.

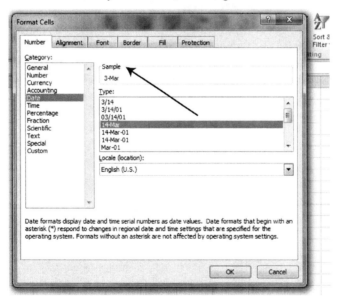

Figure 5–65. *What you see is what you are going to get: Previewing a data format. The Sample area reveals the preview (see arrow).*

Here's another tip: instead of directly entering 1/15 in a cell, you could have also entered 1-15. Excel's general format will also treat that expression as a date. And if you enter a date from the current year, you don't need to enter any reference to the year; 1/15 will be read as 1/15/11. But if you want to enter the same date from, say, two years ago, you'll need to enter 1/15/09.

Customizing Number Formats

If you're not quite happy with any of the formatting suggestions supplied by the **Number Format** drop-down menu, there are still more ways to remake the appearance of values.

The Special Formats Option

The **Format Cells** dialog box lists a **Special** option, which automatically formats values with four built-in looks that you can apply to values (see Figure 5–66).

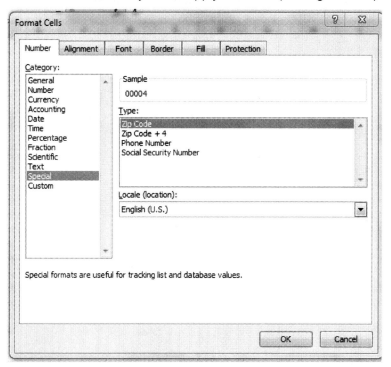

Figure 5–66. *The Special formatting option*

The **Social Security Number** option, for example, lets you type the nine-digit numbers without those pesky dashes that punctuate the numbers. Thus, if you select the desired cells and click **Social Security Number**, you'll be able to type 123456789, and have it automatically rewritten as 123-45–6789, sparing you the slightly odious task of remembering exactly where to enter those dashes.

Similarly, the **Phone Number** option will allow you to type 1234567 and immediately revise it to 123-4567.

The Custom Option

But there's still more. Excel's **Custom** option gives you the freedom to fine-tune numerical appearances precisely to your liking. While some **Custom** options are rather complex, there's one I use often that's quite simple.

You've probably noted by now that when you type a decimal value—say, .37—Excel ascribes this default format to it in its cell:

0.37

I don't know about you, but I don't like that leading zero; I want to see .37, and nothing more.

1. To achieve that appearance, select the cells you want to reformat and select **Custom**. You'll see the dialog shown in Figure 5–67.

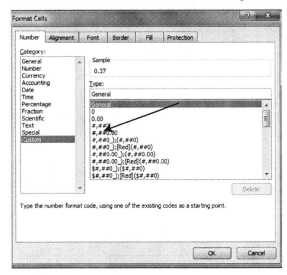

Figure 5–67. *Decimal derring-do: About to excise that leading zero*

2. Then click the 0.00 option, the third one down the **Type** list (see the arrow in Figure 5–68).

Figure 5–68. *Note that the Type field records the current format in the cell, with the leading zero in place.*

3. Then click in the **Type** field and simply delete the leading zero. Note the **Sample** area shown in Figure 5–69.

Figure 5–69. *The zero has been zapped.*

4. Click **OK**, and all decimal values in the selected cells will lose that zero.

> **NOTE:** The preceding customization won't change a value such as 3.37; it will only eliminate the zero on decimals that have no values to the left of the decimal point (e.g., 0.37 or 0.98).

Experimenting with the **Custom** options and observing how the content in the **Sample** area changes should prove instructive and useful.

Copying Formats (Not Data) with the Format Painter

Let's say you've formatted a cell with these characteristics:

- Using an Algerian 19-point font
- Colored red
- Italicized
- Festooned with an orange background

Something like Figure 5-70.

Figure 5-70. *Have it your way: Your customized format*

Hey—it's your worksheet. And you're so enamored with this collection of embellishments that you want to bring it to other cells. Of course, you could select those cells and then click the various options that gave rise to that thing of beauty in the preceding screenshot—but that's a lot of clicks. What you can do instead is copy and paste the format of that cell to other cells with the format painter. Here's how:

1. Select a source cell containing the formats you want to copy to other cells, as in Figure 5-71.

Figure 5-71. *The source and destination cells*

2. Click the **Format Painter** button in the **Clipboard** button group (on the **Home** tab). The cursor will be accompanied by a paintbrush icon, as in Figure 5-72.

Figure 5-72. *Given the brush-off: The format painter cursor*

3. Click and drag onto destination cells, as in Figure 5-73.

Figure 5-73. *Paint job: The format painter at work*

4. Release the mouse. The destination cells should display the source formatting, as in Figure 5-74.

Figure 5-74. *The destination cells, after the source format has been copied to them. You might now want to widen their column.*

The format painter copies *only* the formats characterizing the source cell, not the cell's data. It provides a handy way to export the formats into other cells, while leaving the destination-cell data intact.

> **NOTE:** After you apply the format painter once to destination cells, the paintbrush disappears, and you're back to the normal data entry mode. If you want to use the format painter to copy formats repeatedly to different ranges of cells, double-click the **Format Painter** button. The paint brush will remain in effect, and you can drag on as many different ranges as you wish. To turn the paintbrush off, just press the Esc key.

Applying Ready-Made Formats with Styles

There may be times when you're having difficulty coming up with a nicely designed format that suits your data, and you may need something quickly—say, for a meeting or a presentation. Excel's **Cells Styles** option presents a large series of style options at the click of a mouse.

1. First select the cell(s) you want to restyle.

2. Click the **Cell Styles** drop-down arrow in the **Styles** button group, and you'll be presented with the dialog shown in Figure 5–75.

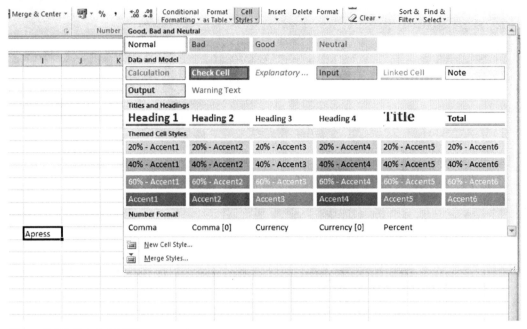

Figure 5–75. *Out of style? Choose one here.*

3. Click any of these and see how your data looks (or just hover your mouse over the style option that interests you; the cell preview mode operates here, too).

4. If you reconsider your style selection, just summon that style gallery again and click another one (see Figure 5–76).

Figure 5–76. *Just click a different style if you're not happy with the first one.*

Customizing Your Own Style

You can also design your own styles. Let's say you want to turn that lovely Algerian, 19-point concoction into a style:

1. Format a cell as you wish. Here I've used

   ▪ An Algerian 19-point font

   ▪ The color red

   ▪ Italics

   ▪ An orange background

2. Select it.

3. Click the **Cell Styles** ➤ **New Cell Style…** option (in the lower left of the **Cell Styles** dialog box). You'll see the dialog shown in Figure 5–77. Note that the cell's formatting attributes are recorded in the **Style Includes** area.

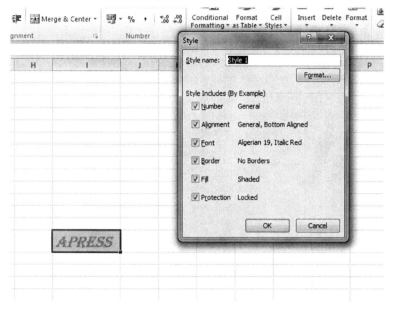

Figure 5–77. *DIY style*

4. Type your own style name in the **Style name** field and click **OK**.

5. Click the **Cell Styles** button again and you'll see the dialog in Figure 5–78.

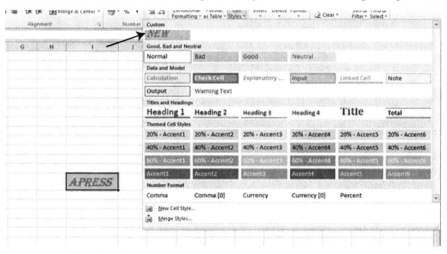

Figure 5–78. *My style, duly recorded*

Not a catchy name, but you see the style listed under the **Custom** heading at the top of the dialog box. To delete a user-devised style, right-click its name and click **Delete**.

Applying Styles Quickly: Another Way to Access Formatting Options

As already stated, Excel isn't stingy about providing the user with various ways to do the same thing, and one way to carry out important formatting options uses the right mouse button click. Right-click a cell you want to format and you'll see what's shown in Figure 5–79.

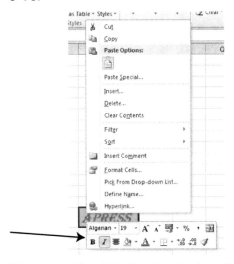

Figure 5–79. *The mini-toolbar, featuring formatting's greatest hits*

Two objects suddenly appear:

- What's called the context menu, that tall column listing various command options, which by and large you can also access on the ribbon (e.g., **Cut** and **Copy**)

- The mini-toolbar, a collection of commonly applied formatting options gathered from various button groups. Just click the one you need (with the left button, by the way).

Note that the previewing feature described previously works here, too—rest your mouse over a formatting command before you click it, and the selected cells will show what the formatting change will look like.

Conditional Formatting

There may be times when you want to call special attention to certain cells. For example, you may be working with a list of test scores and want to quickly be able to tell which tests exceed a certain score, fall below that score, or both. Excel's conditional formatting feature lets you format cells so that they change their appearance *only when they meet conditions you specify.*

To continue with our example, with conditional formatting you can instruct any cell with a value greater than, say, 90 (a high test score) to turn blue—but *only* if it tops 90. Otherwise, the cell will continue to exhibit its original appearance. Thus, conditional formatting is an effective, and pretty easy, way to highlight certain cells scattered among a large mass of data (imagine reviewing 5,000 test scores!).

In fact, Excel gives the user many different ways to engineer conditional formats, some more complex than others. But many can be quite simple, even almost self-evident. Let's demonstrate one now, by turning to our test example.

1. Start by entering the test results from Figure 5–80 in cells C5:D15.

Student	Score
Ted	77
Jane	81
Bill	90
Janice	82
Bob	71
Ed	68
Edith	79
Quincy	93
Sally	80
Rob	75

Figure 5–80. *Testing, testing . . . looking for scores above 90*

> **NOTE:** Remember our objective: we want to be able to quickly identify all those scores that have achieved 90 or higher by having their cells turn blue.

2. Select the range of scores we want to conditionally format: D5:D15.

3. Click the **Conditional Formatting** button in the **Styles** button group on the Home tab (see Figure 5–81).

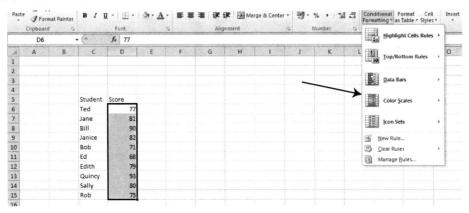

Figure 5–81. *The Conditional Formatting drop-down menu*

4. Click the first option, **Highlight Cells Rules**. You'll see the conditional formatting rules shown in Figure 5–82.

Figure 5–82. *Conditional formatting rules*

5. Select **Greater Than…**, and you'll see the dialog in Figure 5–83.

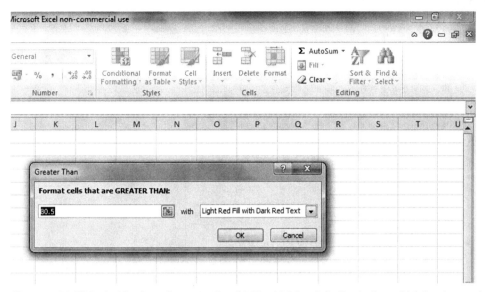

Figure 5–83. *We're looking for cells greater than 90. The 80.5 is a default selection, which Excel computed by averaging the highest and lowest scores in the range.*

6. Type **90** in the **Format Cells that are GREATER THAN:** field. We've established our condition: test scores above 90.

7. Click the drop-down arrow along the **Light Red Fill with Dark Red Text** entry. That's Excel's default, telling you that if any selected cell meets your condition, it will turn light red, and its text will appear as dark red. But we want our cells to turn blue instead, so click the **Custom Format...** option. You'll see the **Format Cells** dialog box, as shown in Figure 5–84.

8. Click the **Fill** tab, because we want the cells that meet our condition to turn blue, not the text in those cells.

9. Click a blue color in the resulting palette. Click **OK**.

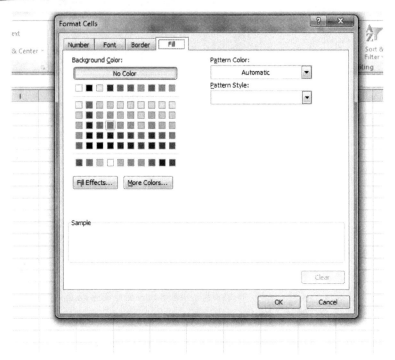

Figure 5–84. *Color scheme: Selecting a cell formatting color*

10. You'll be brought back to the **Greater Than** dialog box. Click **OK**.

11. Turn off the blue selection color surrounding the test score range D6:D15. You'll see the content shown in Figure 5–85.

Student	Score
Ted	77
Jane	81
Bill	90
Janice	82
Bob	71
Ed	68
Edith	79
Quincy	93
Sally	80
Rob	75

Figure 5–85. *Well done, Quincy!*

To summarize, we used the conditional formatting feature to highlight all the cells that meet a condition we specified—in this case, all test scores over 90. We selected the cells we wanted to analyze, clicked the appropriate conditional formatting option (in this case the **Greater Than...** option), entered our greater-than-90 criterion, and then chose the color we wanted to apply to the cells that met the condition. And we see that only Quincy surpassed the 90 mark.

Looking for Scores Equal to or Greater Than 90

Now, what if we're looking instead for all scores equaling or bettering 90? There's more than one option here. We could click **Highlight Cells Rules ➤ Between…** instead of the original **Greater Than…**, which would reveal the dialog box shown in Figure 5–86.

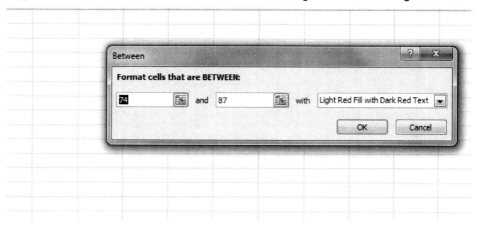

Figure 5–86. *One approach to looking for scores equal to or greater than 90*

We'd then enter 90 in the first field, and 100 in the other, and then click OK. The rest of the process would be identical to the first exercise.

An Alternative Approach to the Same Result

The second option would take us to this command sequence:

1. Select **Highlight Cells Rules ➤ More Rules…**, as shown in Figure 5–87.

Figure 5–87. *Rules are made to be . . . followed.*

2. Then select **Format only cells that contain**, and then **greater than or equal to**, as in Figure 5–88.

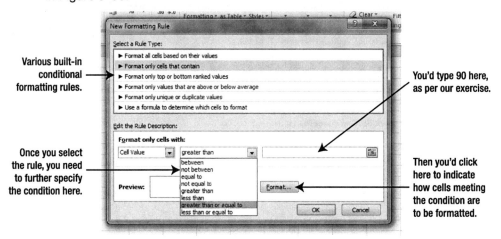

Various built-in conditional formatting rules.

You'd type 90 here, as per our exercise.

Once you select the rule, you need to further specify the condition here.

Then you'd click here to indicate how cells meeting the condition are to be formatted.

Figure 5–88. *Plan B*

3. Click and then type **90** in the blank field to the right of greater than or equal to.

4. Then click **Format** and **OK**, and once again you'll be brought back to the **Format Cells** dialog box. And as with the other examples, you need to decide which sort of formatting change to introduce.

Just keep in mind that when you institute a conditional format, you can change the appearance of the *text* in cells (e.g., its font, color, or boldface/italics status) that meet your condition, as well as the color of the cell itself.

Some Additional Conditional Formatting Options

Again, Excel makes many other conditional formatting options available. Let's just look at two more.

1. Select the test data cells again and click **Conditional Formatting** ➤ **Top/Bottom Rules**. You'll see the options shown in Figure 5–89.

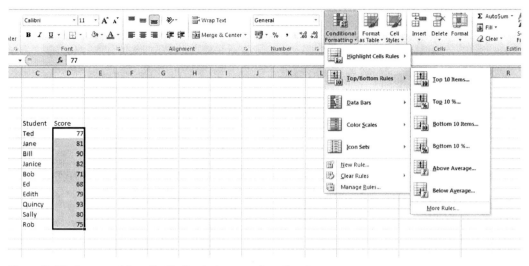

Figure 5–89. Average white cells: Finding test scores above the class average

2. Click **Above Average…**, and you'll be brought to the dialog shown in Figure 5–90.

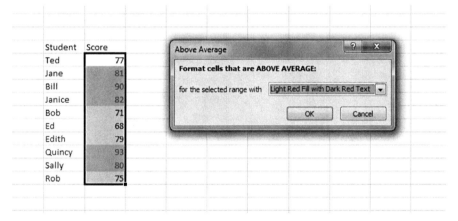

Figure 5–90. Note that the above-average scores are tinted red in preview mode even before you click OK.

3. Click OK now, meaning that you're accepting Excel's **Light Red Fill with Dark Red Text** default conditional format. You'll see that all test scores exceeding the class average will exhibit exactly that—their cells will appear in light red, and the text in those cells will appear in dark red.

And conditional formats are dynamic, meaning that if you change the data with which you're working, the formats will change correspondingly. If you enter 100 for Edith's grade, for example, her cell will immediately turn light red with dark red text, because it now exceeds the class average—and Sally's grade of 80 will lose that formatting, because her grade will now fall below the average.

Turning Off Conditional Formatting

If you want to turn off your conditional formats and restore the cells to their original, black-text-on-white-background appearance, do the following:

1. Select the cells.

2. Click **Conditional Formatting** ➤ **Clear Rules** ➤ **Clear Rules from Selected Cells** (or from **Entire Sheet**, if that's what you want to do).

Using Data Bars: A Different Kind of Conditional Format

1. Here's one more conditional format option of a very different sort. Instead of coloring cells or their backgrounds on the basis of specified conditions, data bars occupy conditionally formatted cells with mini bar charts, which are proportioned to the values in those cells.Select the test data.

2. Click **Conditional Formatting** ➤ **Data Bars**.

3. Hover the mouse over the first **Gradient Fill** option, and you'll see the options shown in Figure 5–91.

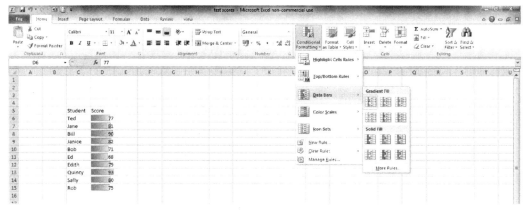

Figure 5–91. *Grades and gradients: Applying gradient bars to the test scores*

What's happened—or what *will* happen if you go ahead and click—is the application of a mini–bar chart inside each cell displaying a test score. Note that the bar in Quincy's 93— the highest score in the class—fills the entire cell, and the other bars are sized in proportion to that 93. If you enter 100 in Edith's cell again, *her* bar that will occupy the entire cell, with the other cells proportioned to her grade.

> **NOTE:** If you widen the column in which the data bars appear, the disparity in bar lengths between various grades will seem more pronounced.

Summary

Making your worksheets look good is an important part of the spreadsheet-building process. Excel's formatting options provide you with a heap of ways to do just that. Now we can move to another way—really, a group of ways—to present your data with striking visual appeal. The next chapter will introduce you to the world of charts.

Chapter 6

Charting Your Data

People like to see information presented visually. Looking at data in graphical form lets readers—and spreadsheet viewers—quickly and vividly understand what's going on, in a way that hundreds or thousands of rows worth of data can't. Compare the two portrayals of test scores shown in Figure 6–1.

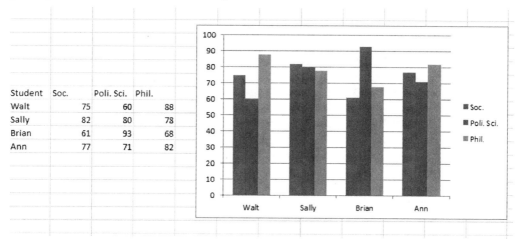

Student	Soc.	Poli. Sci.	Phil.
Walt	75	60	88
Sally	82	80	78
Brian	61	93	68
Ann	77	71	82

Figure 6–1. *Two points of view*

Same data, two different looks. The column chart (that's what shown in Figure 6–1, and once you learn a bit about how charts are constructed, you'll be able to fashion one in about 10 seconds) conveys a sense of proportion among the scores that the cells to its left can't.

Excel makes it easy to conjure charts that can embellish your worksheets in productive and appealing ways. Needless to say, the more you know about its wide inventory of charting options the better, but Excel's charting basics are simple and will enable you to make crisp, lucid presentations of your data—even if you don't get to the all the bells and whistles.

Defining Chart Elements

In order to better understand how Excel charting works, let's take a closer look at some of charting elements (see Figure 6–2).

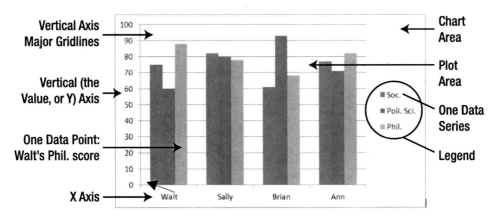

Figure 6–2. *Basic chart elements*

Table 6–1 describes these in more detail.

Table 6–1. *Basic Chart Element Descriptions*

Chart Element	What It Does
Vertical value (y) axis	Draws up a scale measuring the source data to be charted. In our example, the values on the y-axis represent the span of test scores in the source data.
Horizontal category (x) axis	Lists the variables by which the data is being plotted. In our case, the x-axis consists of the names of the students whose grades are being plotted.
Data series	Groups of the data being plotted. Figure 6–2 displays three data series, each representing a subject and denoted by a different color: blue for Soc., red for Poli. Sci., and green for Phil.

Chart Element	What It Does
Legend	Lists the chart data series in color-coded form.
Chart area	Provides the background of the chart.
Data point	An individual value in the data series. For example, Walt's philosophy score is a data point in the Phil. data series.
Plot area	The area in which the data is actually charted.
Vertical (value) axis major gridlines	The lines that intersect the values on the vertical axis and run across the plot area.

TIP: The data series are always identified in the chart legend. But as you'll see, the same data can be reorganized into different data series.

Note that when you rest your mouse over any chart element, Excel supplies an identifying caption, as in Figure 6–3.

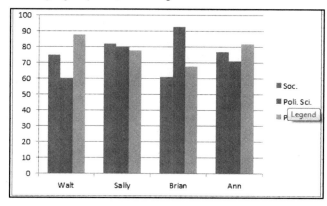

Figure 6–3. *Identifying the chart legend*

Choosing a Chart Type

Perhaps the first thing you need to do once you start chart-making is identify exactly what type of chart you want to use. Click the **Insert** ribbon tab and you'll be brought to the **Charts** button group (see Figure 6–4).

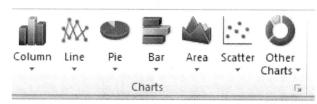

Figure 6–4. *The Charts button group*

Here you're shown a collection of basic chart types, each of which offers several subtypes that let you portray your data in different ways, with different looks. Table 6–2 briefly describes them.

Table 6–2. *Chart Types*

Chart Type	What It Does	When to Use It
Column	Depicts data as vertical bars; perhaps the most commonly used type	When you need to present individual sets of data (e.g., sales totals by different departments)
Line	Depicts data as a series of lines	When you want to present data that varies over time (e.g., a student's test scores)
Pie	Characterizes only *one* data series as a series of slices, each contributing to a whole	If, for example, you need to portray different departments' percentages of an overall company budget
Bar	Basically depicts a column chart whose data series are presented horizontally instead of vertically	As per a column chart, but here the data bars extend sideways
Area	Depicts a line chart whose data fills in the areas between the lines and the x-axis (take a look at the **Area** button)	When you want to convey the relative depth of data (e.g., a test score of 90 will cover more area than a score of 75)
Scatter	Portrays data along *two* value axes (that term will be defined shortly), thus treating data as paired values.,	When you want to look at data organized by two quantitative variables at the same time, e.g., plotting marathon times by age of the runners.
Other	Encompasses a collection of less-commonly used charts.	When you need a specialized chart, such as for a stock market comparison

Creating a Column Chart

Now that we've gotten oriented, let's try our hand at producing a column chart. First, open the Test Scores workbook, and then perform the following steps:

1. Click anywhere within the data. There's no need to select the whole range of data, and in fact you shouldn't.

2. Click the **Insert** tab, and then choose **Column** from the **Chart** button group. You'll see the options shown in Figure 6–5.

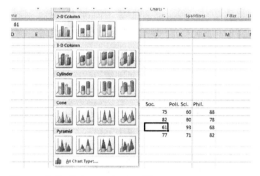

Figure 6–5. *Column chart subtypes*

3. Click the chart subtype you want to choose. We'll click the first option, in the upper-left corner of the menu. You'll see the chart that was shown in the earlier figures.

For starters, that's all there is to it; click in the data to be charted, select a chart subtype, and you're done—maybe. If you're happy with what you see, then you *are* done. Note that the chart looks at the grade data and makes some decisions on its own about how the vertical value axis will be scaled—in this case, with values ranging from 0 to 100, spaced at 10-point intervals (see Figure 6–6).

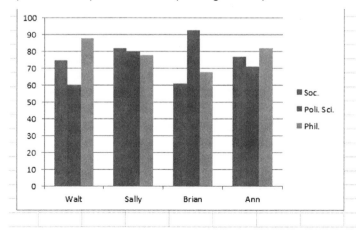

Figure 6–6. *Note the vertical value axis scaled at 10-point intervals.*

NOTE: You can delete a chart by clicking in the chart area and pressing the Delete key.

Creating a Chart in 2 Seconds

No, that heading isn't a typo. You really *can* drum up a chart in about 2 seconds, give or take a millisecond, like this: just click in the data you want to chart, and press the F11 key. You'll see something like Figure 6–7.

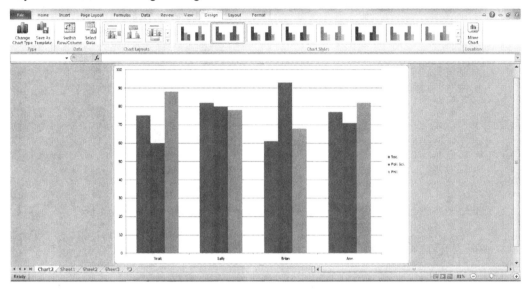

Figure 6–7. *Where's the stopwatch? There's the chart. Note the new worksheet on the far left.*

It's done. Excel latches onto the data and launches a column chart pronto. Note that Excel throws the chart onto a new worksheet, here called Chart2 (because we've already produced a chart in the workbook).

Changing a Chart

If you want to change some or all of the aspects of your chart, all those options await; and while some of these changes are purely aesthetic, other options will let you bring about a real change in the way in which the chart communicates its data, as you'll see. And Excel gives you the tools to change virtually any aspect of your chart.

Moving and Resizing the Chart

Possibly the two simplest ways in which you can change a chart is to move it and resize it. You can move a chart by clicking in the chart area only (but nowhere else) and dragging the chart to a new location in the worksheet. Clicking anywhere else in the chart will only select the element on which you clicked, and you won't be able to drag the chart. You'll know that you've selected the entire chart when the chart acquires that thick border, as shown in the right of Figure 6–8.

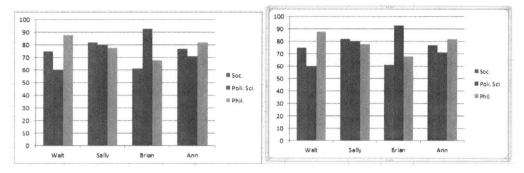

Figure 6–8. *The chart on the right displays the selection border.*

You can also move the chart to a more distant location, such as a different worksheet or even a different workbook, by clicking the chart area so that it's selected in its entirety, and then clicking the standard **Cut** command, clicking in the destination worksheet or workbook, and clicking **Paste** (or pressing Ctrl+V).

You can resize the chart by selecting it and releasing the mouse, and then clicking back a second time in one of the chart borders' dotted areas (in the center (see arrow) and at the corners of the borders, which are characterized by a set of dots), and dragging in the desired direction, as you would with any graphic object in the Microsoft Office suite. You should see a double-sided arrow atop the border when you're about to click to start dragging (see Figure 6–9).

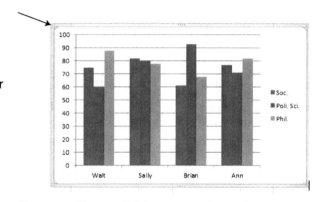

Figure 6–9. *Where to click in order to begin to resize the chart*

If you select the chart and then click one of its corners and drag, you'll maintain the current proportion of chart height to chart width. Resizing a chart can distort the appearance of the data, thus skewing the impression you want the chart to make. Resizing your chart by narrowing it can engineer the kind of look shown in Figure 6–10.

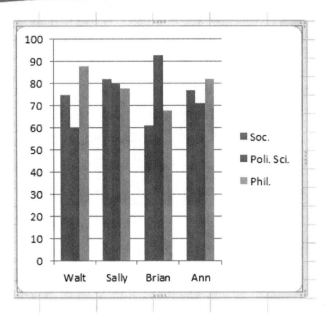

Figure 6–10. *Tight squeeze: Pinching the chart can make Brian's 93 in Poli. Sci. look more impressive.*

There are other ways in which you can introduce chart distortion too (see the "Reformatting the Vertical Axis section" later in this chapter for another example).

Changing the Chart by Changing Its Data

Another way to change the chart is by changing the data that's contributing to it. Excel charts are dynamic; in our case that means that if you change any of the test scores in the original set of scores, the column bar(s) will change accordingly. If, for example, Brian's 93 had been entered by mistake and he had really scored a 63, typing that 63 would automatically resize Brian's Poli. Sci. score (see Figure 6–11). This dynamic feature remains in force even if you move the chart to another worksheet.

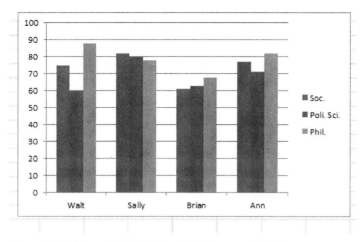

Figure 6–11. *Sorry about that, Brian; that 93 was really a 63.*

Changing the Chart Type

Of course, there are more dramatic ways to change a chart than simply relocating or resizing it. You can also change the chart type—or chart subtype—at the click of a mouse.

When we composed our grade column chart, we encountered a drop-down menu sporting a wealth of column subtypes, each equally accessible via one click (see Figure 6–12).

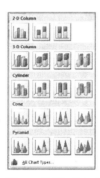

Figure 6–12. *Note the various column motifs.*

But our chart is already on the worksheet. How do we change what's already there? As usual, there's more than one way.

1. Click anywhere on the chart. Then take note of what are called *contextual tabs*. These are tabs that spring onto the screen only when you click a specific object, in this case a chart (see Figure 6–13).

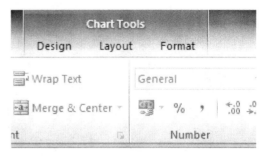

Figure 6–13. *The Chart Tools button groups, appearing beneath the Chart Tools contextual tab*

2. Click the **Design** tab.

3. Click the **Change Chart Type** button in the **Type** button group. You'll see the **Change Chart Type** dialog box (Figure 6–14).

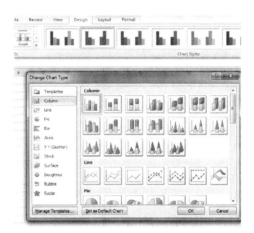

Figure 6–14. *Spoiled for choice: Change Chart Type options*

NOTE: The current chart subtype is selected. Click any of the other column subtypes or scroll down the dialog box to see the other chart options and their respective subtypes.

4. Click your selection, click **OK**, and the chart will be changed.

You can also change chart types by right-clicking in the chart area (again, click only there, not on any other element in the chart) and clicking **Change Chart Type...** in the resulting context menu (not to be confused with the context tabs described previously). You'll be brought to the **Change Chart Type** dialog box, as shown in Figure 6–15.

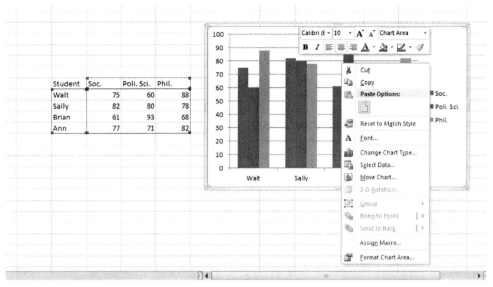

Student	Soc.	Poli. Sci.	Phil.
Walt	75	60	88
Sally	82	80	78
Brian	61	93	68
Ann	77	71	82

Figure 6–15. *An alternative route to the Change Chart Type dialog box. Just click Change Chart Type… in the context menu.*

As you experiment with the chart options, you'll discover that many offer a 3D look, as in Figure 6–16.

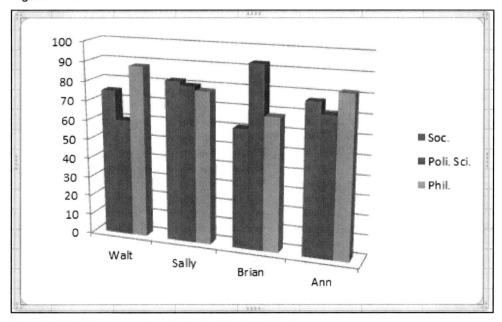

Figure 6–16. *Adding a new dimension to the data: The 3D look*

That's cool, but again, prudence is the watchword when you start getting fancy. Sometimes a cool head should outweigh a cool effect.

Now let's quickly see what happens when we call on the other major chart types to depict the data, as shown in Figure 6–17.

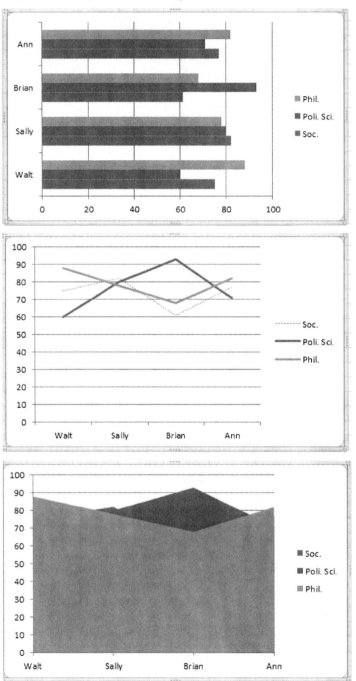

Figure 6–17. *The major chart types (from top to bottom, a bar chart, a line chart, and an area chart)*

Where's the Pie Chart?

Good question. I've omitted that chart type quite intentionally here because of the observation I made in Table 6–2, back when I defined a pie chart. Pie charts can only capture data *one* data series at a time, and our data has three series—Soc., Poli. Sci., and Phil. You could construct a pie chart of only Walt's grades, for example, as in Figure 6–18.

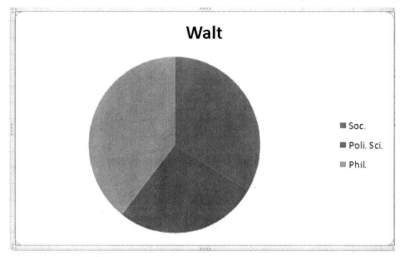

Figure 6–18. *The higher the grade, the larger the slice*

Here Walt's grades are treated as a data series (we'll look past the question of whether grades are the sort of thing you'd best portray with a pie chart; but just note that it can be done)—and that means if we're pie-charting Walt's grades, we *can't* chart Sally's, Brian's, and Ann's as well on the same chart. Pie charts treat their slices as parts of one whole—and that whole consists of one data series.

> **NOTE:** The pie chart automatically adds a title to the chart. You'll soon see how you can add a title to any chart.

Changing the Default Chart

What you should have learned from this exercise is that the standard column chart shown previously serves as Excel's default chart. After all, *we* didn't select that chart when we pressed F11; Excel chose it for us. But what if you want to see a different chart by default?

It's easy. Recall that when you execute the Change Chart Type sequence you trigger the dialog box shown in Figure 6–19. To change the default chart, just click the chart you want to designate and click **Set as Default Chart**. Then click **OK**, and the chart you've chosen will appear from now on when you press F11.

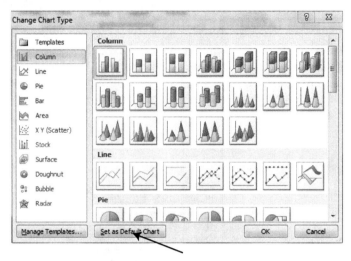

Figure 6–19. *Second thoughts: Where to reset your default chart*

Switching Rows with Columns: A Different Kind of Change

Here's another way to change your charts—one that doesn't change chart types or their colors, but rather does something very different. It's called the *Switch Row/Column option*. Switching a chart's rows and columns flips the chart's axes at right angles to one another, so that the current data series switches places with the data on the horizontal axis. For example, in our charts so far, the student names have occupied the horizontal axis, and the subjects have served as the data series and appear in the legend. By switching the row and column, the *subjects* will now populate the horizontal axis, with the student names holding down the legend.

So why would you want to do this? To give the data a different perspective. Instead of seeing how each student has performed in the three subjects—as with the original chart setup—by switching row and column you can see how the four students' grades are bundled by each subject instead.

Now, if that still leaves you dazed and confused, actually trying the option out on our chart should clarify.

1. Click the chart.

2. Turn it back to a column chart if you need to.

3. Click the **Chart Tools** tab and then the **Design** tab, and then click the **Switch Row/Column** button in the **Data** button group. You'll see what's shown in Figure 6–20.

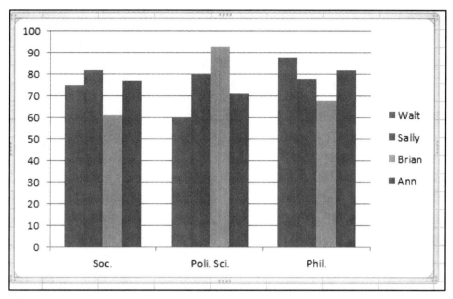

Figure 6–20. *Trading places: The student names now serve as the data series, replacing the subjects. Remember that the legend always records the data series.*

See the effect? The chart has been stood on its head, so to speak, or maybe its side. While it was the test subjects that served as the chart's original data series, now it's the student names playing that role—each *student* is now a data series. The data being charted is exactly the same as before, but it's being characterized by a new perspective—sort of at a right angle to itself. Of course, if you click the **Switch Row/Column** button a second time, you'll be back where you started, and the subjects will be reinstated as the data series.

Formatting Charts

Just as you can format your data, you can format and reformat your charts. And as with data in cells, there are plenty of ways to modify chart appearances: by changing colors, text fonts, or borders around the plot area, or by introducing data labels, chart titles, and the like.

Of course, you need to know how to get to all these options—and in keeping with Excel's general approach, there are several ways available. Let's take a look at them.

The first step in the formatting process, as usual, is to click the object you want to format (depending on which approach you use, that click might utilize the left or right button, as I'll discuss). You need to be clear about exactly which object you have in mind, because it's easy to think you're about to click the major gridlines when you've really hovered your mouse over the plot area. That's where Excel's chart captions come in; again, resting your mouse over a chart object triggers an identifying caption.

Formatting with the Mini-Toolbar

I introduced the mini-toolbar in Chapter 5. Note that the same-right-click that brings the context menu onto the screen takes the mini-toolbar along for the ride in chart formatting. The mini-toolbar provides a selection of popular formatting options. In fact, the options shown on the mini-toolbar are always the same, no matter which object you click (see Figure 6–21):

- The Font and font size buttons
- The increase- and decrease-font-size buttons
- A chart element button (which reads **Chart Area** in Figure 6–24), whose drop-down arrow allows to you select any other chart object
- The bold and italic font options
- The three basic cell alignment options: left, right, and center
- The font color button
- The shape fill button, which lets you color the object you've selected.
- The shape outline button, which lets you select a color for the *border* of the object.
- The format painter button

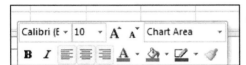

Figure 6–21. *Mini-toolbar options*

Which of the toolbar's options will be *active* on the toolbar, however, depends on the object you click. Thus, if you click column bars, for example, you won't be able to change any fonts with the mini-toolbar, because there's no text on the bars to change.

NOTE: When you want to select a particular data series, just click *one* of the series' bars. All the other bars will be selected as well. And keep in mind exactly what gets selected. If you select the Phil. data series, you'll see something like Figure 6–22.

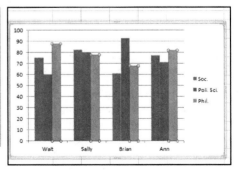

Figure 6–22. *Select group: Note the selection handles at the corners of each Phil. bar.*

Formatting with the Context Menu

We visited the context menu back when we explored that alternative way to access the **Change Chart Type** dialog box. Again, right-clicking the object you want to format calls up that menu, the *last* option on which is always the format-object option (see Figure 6–23).

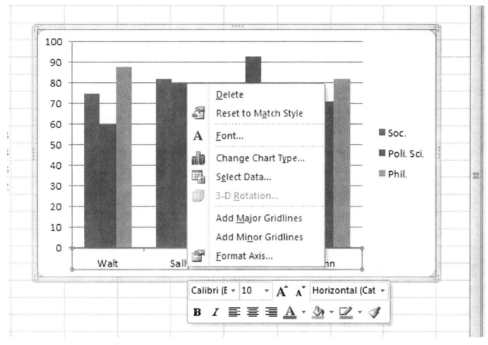

Figure 6–23. *Note the last option. Here we're about to reformat the x-axis.*

Formatting with the Current Selection Button Group

Clicking the **Layout** tab beneath the **Chart Tools** context tab heading calls up the **Current Selection** button group on the tab's left edge, as shown in Figure 6–24.

Figure 6–24. *The Current Selection button group. Note that the vertical (value) axis has been selected.*

Click **Format Selection** to work with that object's formatting options; and whether you bring up the context menu or turn to the **Current Selection** button, you'll be brought to the same dialog box.

Say you want to reformat the chart area. Either of the two methods described previously will bring you to a format dialog box (see Figure 6–25);

Figure 6–25. *Take your choice: you'll get here either with the context menu and the Current Selection button group.*

That's how the standard format-any-chart-object dialog box looks.

Exploring the Format Dialog Box

The contents of the format dialog box will vary with the object you've selected. The formatting options for data series, chart, and plot areas are basically of the change-their-color variety. For example, if you want to recolor a data series, do the following:

1.   Click one of the data series' bars to select it.

2. Then either click
    Format Selection or
    right-click the bar and
    click **Format Data Series**.
    You'll see the dialog
    shown in Figure 6–26.

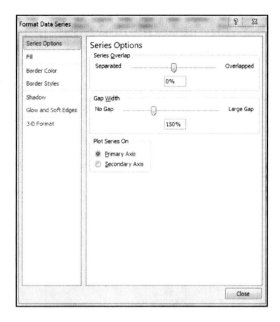

Figure 6–26. *Filling Phil.: Changing that data series' color*

3. Then click **Fill**, click
    the **Solid Fill** radio
    button, and click the
    down arrow by **Fill
    Color**, as shown in
    Figure 6–27.

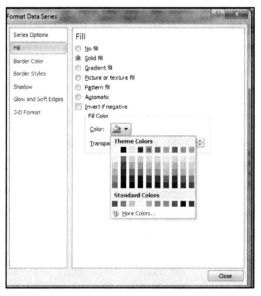

Figure 6–27. *True colors: Select the color you wish.*

4. Select your color, click **Close**, and you're done (note again that your new
    data series color will appear on the chart in preview mode even before
    you click **Close**).

You can also fill data series bars with interesting gradient fills—textured sweeps of color that spread across the bars. Clicking **Gradient fill ➤ Preset colors** instead of **Solid fill** will give you the options shown in Figure 6–28.

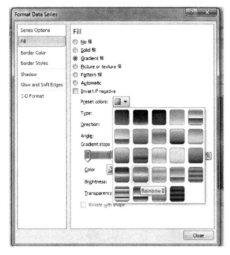

Figure 6–28. *An alternative to solid fills*

After you've selected one of those built-in options (here, **Rainbow II** was clicked) and clicked **Close** you'll get something like Figure 6–29.

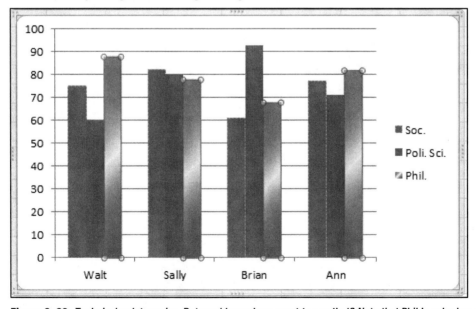

Figure 6–29. *Technicolor data series. But would your boss want to see that? Note that Phil.'s color has also changed accordingly in the legend.*

Try playing around with the other gradient options, too.

NOTE: You can also access the gradient and other options with the mini-toolbar, by clicking the arrow to the right of those toolbar buttons accompanied by the arrow. In our example, if you click the arrow by the fill button, you'll see what's shown in Figure 6–30.

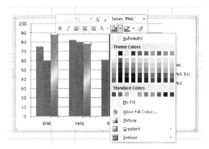

Figure 6–30. *Note the gradient option.*

NOTE: If you've introduced all kinds of formatting variations into the chart and are beginning to have second thoughts about it all, return to the **Current Selection** button group, select the changed object(s) in sequence, and click **Reset to Match Style**. All the default formatting settings will be restored.

Reformatting the Vertical Axis

Now that we've talked about some of those color-based formatting options, we need to turn to some different kinds of formatting possibilities. Let's turn to the vertical (value) axis, the leftmost area of the chart, which lists the values against which the chart data is measured. When you devise a chart, Excel makes an educated guess as to which values best characterize the data. In our chart we see a scale of values running from 0 to 100 at 10-point intervals, reflecting the test scores we're charting.

But you can change the scale. For example, you could space the intervals differently— say, at 5-point intervals, so that the 0 to 100 scale could display 0, 5, 10, 15, and so on, instead.

Say you wanted the value axis to read 0, 20, 40, 80, and 100.

1. Right-click right atop the axis and click **Format Axis**, and you'll be taken to the dialog shown in Figure 6–31.

Figure 6–31. *Value axis options*

NOTE: The fact that **Major Unit** field is dimmed means that the 10.0 value was automatically selected by Excel.

2.   Click the **Fixed** radio button by the **Major Unit** field.

3.   Enter **20** to replace the 10.0.

4.   Click **Close**, and you should see the chart shown in Figure 6–32.

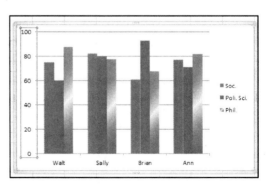

Figure 6–32. *A decent interval: Each value on the axis is now spaced at 20 points apart.*

Also notice that you can change the maximum and minimum values at either end of the scale. Thus, if you click the **Fixed** radio button alongside **Minimum** (it's called "fixed" because you've chosen and fixed that value, overriding Excel's automatic decision) and type **40**, your chart will look like Figure 6–33.

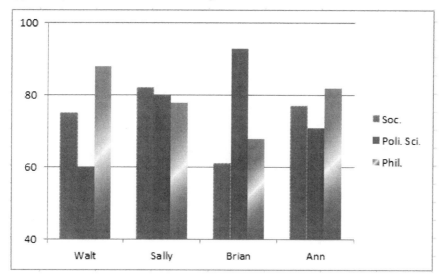

Figure 6–33. *Raising the bottom line: A new minimum chart value*

OK—why would you want to do this? The fact is that many charts adopt a minimum value greater than 0, because the values being charted aren't likely to go anywhere near that numerical point. Think about the stock market charts you've seen; they'll practically never start at 0, because the Dow Jones index is up there in the five figures (at least it is now), and a daily change of 100 points looks far more striking when the chart minimum is set at 10,000 than it would if it were 0. On the other hand, establishing a new minimum will change the visual relation of the bars to one another. Brian's 93 will seem even more masterly as a result. You need to think about how, or if, that distortion will impact your audience.

Color-Coordinating Your Data Using Chart Styles

Remember I stated a while back that virtually every element of a chart can be changed, and changing chart colors is probably one of the principal changes you're likely to make. Excel gives you plenty of opportunities to fine-tune your chart, one element at a time. But you can also revamp the appearance of a chart in one fell swoop with the **Styles** option, a very easy-to-apply feature that recolors all the chart data series and, depending on the option you choose, the plot area too. Just click **Chart Tools**, and click **Chart Styles** on the **Design** tab (click the **More** drop-down arrow—the third of the three drop-down arrows) to reveal all the selections (see Figure 6–34).

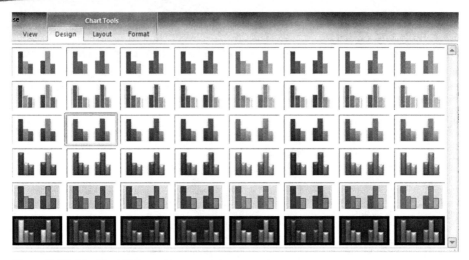

Figure 6–34. *The Chart Styles option*

Just click the style you want, and that's it. Note that the options in the last two rows of styles will also recolor the plot area, in addition to the data series. Just remember that even if you do use styles, you can still continue to make additional changes to any element of the chart on your own, including the colors of a style.

Formatting a Chart Object Using Shape Styles

Don't confuse *shape styles* with *chart styles*. Unlike chart styles, shape styles enable you to reformat just *one* chart object in particular (axis text, plot area, one data series, etc.). Also unlike chart styles, the **Shape Styles** option shows you how the reformatted object will look in preview mode, when you rest your mouse over a style before you click it.

Let's see how shape styles are used:

1. Select the chart element for which you want to add a shape style. In this case, let's format the horizontal (category) axis, so select it.

2. Click **Chart Tools**, click the **Format** context tab, and then click the **Shape Styles More** drop-down arrow (that's the third of the three arrows in that button group). **Shape Styles** will reveal the options shown in Figure 6–35.

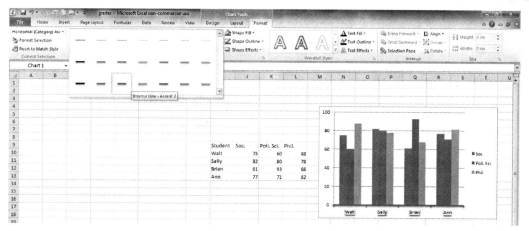

Figure 6–35. *Shapes of things to come: The Shape Styles option*

3. Click the style you want to apply. In this case, let's use Intense Line -
   Accent 2 (see Figure 6–36).

Figure 6–36. *Notice the embossed names. The axis line above the names has been recolored, too.*

Formatting Text Elements with WordArt

If you select a text-based chart element, you can try out the **WordArt Styles** options to the
right of **Shape Styles**. If you select the horizontal (category) axis again and then click the
WordArt More down arrow, you'll see the options shown in Figure 6–37.

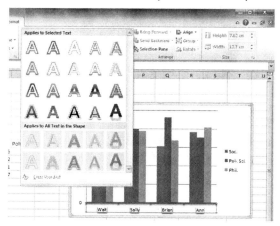

Figure 6–37. *The next text option: WordArt*

Try out these effects.

Adding Extra Chart Elements with Chart Layouts

The Chart Layouts button group is to the immediate left of Chart Styles on the Design tab. Chart layouts introduce an array of elements to your charts above and beyond color changes (see Figure 6–38).

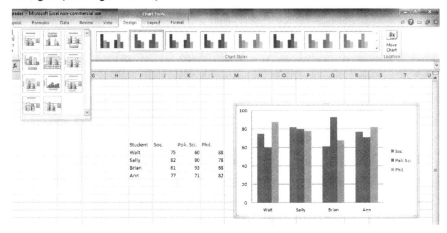

Figure 6–38. *Chart Layout options*

Experiment with these and you'll discover some new and informative ways to tweak your chart. For example, layout 5 (each layout is identified by a numbered caption; just rest your mouse above any layout choice to see it) presents the chart variation shown in Figure 6–39.

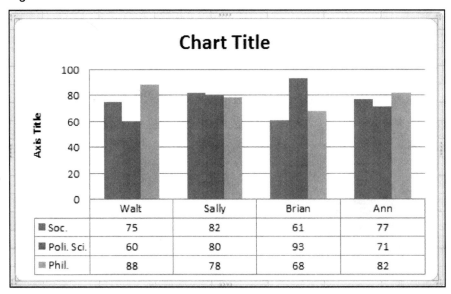

Figure 6–39. *The chart, accompanied by what's called a data table*

This layout exhibits a *data table,* which displays all the data contributing to the chart on the chart itself. It also adds two title boxes—one to describe the chart, and the other to identify the vertical (value) axis. To replace the title text with titles of your own, just click the titles (you'll see a selection border around it), type your title, and press Enter.

> **NOTE:** Data tables and other extras take space from the actual chart in order to make room for themselves. That means the chart itself will shrink as the extras surrounding it (such as titles and data tables) are added. As result, you'll have to resize the chart yourself if you want the original chart size to be restored with its new additions. Needless to say, if you don't like how the chart looks in its resized state you can execute an undo, or you can simply delete the extras.

Adding Extra Chart Elements with the Layout Tab

The buttons on the Layout tab let you add and modify many of the chart elements already discussed, such as chart and axis titles, data tables, and legends, as well as some objects we've yet to discuss, such as data labels. Each button sports a drop-down menu whose options are pretty clearly explained in caption form. And if the captions don't help, simply clicking each option should answer all your questions. Let's survey these buttons.

Chart Title

To add a chart title, go to the Layout tab and click Chart Title, as shown in Figure 6–40.

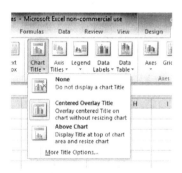

Figure 6–40. *Title search: The Chart Title button*

As its name suggests, **Chart Title** lets you install a title on the chart in one of two positions:

- As a *centered overlay*, in which the chart superimposes the title right on top of the chart (see Figure 6–41).

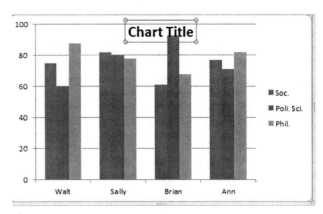

Figure 6–41. *Atop the charts: The centered overlay position*

- Above the chart. This one is pretty obvious, but note that the caption says that this option resizes the chart—that is, it grabs territory from the chart itself and downsizes it (see Figure 6–42).

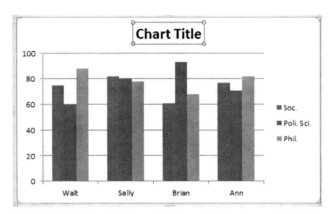

Figure 6–42. *Unobstructed view: The chart title is placed above the data.*

Now, you're not going to be happy with a chart title whose text declares "Chart Title." to substitute your own title, just click the title to select it, type your title in the formula bar, and press Enter.

TIP: You can always delete a title (and most other chart objects) by selecting it and pressing the Delete key.

Axis Titles

This option lets you enter and position a title for the vertical (value) axis and/or the horizontal (category) axis.

The vertical axis choices are shown in Figure 6–43.

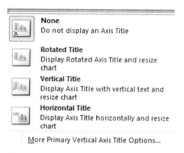

Figure 6–43. *Vertical axis title options. Note that all of these will contract the actual chart size by grabbing space for themselves.*

The rotated, vertical, and horizontal titles look like Figure 6–44.

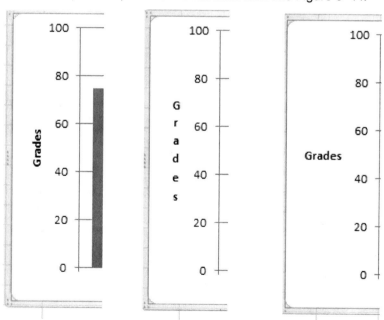

Figure 6–44. *From left to right, the rotated, vertical, and horizontal title orientations*

Legend

The **Legend** options (shown in Figure 6–45) let you position the legend at various points across the chart.

Figure 6–45. *The stuff of which legends are made*

Data Labels

The **Data Labels** options allow you to post on the chart the actual values that contribute to the chart, in various positions. Figure 6–46 shows an example.

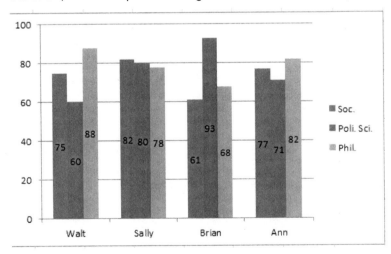

Figure 6–46. *Designer labels: Data labels, placed inside column bars*

TIP: Just remember that if you find that black-text-on-blue-bar color contrast too weak (as per the Soc. data series in our chart), you can always recolor the bar by reformatting that data series. You can also recolor the data labels by right-clicking any one of the values in that data series, and recoloring the font via the mini-toolbar.

Data Table

We've discussed data tables before; they're included in some of the chart layouts we reviewed earlier, and they display the data from which the chart is fashioned onto the chart in table form. For example, the **Show Data Table with Legend Keys** option installs the table in the position shown in Figure 6–47.

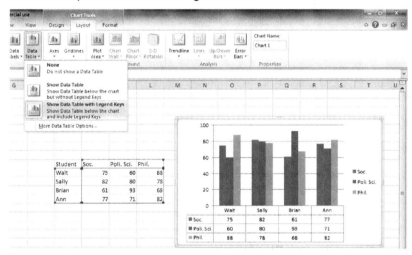

Figure 6–47. *Setting the Table: Where the data table goes*

The legend keys are the identifying text at the data table's left, which you may find a bit redundant, because the legend itself is out there as usual to the right of the chart. That's why Excel offers the Show Data Table option as well, which omits the legend keys.

NOTE: Again, adding a data table to the chart reduces the size of the actual chart.

Axes

The **Axes** option contains some selections you'll likely never use, and some you very well might. The **Axes ➤ Primary Horizontal Axis ➤ Show Right to Left Axis** option switches the vertical axis to the right edge of the chart, *and* reverses the order of the names shown beneath the horizontal axis (see Figure 6–48).

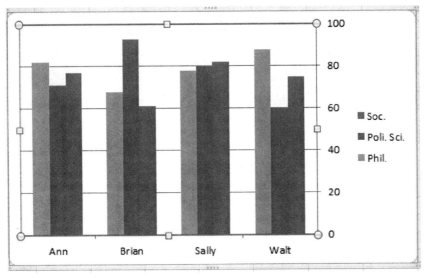

Figure 6–48. *Spinning the axis: Compare the order of the names beneath the axis to the previous screenshot.*

OK—that's one you're likely *not* to use—unless you're working with a right-to-left language such as Hebrew or Arabic. However, the **Primary Vertical Axis** options are ones you may want to know, even in English (see Figure 6–49).

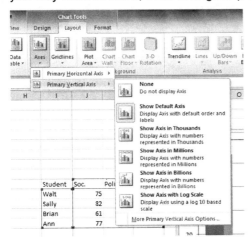

Figure 6–49. *Orders of magnitude: Options for displaying large values on the vertical axis*

Let's see an example of what these options do:

1. Start by typing the set of data shown in Figure 6–50, listing the top ten tourist locations.

Countries	Amount
France	67,310,000
United States	47,752,000
Spain	43,252,000
Italy	34,087,000
United Kingdom	25,515,000
China	23,770,000
Poland	19,520,000
Mexico	19,351,000
Canada	17,636,000

Figure 6–50. *Parlez-vous Francais? Top tourist countries*

2. Chart this and you get what's shown in Figure 6–51.

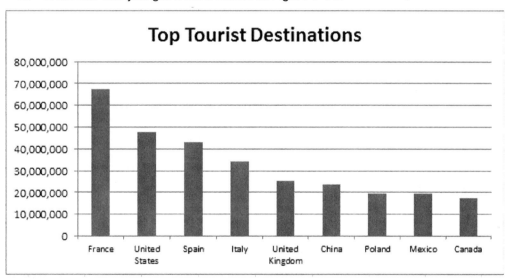

Figure 6–51. *The tourist data charted*

3. The problem is that the chart is congested with all those zeros. To remedy this, select **Show Axis in Millions** from the **Vertical Axis** drop-down, and you'll see the version in Figure 6–52.

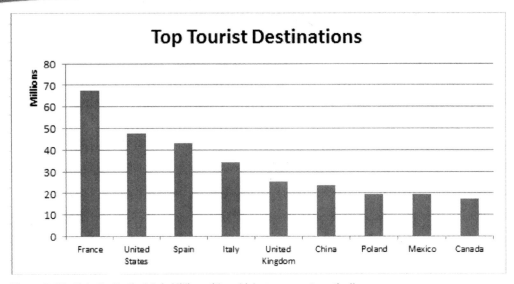

Figure 6–52. *Note the Vertical Axis Millions title, which appears automatically.*

All those millions have been trimmed from the axis, but that change is purely formatting in nature. The axis title reminds the viewer that 50 really still means 50 million, expressed in neat charting shorthand.

Plot Area

The **Plot Area** options (see Figure 6–53) are rather simple, comprising two basic selections, though the second of the two requires a bit of explanation.

Figure 6–53. *The Plot thickens: Plot Area options*

Clicking **None** restores the fill area color to its original, native white. The caption to the second option, **Show Plot Area**, states that it will "Show Plot Area with default color fill." That sounds like the **None** option, doesn't it? But it isn't—not quite. What **Show Plot Area** does is return the plot area to the color it acquires *if* you select one of the chart styles discussed earlier (i.e., one of those styles that recolors the plot area in *addition* to the data). It's only when you go ahead and recolor *this* plot area that **Show Plot Area** comes into play, as it reprises the chart style plot color you selected—not the original, default white.

Introducing Sparklines: Mini-Charts Placed in Cells

One of the most celebrated new features of Excel 2010 is the *sparkline*, a charting tool that enables you to capture your data with a different, cell-based approach. The brainchild of renowned visual information expert Edward Tufte, sparklines have actually been around for a while, but they made their Excel debut with this version.

Sparklines are unlike standard Excel charts in that they actually occupy cells in the worksheet. Standard charts are slapped on top of the worksheet like sticky notes — that's why you can drag them around when you want to move them. Sparklines, on the other hand, lock themselves into individual cells, so they actually have addresses. And because each sparkline occupies one cell, it tends to be rather small, at least for starters. The only way to enlarge one is to either widen its column or heighten its row.

But what can sparklines do for you that Excel's standard charts can't? The answer is that with sparklines you can select a range consisting of rows of data, such as our grades, and batch up a sparkline for each row — something like Figure 6–54.

Student	Soc.	Poli. Sci.	Phil.	
Walt	75	60	88	
Sally	82	80	78	
Brian	61	93	68	
Ann	77	71	82	

Figure 6–54. *Mini-charts, one per student*

That's the sparkline advantage — allowing the user to chart many sets — or rows — of data individually. Let's have a go:

1. First, select the range in which you want the sparklines to appear — in this case M10:M13 (see Figure 6–55). (You can either delete or move any existing charts on your workbook that may be obscuring your view of the range.)

Student	Soc.	Poli. Sci.	Phil.	
Walt	75	60	88	
Sally	82	80	78	
Brian	61	93	68	
Ann	77	71	82	

Figure 6–55. *We'll place a sparkline alongside each student's set of grades.*

2. Click the **Insert** ribbon tab, and click the **Line** button in the **Sparklines** button group (see Figure 6–56; note the **Win/Loss** option, which I'll explain later). You'll then see the dialog in Figure 6–57.

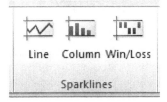

Figure 6–56. *The Sparklines button group*

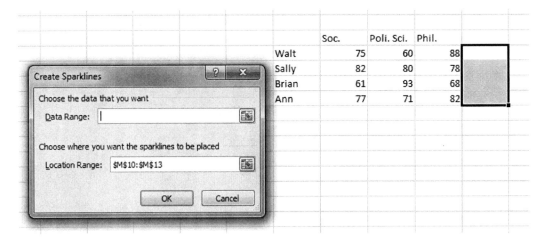

Figure 6–57. *Selecting the data: Each row will yield its own sparkline.*

3. Now select the range containing all the test data, as shown in Figure 6–58.

Figure 6–58. *Selecting the data that will contribute to each sparkline*

NOTE: You may see the name Student posted to the **Data Range** field. That's a range name we produced in the course of the create-from-selection range-naming exercise we carried out in Chapter 3. It stands for cells J10:L13, the cells we need to select now.

4. Click **OK**. The sparklines should appear alongside each student's grades in the location range, as shown previously in Figure 6–54.

Now imagine 1,000 rows of data instead of our 4, each one representing a student's test scores. It would be no problem to establish a sparkline corresponding to each set of grades, affording a teacher or administrator a quick, enlightening read on every student's progress.

Modifying Sparklines

There are several ways you can change the sparklines you've ushered into your workbook. Click any sparkline and you'll fire up the **Sparkline Tools** context tab. Click the tab, and the roster of sparkline options will report for duty (see Figure 6–59).

Figure 6–59. *Sparkline styles*

Note the **Style** option, which emulates the **Chart Styles** drop-down menu; clicking here will enable you to recolor the sparklines.

> **NOTE:** By default, sparklines are *grouped*, meaning that any changes you carry out will affect all the sparklines in the range. If you want to reformat just one sparkline, click the individual sparkline and then click the **Ungroup** button in the **Group** button group (if that doesn't sound too redundant).

The **Show** button group lets you post markers (dots, actually) that denote key data points on the sparklines. For example, if you click the **High Point** option, the sparkline will mark the highest test score for each student (see Figure 6–60).

Figure 6–60. *Dotted lines: Each student's highest grade is punctuated by a dot.*

> **TIP**: You can also change a sparkline color by clicking the **Sparkline Color** drop-down arrow and selecting from the color palette. You can also change the sparkline background by clicking the standard **Font Fill Color** button on the **Home** ribbon.

Representing Binary Values with Sparklines

Sparklines come in only three chart types: line, column, and what's called the win/loss type (see Figure 6–61).

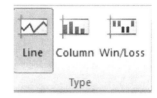

Figure 6–61. *Sparkline chart types*

We've been working with the line type, and clicking the column button generates, well, columns of data. But what if you wanted to capture a strictly binary, one-or-the-other data relationship, such as whether each of a series of transactions yields a profit or a loss, or whether each of the games a team plays across a season results in a win or loss? That's where the win/loss sparkline comes in.

Win/loss represents all positive values as columns above a virtual horizontal axis, and all negative values as below-the-axis columns. Thus, values such as these:

5, –6, 9, 11 –3

would be translated by the win/loss chart as shown in Figure 6–62.

Figure 6–62. *Can't win 'em all: How the win/loss chart captures data*

There's no proportion here either; all the positive and negative values are characterized by identically sized columns.

So when would you use win/loss? You could turn to win/loss when you need to depict data in up/down or yes/no terms—say, for profit/loss data comparisons, or pass/fail test scores; you could enter a 1 for every passed exam, and a –1 for a failure, for example. This chart type is called "win/loss" because it was inspired by sporting outcomes. With win/loss you could chart a team's fortunes across a season by entering 1 (or really any positive value) for every victory, and –1 (or any negative value) for every loss. After all, wins and losses are either/or.

> **NOTE:** You can delete one sparkline by clicking its cell, clicking the **Clear** drop-down arrow in the **Group** button group, and clicking **Clear Selected Sparklines**. To delete the entire sparkline group, just click **Clear Selected Sparkline Groups** instead.

Summary

As with most Excel capabilities, charting is an acquired taste, and learning its subtleties takes a bit of practice. But just the same, knowledge of charting essentials will empower you to cook up a perfectly presentable chart in about 10 seconds. Next, we'll take a look at Excel's database features.

Chapter 7

Sorting and Filtering Your Data: Excel's Database Features

You hear the term *database* all the time, even in everyday conversation, but the concept is rarely defined. People tend to rely on a common sense understanding of databases, and that's usually good enough—and the reality is that even Excel has found the task of deciding what it really means by *database* a bit troublesome. That doesn't have to concern us, but on the other hand, since we need to use the term throughout this chapter, we'll plunge ahead and define a database as a collection of records (i.e., rows) organized into fields, all of which are topped by titles.

And as it turns out, that's pretty close to the common sense understanding. Thus, the very standard collection of data shown in Figure 7–1 would qualify as a database.

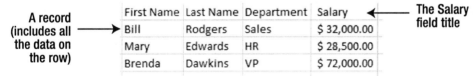

A record (includes all the data on the row)

The Salary field title

First Name	Last Name	Department	Salary
Bill	Rodgers	Sales	$ 32,000.00
Mary	Edwards	HR	$ 28,500.00
Brenda	Dawkins	VP	$ 72,000.00

Figure 7–1. *A garden-variety database*

Pretty standard, no? Note that the first row—called a *header row*—contains the titles of each field, or column. And it doesn't matter if the database contains 30,000 records or 3. Either way, it's a database.

Databases serve as the starting point for many of the tasks users can carry out in Excel. For starters, databases can be sorted, either in numerical or alphabetical order, and either ascending or descending—that is, A to Z, or Z to A, or 1 to 100, or 100 to 1. And the same can be done with dates that you want to sort in chronological order, because remember, dates are values.

In addition, users can pose all sorts of questions of databases, such as

- How many people work in HR?

- What's their average salary?

- How many people in the company make more than $50,000?

- How much money did each salesperson earn each month?

In order to answer these questions, databases can be asked to produce a subset of their records—that is, only those records that meet a certain criterion or criteria that the user establishes. Excel offers a range of ways in which these kinds of questions can be asked—and answered—and we'll look at some of them in this chapter.

And because databases depend on accurate data entry, Excel provides a set of controls on the data entry process, through which the user can at least minimize the likelihood of making mistakes. Called *data validation* techniques (introduced previously in Chapter 2), these are fast and easy ways to place limits on the kinds of data that can be entered in cells. You'll learn about some of these too. But first, let's take a look at sorting.

Sorting Data: Instilling Order in Your Data

When I did my thing as a corporate trainer in New York, our in-house training manuals described sorting as an advanced topic. It isn't. Spreadsheets nowadays make the job of arranging values and/or text in order an easy task. Here's an example:

1. Enter the records from Figure 7–2 in a blank workbook, starting at cell H7 (note the header is formatted differently from the rest of the database; this will be important later).

First Name	Last Name	Department	Salary
Bill	Rodgers	Sales	$ 32,000.00
Mary	Edwards	HR	$ 28,500.00
Brenda	Dawkins	VP	$ 72,000.00
Walter	Barton	HR	$ 25,000.00
Quincy	Zachary	VP	$ 75,400.00
Don	Albert	Sales	$ 31,458.00
Donna	Lee	HR	$ 27,600.00
Carl	Nunez	Marketing	$ 48,100.00
Nora	Barnacle	Sales	$ 33,000.00
Greg	Heinz	HR	$ 42,568.00
Kate	Vinson	VP	$ 72,451.00
Ted	Harris	Marketing	$ 30,000.00
Ned	Paulson	Sales	$ 40,000.00
Alan	Dreiser	HR	$ 29,563.00
Inez	Greer	Sales	$ 31,000.00

Figure 7–2. *Out of sorts: Our workforce, ready to be sorted*

2. Save the workbook as Sort. Note that the first and last names have been assigned separate fields; this is a good thing to do when working with databases.

3. Now let's suppose we want to sort this database by the last names of the staff. Start by clicking anywhere in the Last Name column. *Don't* try to select the entire database; that's totally unnecessary at best and will cause problems at worst. Then click **Home ➤ Sort & Filter** in the **Editing** button group. You'll see the drop-down shown in Figure 7–3.

Figure 7–3. *Where to start sorting*

4. Click **Sort A to Z**, and you'll see the content shown in Figure 7–4.

First Name	Last Name	Department	Salary
Don	Albert	Sales	$ 31,458.00
Nora	Barnacle	Sales	$ 33,000.00
Walter	Barton	HR	$ 25,000.00
Brenda	Dawkins	VP	$ 72,000.00
Alan	Dreiser	HR	$ 29,563.00
Mary	Edwards	HR	$ 28,500.00
Inez	Greer	Sales	$ 31,000.00
Ted	Harris	Marketing	$ 30,000.00
Greg	Heinz	HR	$ 42,568.00
Donna	Lee	HR	$ 27,600.00
Carl	Nunez	Marketing	$ 48,100.00
Ned	Paulson	Sales	$ 40,000.00
Bill	Rodgers	Sales	$ 32,000.00
Kate	Vinson	VP	$ 72,451.00
Quincy	Zachary	VP	$ 75,400.00

Figure 7–4. *All done!*

That's it. The last names are sorted in A-to-Z order, and the deed is done.

NOTE: You'll find another set of sort buttons with a slightly different appearance on the **Data** tab, as shown in Figure 7–5.

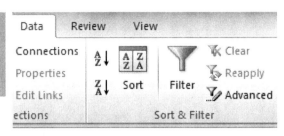

Figure 7–5. *Sort of the same: Another set of sort buttons*

Any questions? You may well have a few. To answer one right away: Yes, when you sort by a field, all the other fields in the database get sorted too, so that all the data fields will continue to be aligned with each other. Thus, Zachary will still lined up with Quincy; he won't be randomly paired with someone else's first name.

Another question might involve the header row, which remains in position. Why wasn't that row sorted along with the others? How does Excel know that the phrase *Last Name* really doesn't signify someone's last name?

There are two answers to this question:

- Excel won't sort the first row in a database if it's formatted differently form the other database rows.

- In addition, Excel won't sort a top row if there's a data type disparity somewhere in the database. That means that if a heading in the database is text and the cells beneath it consist of values, Excel assumes the heading is just that—a heading, not data—and is not to be sorted. As you can see, there's a data-type disparity in our database—in the Salary field.

Once you understand how sorting works, you should be able to sort any field in either direction. Thus, if you want to sort salaries in descending order, just click anywhere in the Salary range and click **Sort Largest to Smallest** on the **Sort & Filter** drop-down menu. And yes, we've just seen something new. When Excel recognizes a field filled with values, it converts its sort options into the largest-to-smallest variety. Sort a text field and Excel presents you with its A-to-Z choices instead. Just note that if you happen to click the *header* cell of a value field that happens to be text (e.g., Salary), the drop-down will state **Sort A to Z**, even though the actual *data* consists of values.

NOTE: Remember that although we're working with a small database, the principles of sorting I describe here work equally as well with 15,000 records as they do with just 15.

Sorting by Two Fields: The Hows and Whys

Consider this scenario: you're the instructor of a large, lecture-hall-sized class, and you've entered the names of all your students on a worksheet. You want to sort them in the standard last-name alphabetical order, but a quick scan of the data turns up several students with identical last names. You'd then probably want to sort the *first* names as well, so that Edna Arnold will appear in the sort before Gary Arnold.

And that introduces a classic sorting issue. Sorting by a second field is something you may want to do when, and only when, you have duplicate data in the first field—that is, when you discover at least two entries in that field with the same contents. There's simply no point in sorting by a second field unless you have duplicate data in the first.

And as it turns out, our own database exemplifies this point. Suppose we want to sort our records by department. The Department field exhibits numerous duplicates, so we could sort by a second field as well—say, salary. In other words, we want to wind up with the results shown in Figure 7–6.

First Name	Last Name	Department	Salary
Greg	Heinz	HR	$ 42,568.00
Alan	Dreiser	HR	$ 29,563.00
Mary	Edwards	HR	$ 28,500.00
Donna	Lee	HR	$ 27,600.00
Walter	Barton	HR	$ 25,000.00
Carl	Nunez	Marketing	$ 48,100.00
Ted	Harris	Marketing	$ 30,000.00
Ned	Paulson	Sales	$ 40,000.00
Nora	Barnacle	Sales	$ 33,000.00
Bill	Rodgers	Sales	$ 32,000.00
Don	Albert	Sales	$ 31,458.00
Inez	Greer	Sales	$ 31,000.00
Quincy	Zachary	VP	$ 75,400.00
Kate	Vinson	VP	$ 72,451.00
Brenda	Dawkins	VP	$ 72,000.00

Figure 7–6. Tilling two fields: Sorting by Department and Salary

Note that Department is sorted in A-to-Z sequence but Salary is sorted largest to smallest—kind of the opposite direction—because we wanted to see who were the highest earners in each department. And how do we do all this? Here's how:

1. First click in the first field by which you want to sort. You need to decide which field gets sorted first. In our case, we want to sort the Last Name field first, and then Salary, so click in the Last Name field.

2. Click **Home** ➤ **Sort & Filter** ➤ **Custom Sort**, and you'll see the dialog shown in Figure 7–7.

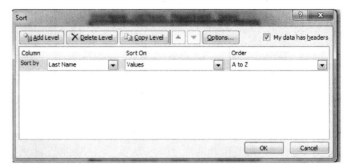

Figure 7–7. The Sort dialog box

NOTE: The **Sort by** field is filled with **Last Name**, because that's the field in which we click to start the process. If you click in the wrong field by mistake, you can just click the accompanying drop-down arrow, which lists all the fields in the data base. Note in addition the **Order** field displays **A to Z**, the default sorting option selected by Excel. If you want to sort the field as per the Z-to-A ordering, click the drop-down arrow and select that option (there's a bit more to say about the other **Sort On** options; we'll get to that a bit later).

3. We want to sort by *two* fields—so where's the second one? Click the **Add Level** button, and you'll see a second entry beneath the **Column** entry, entitled **Then by**.

4. Click the drop-down arrow and click **Salary**, the second field by which we want to sort (see Figure 7–8).

Figure 7–8. *The second sort field comes into view.*

NOTE: By default, Excel checks the **My data has headers** check box, thus telling the application not to sort the first row in the database.

5. Now that we've added the second field to be sorted, we need to look at **Order**, which reads **Smallest to Largest**. Click that down arrow and select **Largest to Smallest**, the direction in which we want to sort Salary.

6. Click OK.

You can also click any field in the dialog box and click **Delete Level** if you decide you want to remove it as a sorted field. The up and down arrows alongside the **Copy Level** button allow you to promote or demote fields in the sort order. Thus, if you wanted to sort Salary first you'd click in that field and then click the up arrow. **Salary** will move above **Department** in the dialog box and be sorted first.

> **NOTE:** The Copy Level button concerns yet another level of sorting, where you can sort by the format of a cell as well as its value. That is dealt with in the next section.

Sorting by Cell Format

Now what about those additional options on the **Sort On** drop-down menu—namely, **Cell Color**, **Font Color**, and **Cell Icon**? These are choices you're far less likely to select; they relate to *conditional formatting*, allowing you to tell Excel to sort cells (or the text in them) that have been, for example, formatted green before cells that have been formatted red.

Thus, if you were to click **Cell Color**, additional buttons asking you to identify which color is to be sorted first would appear in the dialog box; or in the case of **Cell Icon**, which conditionally formatted icon would receive sorting priority (see Figure 7–9).

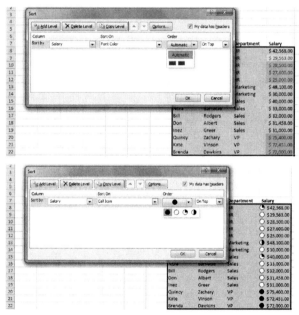

Figure 7–9. *Two different sorts of sorts based on conditional formats (the first by cell color and the second by cell icon)*

NOTE: What about the **Copy Level** button? If you click **Copy Level** on a field in the dialog box, that *same* field will be instated again in the **Sort** dialog box. That's right—the same field will appear twice. But how can you sort the same field twice?

Again, the answer takes us back to conditional formats. If, say, you wanted to sort the database by Salary in largest-to-smallest direction, and at the same time you conditionally formatted the data so that some of the Salary cells turned red and others didn't (for whatever reason), you could instruct Excel to sort the red $50,000 cells before the uncolored $50,000 cells in that copied level. (No, you're not likely to use this one.)

Finding What You Want with Filters

In the introduction of this chapter I pointed out that a great deal of the work people do with databases involves asking questions of a database's records; questions whose answers are usually supplied by just *some* of the records—such as which people in the company earn more than $50,000, or who works in the Sales department. Excel offers a very easy way to ask and answer these kinds of questions—through its *filter* feature.

Filters have been around in Excel for quite some time, but they've been improved, without compromising ease of use—as you're about to see.

1. To begin filtering your data, just click anywhere in your database, and then click the **Filter** button in the **Data** tab's **Sort & Filter** button group (see Figure 7–10).

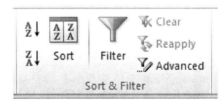

Figure 7–10. *Where to start the filtering process*

2. Click the **Filter** button and you'll see the results from Figure 7–11.

First Name	Last Name	Department	Salary
Don	Albert	Sales	$ 31,458.00
Nora	Barnacle	Sales	$ 33,000.00
Walter	Barton	HR	$ 25,000.00
Brenda	Dawkins	VP	$ 72,000.00
Alan	Dreiser	HR	$ 29,563.00
Mary	Edwards	HR	$ 28,500.00
Inez	Greer	Sales	$ 31,000.00
Ted	Harris	Marketing	$ 30,000.00
Greg	Heinz	HR	$ 42,568.00
Donna	Lee	HR	$ 27,600.00
Carl	Nunez	Marketing	$ 48,100.00
Ned	Paulson	Sales	$ 40,000.00
Bill	Rodgers	Sales	$ 32,000.00
Kate	Vinson	VP	$ 72,451.00
Quincy	Zachary	VP	$ 75,400.00

Figure 7–11. *Note the filter arrows.*

NOTE: The filter drop-down buttons will not print, even if they are visible on the screen. If the arrows obscure part of a field heading, you can widen that column.

3. Now let's say we want to view only those employees who work in Sales. Just click the filter down arrow by Department, as shown in Figure 7–12.

Figure 7–12. *All the departments in the company are listed.*

4. Then click the **Select All** check box, which removes the check marks next to all the department names. Then click the **Sales** check box and click OK. You'll see the results shown in Figure 7–13.

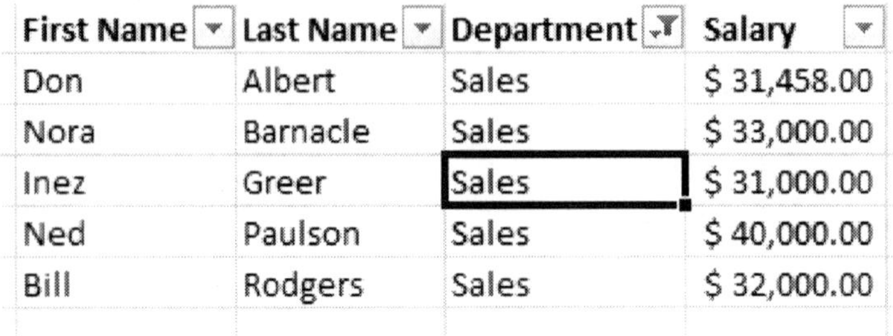

First Name ▼	Last Name ▼	Department ⊤	Salary ▼
Don	Albert	Sales	$ 31,458.00
Nora	Barnacle	Sales	$ 33,000.00
Inez	Greer	Sales	$ 31,000.00
Ned	Paulson	Sales	$ 40,000.00
Bill	Rodgers	Sales	$ 32,000.00

Figure 7–13. *The Sales department*

I told you it was easy. We've just isolated—or filtered—the members of the Sales staff. In order to bring that outcome about, Excel has *hidden* the rows of all the employees in the database who *aren't* in Sales. Note the gaps in row numbers in Figure 7–14.

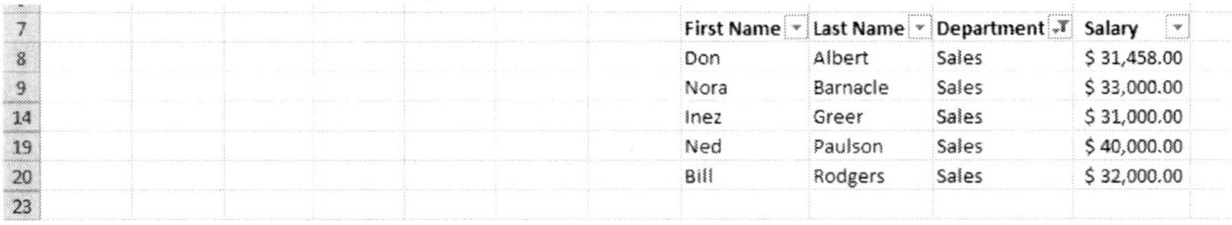

	First Name ▼	Last Name ▼	Department ⊤	Salary ▼
7				
8	Don	Albert	Sales	$ 31,458.00
9	Nora	Barnacle	Sales	$ 33,000.00
14	Inez	Greer	Sales	$ 31,000.00
19	Ned	Paulson	Sales	$ 40,000.00
20	Bill	Rodgers	Sales	$ 32,000.00
23				

Figure 7–14. *Something's missing—rows.*

Notice that the Sales department records occupy rows 8, 9, 14, 19, and 20. The other rows are occupied by members of different departments, and are thus obscured from view.

> **TIP:** You can also filter the Sales staff by typing **Sales** in the search field right above the check boxes shown previously in Figure 7–12, and clicking **OK**.

It's easy to miss, but when you filter a database, the number of records you've pulled out is recorded in the lower left of the status bar, as shown in Figure 7–15.

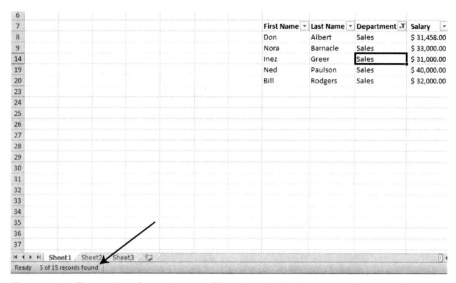

	First Name	Last Name	Department	Salary
	Don	Albert	Sales	$ 31,458.00
	Nora	Barnacle	Sales	$ 33,000.00
	Inez	Greer	Sales	$ 31,000.00
	Ned	Paulson	Sales	$ 40,000.00
	Bill	Rodgers	Sales	$ 32,000.00

Figure 7–15. *The number of records you've filtered is tallied in the lower-left corner of the screen.*

Moreover, you can filter multiple departments simultaneously. If you wanted to filter both Sales *and* HR staff, you could check the boxes in Sales and HR (again, after deselecting **Select All** in order to tell Excel you don't want to see all the staff), and click **OK**. You'll then see both Sales and HR people listed on the screen, but no other staff.

Clearing a Filter

Now it's time for an obvious question: if the filter works by hiding rows that don't meet the current filter criterion, how do you get those hidden rows back on the screen? That's easy, too: just click the **Clear** button to the right of the **Filter** button in the **Sort & Filter** group, and all the database records will reappear. And in order to do this, you don't even have to click in the database first. The **Clear** command works no matter where you've clicked in the worksheet. (And don't be fooled by the word *Clear* here; it doesn't mean *erase* or *delete*—it refers to clearing the filter.)

NOTE: To turn the filter off completely, just click the **Filter** button a second time.

Text and Number Filters: Filters Within the Filter

Sometimes you need to filter a database on the basis of a part of a field. Consider this example: you want to filter all the HR staff, but each employee has a department code that looks something like this:

- HR-103

- HR-561

and so on. The kind of filter we've worked with so far won't corral all these HR members, because each staffer is *uniquely* identified; they're no longer just HR, but rather HR-274, and so on, and our method won't pull all the staffers out in one shot. But Excel's *text filter* will let you filter all staff who have HR *somewhere* in their ID, even of those IDs aren't exactly the same.

1. Start by clicking the filter drop-down arrow and then clicking **Text Filters**. You'll see the options shown in Figure 7–16. Clicking any of these options will take you to what's called the **Custom AutoFilter** dialog box, as you're about to see.

Figure 7–16. *Text filters: Giving you more filtering options*

2. In view of the preceding example, let's say that you're interested in filtering all the department records that contain the letters *HR*—no matter what other text appears in each record. In that case, select **Contains...** in the **Text Filters** drop-down menu, and you'll see what's shown in Figure 7–17.

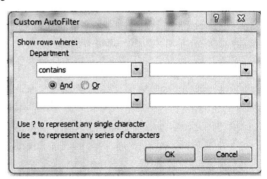

Figure 7–17. *This one's pretty easy too. Just enter the text the filter needs to look for.*

3. Type **HR** in the field to the right of the field with the word *contains*, and click OK. Doing so will filter all the records containing the *HR* letter sequence, even if it appears with other letters (e.g., HR-403).

NOTE: The term *AutoFilter* is really equivalent to the term *filter*, even though Excel switches between the two.

And once you see how that works, you'll see that the other text filter options (**Equals...**, **Does Not Equal...**, etc.) are easy to figure out. Clicking any of these takes you back to that same **Custom AutoFilter** dialog where the appropriate option appears. In fact, if you click the down arrow to the right of the **contains** entry (shown previously in Figure 7–17), you'll see all the text filter options, as shown in Figure 7–18.

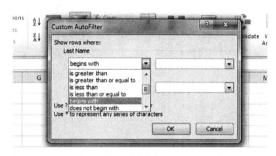

Figure 7–18. *No matter which text filter option you choose, the drop-down menu can always take you to the others.*

NOTE: If you take a close look at Figure 7–18, you'll notice the **is greater than** option, which sounds like an odd choice to be offered when you're filtering text. But here, "greater than" refers to text in the field starting with letters in the alphabet coming *after* the text you've specified. For example, if you enter the letter *D* under the **is greater than** option, the text filter will locate all names starting with letters appearing after *D* in the alphabet, as well as names such as Dreiser—because *Dre* . . . is more than, or greater than, just plain *D*.

But what's probably going to serve you more productively than text filters are the *number filters*. These let you filter all workers earning more than $30,000, or all employees making more than the company salary average, for example.

The following steps show you how to apply a number filter.

1. Click in a field populated with values such as salaries, and then click the field drop-down arrow (again, after you've clicked **Clear** to return all the records to the screen). You'll see the options shown in Figure 7–19.

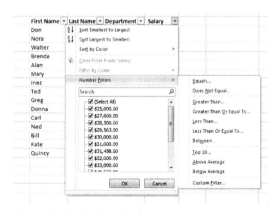

Figure 7–19. *Number filters*

2. These are pretty easy, too. Clicking any of these options will again unfurl the **Custom AutoFilter** dialog box (except the **Top 10...** option, which will call up its own distinct dialog box), as shown in Figure 7–20.

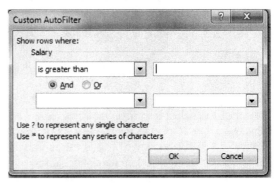

Figure 7–20. By the numbers: Just type a value and click OK.

3. This should be pretty self-evident by now. If you want to see all the staffers earning more than $30,000, just type **30000** and click OK.

You may also want to take special note of the **Top 10...** option, which lets you filter the top (or bottom) 10 values in the field—or the top 20, or the top 5, or any value you specify (see Figure 7–21).

Figure 7–21. The Top 10... option: Better than a Letterman list

Just click (or type) in the field exhibiting the default **10** and replace it with any other value, if you want to. And think big: imagine a set of test grades for a lecture class of 200 students, and think how simple would be to determine its top 10 highest scores. Also, if you click the drop-down arrow by **Items** field, you'll call up a **Percent** option, which lets you find out the top 10 percent of all scores instead.

Filtering Multiple Fields

In addition, you can filter the filter results. That means, for example, that starting with the result in which the Sales staff has been filtered, we could then execute a *second* filter— say, to find all the Sales personnel who earn more than $35,000. We'd do that by next clicking the Salary drop-down arrow and filtering for salaries above $35,000—using the number filters from the previous section. After that double filter is completed, only Ned Paulson would remain on the screen, because he's the only salesperson who earns over $35,000 (see Figure 7–22).

First Name	Last Name	Department	Salary
Don	Albert	Sales	$ 31,458.00
Nora	Barnacle	Sales	$ 33,000.00
Inez	Greer	Sales	$ 31,000.00
Ned	Paulson	Sales	$ 40,000.00
Bill	Rodgers	Sales	$ 32,000.00

First Name	Last Name	Department	Salary
Ned	Paulson	Sales	$ 40,000.00

Figure 7–22. *First we filter the Sales personnel, and then we filter those results by Salary.*

Tables: Adding User-Friendliness to Your Database

Working with a database and adding records to it is generally a pretty easy task, but Excel provides the user with a way to make the process even easier—by transforming the database into a *table.* A table is a database to which some ease-of-use features have been added—features that spare the user from some of the drudgery associated with data entry (e.g., automatically copying a new formula to all the rows in the table). Let's turn our database into a table, and we'll see how it works:

1. Click anywhere in the database. Then click the **Insert** tab and select **Table** from the **Tables** button group. Doing so brings up the dialog box shown in Figure 7–23.

Figure 7–23. *Turning the tables on a database*

2. Click **OK**, and then click anywhere in the worksheet to deselect the database. You'll see the results shown in Figure 7–24.

First Name ▼	Last Name ▼	Department ▼	Salary ▼
Don	Albert	Sales	$ 31,458.00
Nora	Barnacle	Sales	$ 33,000.00
Walter	Barton	HR	$ 25,000.00
Brenda	Dawkins	VP	$ 72,000.00
Alan	Dreiser	HR	$ 29,563.00
Mary	Edwards	HR	$ 28,500.00
Inez	Greer	Sales	$ 31,000.00
Ted	Harris	Marketing	$ 30,000.00
Greg	Heinz	HR	$ 42,568.00
Donna	Lee	HR	$ 27,600.00
Carl	Nunez	Marketing	$ 48,100.00
Ned	Paulson	Sales	$ 40,000.00
Bill	Rodgers	Sales	$ 32,000.00
Kate	Vinson	VP	$ 72,451.00
Quincy	Zachary	VP	$ 75,400.00

Figure 7–24. *The database, now a table*

TIP: You can also begin the table-making process via its keyboard equivalent, Ctrl+T.

You'll also see a **Table Tools** contextual tab, which we'll discuss shortly. The most obvious change produced by the table is the data's new format, in which the database records are colored alternately blue. These are called *banded rows*, an effect that makes the records easier to read. But there are features to a table that aren't quite so obvious, including these:

- The filter is turned on (although you can still turn it off in the standard way by clicking the **Filter** button).

- The header row in a table always remains on the screen. That means that if the table contains hundreds or even thousands of rows, and you scroll down the table, that first row will nevertheless stay in view. Take a look at the example shown in Figure 7–25.

Client	Date	Invoice
58 Callahan	5/22/04	£2,222.20
59 Callahan	5/23/04	£1,504.50
60 Buchanan	5/30/04	£3,554.27
61 Callahan	6/9/04	£1,072.42
62 Callahan	6/18/04	£ 639.90
63 Callahan	6/26/04	£ 210.00
64 Buchanan	6/30/04	£2,147.40
65 Callahan	7/4/04	£ 550.59

Figure 7–25. The header row's still on the screen—but look at the row numbers!

■ The table receives a name—by default, Table1. (These names proceed in sequence; your second table will be called Table2, your third Table3, etc.) Whenever you click in the table, its name will appear in the **Table Name** field in the **Properties** button group on the **Table Tools Design** tab. You can also rename a table by clicking in the table and clicking in the **Table Name** field, typing a new name, and pressing Enter. The table name will appear when you click the drop-down arrow in the Name box; click the name and the table will be selected.

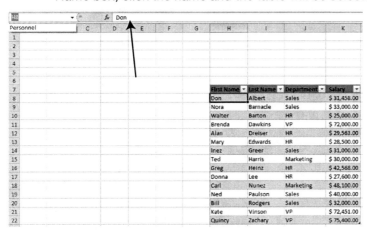

Figure 7–26. A table renamed. Note the Name box.

■ If you enter additional records (or rows) to the table, they too will automatically exhibit the same format.

- If you add a new *field* (or column) to the table, it too will display the new format.

- This one is important. If a field has formulas in it, any new records added to the table will automatically receive the formula, too (with the appropriate absolute or relative cell addressing figured in).

For example, suppose our pre-table database had a Raise field, in which every salary was awarded a boost of 5 percent (see Figure 7–27).

f_x	=K8*1.05								
D	E	F	G	H	I	J	K	L	

First Name	Last Name	Department	Salary	Raise
Don	Albert	Sales	$ 31,458.00	$ 33,030.90
Nora	Barnacle	Sales	$ 33,000.00	$ 34,650.00
Walter	Barton	HR	$ 25,000.00	$ 26,250.00
Brenda	Dawkins	VP	$ 72,000.00	$ 75,600.00
Alan	Dreiser	HR	$ 29,563.00	$ 31,041.15
Mary	Edwards	HR	$ 28,500.00	$ 29,925.00
Inez	Greer	Sales	$ 31,000.00	$ 32,550.00
Ted	Harris	Marketing	$ 30,000.00	$ 31,500.00
Greg	Heinz	HR	$ 42,568.00	$ 44,696.40
Donna	Lee	HR	$ 27,600.00	$ 28,980.00
Carl	Nunez	Marketing	$ 48,100.00	$ 50,505.00
Ned	Paulson	Sales	$ 40,000.00	$ 42,000.00
Bill	Rodgers	Sales	$ 32,000.00	$ 33,600.00
Kate	Vinson	VP	$ 72,451.00	$ 76,073.55
Quincy	Zachary	VP	$ 75,400.00	$ 79,170.00

Figure 7–27. *Pay day. Note the formula in the formula bar.*

Once those raise formulas are in place and the database is then converted into a table, any *new* records you enter will also display the 5 percent raise, because the formula in the Raise field will write itself. Moreover, if you edit any one of the formulas in the Raise field, the table will rewrite *all* the formulas in the column correspondingly—a very cool feature.

> **NOTE:** The preceding example assumes you've written the raise formulas *before* you converted the database into a table. But if you write them *after* converting to a table, they may look very different. For example, if you transform your database into a table and *then* add the Raise field, and proceed to write the raise formulas by clicking in the cells in the Salary column, they'll *all* read
>
> =[@Salary]*1.05
>
> without a specific cell reference. That's how tables write formulas—they refer to fields, not cell references. But however the formula appears, its mathematical outcome will be identical.

There are a few other table features that are good to know. For one thing, it's easy to add columns to tables; and for another, when you click anywhere in the table, the **Table Tools** context tab is triggered (see Figure 7–28).

Figure 7–28. *What you see when you click the Table Tools context tab. Note that the entire ribbon is now occupied with table options.*

Note the **Table Styles** button group. Clicking its drop-down arrows reveals a collection of predesigned styles that you can apply to the table (see Figure 7–29).

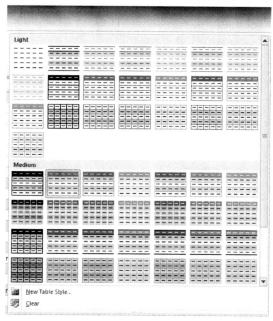

Figure 7–29. *Table styles: Just click one*

You can inspect any of the table styles in preview mode by resting your mouse over it before you click. The table will exhibit the style.

> **NOTE:** You can also click the **Format as Table** button in the **Styles** button group, located on the Home tab. Clicking this will do two things: change a database into a table and let you choose a table style.

To the left of Table Styles, you'll see the Table Style Options button group (see Figure 7–30).

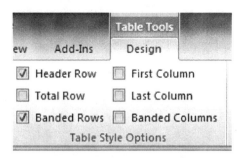

Figure 7–30. *The Table Style Options button group*

Its check boxes let you change specific elements of the table's appearance. If you uncheck **Banded Rows** and check **Banded Columns**, for example, you can realize the effect shown in Figure 7–31.

First Name ▾	Last Name ▾	Department ▾	Salary ▾
Don	Albert	Sales	$ 31,458.00
Nora	Barnacle	Sales	$ 33,000.00
Walter	Barton	HR	$ 25,000.00
Brenda	Dawkins	VP	$ 72,000.00
Alan	Dreiser	HR	$ 29,563.00
Mary	Edwards	HR	$ 28,500.00
Inez	Greer	Sales	$ 31,000.00
Ted	Harris	Marketing	$ 30,000.00
Greg	Heinz	HR	$ 42,568.00
Donna	Lee	HR	$ 27,600.00
Carl	Nunez	Marketing	$ 48,100.00
Ned	Paulson	Sales	$ 40,000.00
Bill	Rodgers	Sales	$ 32,000.00
Kate	Vinson	VP	$ 72,451.00
Quincy	Zachary	VP	$ 75,400.00

Figure 7–31. *Banded table columns*

And if you click the **First Column** and/or **Last Column** options, special effects (e.g., boldfaced text) will be imparted only to those columns, which you may want to emphasize.

The **Table Style Options** group also features an important **Total Row** selection. Click its check box and you'll see something like Figure 7–32.

First Name	Last Name	Department	Salary
Don	Albert	Sales	$ 31,458.00
Nora	Barnacle	Sales	$ 33,000.00
Walter	Barton	HR	$ 25,000.00
Brenda	Dawkins	VP	$ 72,000.00
Alan	Dreiser	HR	$ 29,563.00
Mary	Edwards	HR	$ 28,500.00
Inez	Greer	Sales	$ 31,000.00
Ted	Harris	Marketing	$ 30,000.00
Greg	Heinz	HR	$ 42,568.00
Donna	Lee	HR	$ 27,600.00
Carl	Nunez	Marketing	$ 48,100.00
Ned	Paulson	Sales	$ 40,000.00
Bill	Rodgers	Sales	$ 32,000.00
Kate	Vinson	VP	$ 72,451.00
Quincy	Zachary	VP	$ 75,400.00
Total			$ 618,640.00

Figure 7–32. *The table, with a Total row appended at the bottom. If the total is too large to be seen, just widen the Salary column with autofit.*

By default, the Total row adds the values in the *rightmost* field of the table, as shown in the figure. If that column contains textual data, the number of records is counted instead. And if you click in any other cell in the Total row, a drop-down arrow will appear, letting you select a mathematical operation for the data in that field (see Figure 7–33).

First Name	Last Name	Department	Salary
Don	Albert	Sales	$ 31,458.00
Nora	Barnacle	Sales	$ 33,000.00
Walter	Barton	HR	$ 25,000.00
Brenda	Dawkins	VP	$ 72,000.00
Alan	Dreiser	HR	$ 29,563.00
Mary	Edwards	HR	$ 28,500.00
Inez	Greer	Sales	$ 31,000.00
Ted	Harris	Marketing	$ 30,000.00
Greg	None		$ 42,568.00
Donna	Average		$ 27,600.00
Carl	Count / Count Numbers	arketing	$ 48,100.00
Ned	Max	les	$ 40,000.00
Bill	Min / Sum	les	$ 32,000.00
Kate	StdDev		$ 72,451.00
Quincy	Var / More Functions...		$ 75,400.00
Total			$ 618,640.00

Figure 7–33. *The Total row lets you perform a calculation on any field in the table.*

What Excel is really doing here is enabling you to use one of its functions, which will calculate a result for the field in which you've clicked. Note the array of options made available; in Figure 7–33, in which we've clicked in a text field, we'll be able to tally a count of the number of last names in the table column. Click the down arrow by Salary and you can select a different calculation—say, an average. If you decide you need to add additional records to the table, you can click the **Total Row** check box a second time to remove it. You can then continue adding records.

Finding Duplicate Records in the Table (and Removing Them)

A classic data entry problem, one particularly besetting large databases, is the specter of duplicate records. It's not uncommon to discover the same names appearing repeatedly in large lists, and if you're the person charged with maintaining the database, you'll need to do something about it. Excel's tables are equipped with a *Remove Duplicates* feature, which speeds the task of winnowing those doubles from the data.

The first order of business in removing duplicates is deciding exactly what constitutes a duplicate. After all, Jane Walsh and John Walsh share a last name, but you're not likely to declare them duplicate entries. What you usually want to sift out are entire records that are identical—that is, two John Walshes—although it always isn't that simple. J. Walsh and John Walsh, both of whom record an address of 123 Broadway, might very well qualify as duplicates, too.

1. To see how Excel helps you with this task, pick out an empty area of the worksheet and enter the simple database shown in Figure 7–34. Remember that the size of the database is irrelevant. The Remove Duplicates options works the same way in every case.

First Name	Last Name
John	Walsh
Bill	Enright
Jane	Walsh
John	Walsh

Figure 7–34. Double take: Searching for duplicates

2. Then convert the database to a table. Note that the "My table has headers" check box won't be checked, and that's because all the data in the database, including that in the top row, is text, so Excel can't tell if there's anything special or different about that top row. We thus need to tick the check box in order to let Excel know that we *do* want a header row.

3. Then click the **Remove Duplicates** button in the **Tools** button group, which will bring up the dialog shown in Figure 7–35.

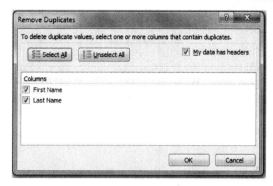

Figure 7–35. *The Remove Duplicates dialog box*

4. You can probably figure out what to do next—just click OK. Because our table contains two people with the same last name but different first names, we leave *both* columns checked, which means that Excel will search the data only for records in which both fields are identical. When you click OK, you'll see the message shown in Figure 7–36.

Figure 7–36. *Yeah, "1 duplicate values" needs a grammar check . . . but it worked!*

5. Click OK and you'll be left with three records, as one of the two John Walshes has been deleted.

Converting a Table to a Range

If you want convert a table back to the standard database with which you started, click **Convert to Range** in the **Tools** button group on the **Table Tools** tab. You'll be prompted to convert the table back to a "normal" range (as Excel puts it)—just click OK. Remember, after all, that a database is also just a range, too.

> **NOTE:** When you convert a table back to a range, any table formatting you may have applied, such as banded rows and/or columns, will remain.

And given the advantages of turning a range into a table, why would you want to return it back to standard range status? That's a good and subtle question, and while you're not likely to convert it back to a normal range, there are some potential reasons why you might. For one, if you delete a record in a table—even the last record—the records on either side of the deleted row still remain in the table, and that means the blank rows will appear in pivot table reports.

Summary

Excel's sorting, filtering, and table features make the tasks of ordering and tracking down information from your data easy. But the techniques discussed so far may not answer all the questions you'd like to ask of your data. For example, what if you want to learn the average salary of your employees not across the whole company, but broken out by department? Or what if you need to know how much money each salesperson has earned per month? Or how much money *you* spend per month by budget category? Or perhaps you need to determine university students' grade point averages by their major. In the next chapter we're going to explore a powerful Excel feature that will help you with these questions and more: pivot tables.

Chapter 8

PivotTables: Data Aggregation Without the Aggravation

PivotTables provide a potent and flexible way to organize—and reorganize—the records in a database or table, by letting you break out the data into a variety of visual arrangements. And once you've done so, you can quickly transform the results into a PivotChart.

PivotTables also let you *group* data; for example, you can bundle test score results in groups of 10 points—that is, tally the number of students who score between 100 and 91, 90 and 81, and so on.

And starting with Excel 2010, Microsoft has introduced a new PivotTable feature called the Slicer, which gives you a clearer presentation of filtered data. I'll explain the Slicer soon, although it's similar to the filters discussed in Chapter 7.

Looking at Some PivotTables

In this section, we'll take a look at some specific examples of how PivotTables are used.

Imagine that you're planning a dinner for your organization and you need to assign the invitees to their tables. You start with a database that looks like Figure 8–1.

Guest	Table
Halladay	16
Martinez	24
Grove	18
Santana	3
Johnson	7
Oswalt	15
Clemens	23
Peavy	6
Sabathia	15
Dean	28
Higuera	16
Zambrano	15
Seaver	23
Schilling	5
Ford	17
Sewell	18
Richard	27
Vuckovich	1
Gooden	5
Webb	26
Hoyt	26
Chandler	5

Figure 8–1. *The A list? Dinner guests and their table assignments*

Now while it's true that you could simply sort the data by table number, that approach won't tell you how *many* guests are seated at each table. What you really want to see is something like Figure 8–2.

Count of Table

Table	Total
1	9
2	4
3	4
4	4
5	4
6	2
7	3
8	3
9	5
10	5
11	6
12	4
13	3
14	1
15	6

Figure 8–2. *Guests per table: One way you can organize data with a PivotTable*

Once you've compiled the data in this way with a PivotTable, you can determine if you've over- or underassigned guests to particular tables. But you may also want to see the data displayed as in Figure 8–3.

Figure 8–3. *Who's where: Guests identified by their table. Note that the guest names are automatically sorted, too.*

Here, you've learned exactly who's seating where.

These are the sort of things that PivotTables (technically called PivotTable reports) can do: they can organize—or again, break out—your data in all sorts of combinations and modes of presentation. They're particularly good for identifying patterns and tendencies in the data that might otherwise escape your attention, particularly when you're working with a large database.

Here's one more example, adapted from a Microsoft practice database. In this example, you have a collection of sales records, each of which cites the salesperson, country in which the sale was transacted, transaction date, and amount of each sale (see Figure 8–4).

Country	Salesperson	Order Date	Order Amount
UK	Buchanan	01/05/09	$440.00
UK	Suyama	12/30/08	$1,863.40
USA	Peacock	01/01/09	$1,552.60
USA	Leverling	01/04/09	$654.06
USA	Peacock	12/31/08	$3,597.90
USA	Leverling	01/05/09	$1,444.80
UK	Buchanan	01/12/09	$556.62
UK	Dodsworth	01/04/09	$2,490.50
USA	Leverling	01/06/09	$517.80
USA	Peacock	01/11/09	$1,119.90
USA	Davolio	01/12/09	$1,614.88
USA	Peacock	01/14/09	$100.80
USA	Peacock	01/18/09	$1,504.65
USA	Peacock	01/19/09	$448.00
USA	Callahan	01/14/09	$584.00
UK	Walters	04/05/09	$1,543.73

Figure 8–4. *Salesperson data, ripe for pivot tabling*

One obvious question you might want to ask of the data is: how much money each salesperson earned? A PivotTable will tell you (see Figure 8–5).

Sum of Order Amount	
Salesperson	Total
Buchanan	$68,792.25
Callahan	$123,032.67
Davolio	$182,500.09
Dodsworth	$75,048.04
Fuller	$162,503.78
King	$116,962.99
Leverling	$201,196.27
Peacock	$225,763.68
Suyama	$72,527.63
Grand Total	$1,228,327.40

Figure 8–5. *Salesperson earnings, with the grand total besides*

There's your answer—or at least *one* answer. But with PivotTables, you can also come up with something like what's shown in Figure 8–6.

Sum of Order Amount	Years		
Order Date	2009	2010	Grand Total
Jan	$23,652.81	$49,406.37	$73,059.18
Feb	$22,771.15	$46,133.07	$68,904.22
Mar	$26,033.70	$48,578.81	$74,612.51
Apr	$44,054.62	$70,261.58	$114,316.20
May	$53,133.04	$46,371.24	$99,504.28
Jun	$31,093.16	$62,680.05	$93,773.21
Jul	$62,086.83	$94,342.96	$156,429.79
Aug	$34,566.55	$106,732.56	$141,299.11
Sep	$45,530.49	$106,177.34	$151,707.83
Oct	$38,615.25	$105,352.87	$143,968.12
Nov	$64,144.30		$64,144.30
Dec	$41,147.35	$5,461.30	$46,608.65
Grand Total	$486,829.25	$741,498.15	$1,228,327.40

Figure 8–6. *Sales data broken out, not by salesperson, but by month and year instead*

Now that's a radically different take on the same sales figures—organized here by time frame, with no mention of the salespersons. But we could also do something like Figure 8–7.

Sum of Order Amount	Order Date					
Years	Jan	Feb	Mar	Apr	May	Jun
2009	23652.81	22771.15	26033.7	44054.62	53133.04	31093.16
2010	49406.37	46133.07	48578.81	70261.58	46371.24	62680.05
Grand Total	73059.18	68904.22	74612.51	114316.2	99504.28	93773.21

Figure 8–7. *Turnabout: Now the years are occupying the rows*

Bet that one got your attention! What you're seeing now is precisely the same data from Figure 8–6, but it's been *pivoted*, or flipped on its side, as it were. Now the years run down the column, with the months streaming across. And that's what PivotTables can do: pivot the information across their rows and columns to give the user a variety of ways of presenting the information.

Pretty impressive—and as with Excel's other data management capabilities, the methods for designing PivotTables are identical for databases of 100 or 100,000 records. And once you get the hang of them, you can batch one up in a matter of seconds.

Now take another look at Figures 8–6 and 8–7, and notice that they organize the sales data by months and years, even though the original source data only records each sale on the particular *day* on which it was transacted. But PivotTables let you *group* the data into larger categories, allowing you to easily see the bigger picture.

Again, you can't really produce these kinds of results with the filters discussed previously. PivotTables afford the user a larger and more effective set of tools for analyzing data, and though some newcomers to Excel view them as mysterious, slightly scary, and perhaps user-hostile, a bit of practice and reflection will pay off—because PivotTables are definitely worth knowing about.

It's true that there's a lot to learn about PivotTables if you're interested in turning yourself into the company guru. In fact, there are two Apress books out there devoted exclusively to the subject, *Beginning PivotTables in Excel 2007* and *Excel 2007 PivotTable Recipes*, authored by PivotTable expert Debra Dalgleish. But as with many of Excel's features, there's a set of the basics you *have* learn in order to make PivotTables do productive work, and I'm going to introduce them here.

NOTE: Because a PivotTable works with a *copy* of the original database, any mistakes you may make in the course of your PivotTable design will nevertheless leave the database intact. And you can always apply the Undo command to PivotTables, just as you can with any other Excel feature.

Creating a PivotTable

So let's try to construct some PivotTables, by working with the first 15 records of the sales data we've been looking at.

1. In a blank workbook, copy the records shown in Figure 8–8, starting in cell A1.

Country	Salesperson	Order Date	Order Amount
UK	Buchanan	01/05/09	$440.00
UK	Suyama	12/30/08	$1,863.40
USA	Peacock	01/01/09	$1,552.60
USA	Leverling	01/04/09	$654.06
USA	Peacock	12/31/08	$3,597.90
USA	Leverling	01/05/09	$1,444.80
UK	Buchanan	01/12/09	$556.62
UK	Dodsworth	01/04/09	$2,490.50
USA	Leverling	01/06/09	$517.80
USA	Peacock	01/11/09	$1,119.90
USA	Davolio	01/12/09	$1,614.88
USA	Peacock	01/14/09	$100.80
USA	Peacock	01/18/09	$1,504.65
USA	Peacock	01/19/09	$448.00
USA	Callahan	01/14/09	$584.00

Figure 8–8. *Sales data: Working with text, date, and currency fields*

2. Save the workbook as PivotTables.

3. To start with, we want to break out the sales figures—that is, the data in the Order Amount field—by salesperson to see how much each has earned. The first step is to click anywhere in the database, as we did with sorting and filtering. Then click the **Insert** tab, and choose **PivotTable** from the **Tables** button group (click the top half of the button). You'll see the dialog shown in Figure 8–9.

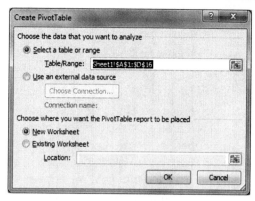

Figure 8–9. *The Create PivotTable dialog box*

4. Note that by default Excel will manufacture a new worksheet in which to place the PivotTable. Click **OK**, and you'll see Figure 8–10. We've put what could be termed the *scaffolding* of the PivotTable in place, but all we see so far is a curious, empty space holding down the left side of the worksheet; we obviously haven't generated any results yet. (Note also that a **PivotTable Tools** contextual tab also appears at the top of your screen.) Now look at the area in the lower half of the **PivotTable Field List**, in the area captioned "Drag fields between areas below." This is where you'll be doing most of the work of designing and redesigning your PivotTables.

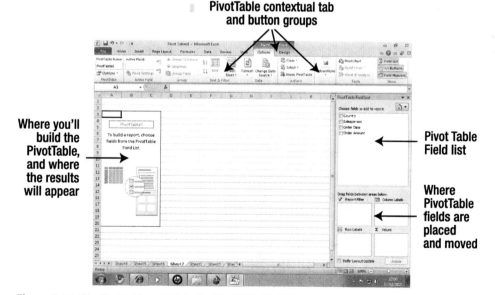

Figure 8–10. *The PivotTable grid. Note the PivotTable Field List on the right.*

NOTE: You can remove the PivotTable Field List from view by clicking PivotTable Tools Options, and clicking the Field List button in the Show button group. Clicking this button a second time will bring the list back onscreen.

5. Next, tick the check box alongside Salesperson in the Choose fields to add to report area near the top right of the PivotTable Field List. Two things will happen, as shown in Figure 8–11: the names of the salespersons will be arrayed in the Row Labels area of the PivotTable on the left, and a bar representing that field will appear in the Drag fields between areas below section in the lower half of the PivotTable Field List. Note also that the salespersons are each listed *once*, no matter how many times they're listed in the source database.

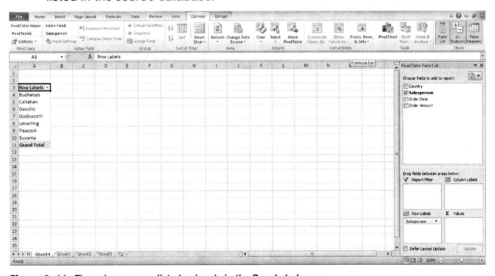

Figure 8–11. *The salespersons, listed uniquely in the Row Labels area*

6. Then tick the check box alongside Order Amount. You'll see the data shown in Figure 8–12.

Row Labels ▼	Sum of Order Amount
Buchanan	996.62
Callahan	584
Davolio	1614.88
Dodsworth	2490.5
Leverling	2616.66
Peacock	8323.85
Suyama	1863.4
Grand Total	**18489.91**

Figure 8–12. *There it is—your first PivotTable*

We've done it. While it may not yet be suitable for framing, the PivotTable tells us what we wanted to know—exactly how much money each salesperson has earned. Note that the data from Order Amount has been automatically shipped to the **Values** area of the **PivotTable Field List,** as shown in Figure 8–13. This was Excel's decision, a point that will be taken up shortly.

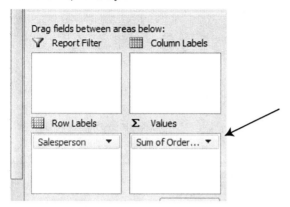

Figure 8–13. *The order amount data inhabits the Values area*

For now, don't worry about how to recast the values into currency format. That's coming up a bit later.

Choosing Which Data to Work On

Note again the four areas occupying the lower region of the **PivotTable Field List: Report Filter, Column Labels, Row Labels,** and **Values.** The idea is to place the information from the database's fields into these areas, with each area doing something different with the data. Since we just worked with the **Row Labels** and **Values** areas—probably the two most important areas—I'll first explain what they do.

The data from any field placed in the **Row Labels** area is *listed uniquely.* And that's exactly what happened in our PivotTable; when we ticked **Salesperson,** all the salespersons in our database were listed in **Row Labels**—and listed once. It makes no difference how often they're actually cited in the original database; place the field in **Row Labels** and each name appears only once.

On the other hand, the data from any field in the Values area is always subject to a *mathematical operation*—it's added, counted, averaged, and the like. And again, this is consistent with our previous example. The Order Amount data—individual sales in dollars—was added, and was broken out by the salesperson data in the Row Labels area.

And that in a nutshell is really what PivotTables are about. Any data in the **Values** area is broken out by the data in the Row Labels area. Consider the collection of PivotTable examples in Table 7-1 (which of course assume you have these kinds of data in a database).

Table 7-1. *Examples of PivotTables: What Data Gets Broken Out, and What Data Does the Breaking Out*

PivotTable Example	Data in Row Labels (What Does the Breaking Out)	Data in Values (What Gets Broken Out)
Sales data broken out by salesperson (our PivotTable)	Salesperson	Order amount
Student aggregate GPAs broken out by major	Major subjects (e.g., sociology, chemistry)	Student GPAs
Total budget expenditures, broken out by budget category	Budget categories	Amount spent on purchases
Dinner seating totals, broken out by table	Table numbers	Table numbers (I'll explain this shortly)

So the essential PivotTable question asks what information you want to see broken out, and by what variable. If you wanted to break out the sales figures by country instead of salesperson, you'd place Country in the Row Labels area, and you'd wind up with what's shown in Figure 8–14.

Row Labels ▾	Sum of Order Amount
UK	5350.52
USA	13139.39
Grand Total	**18489.91**

Figure 8–14. *International comparison: Sales by country*

Getting the Fields Where You Want Them

And how do you move, or place, the field data into either the Row Labels or Values areas? In our first PivotTable, we ticked the check boxes alongside **Salesperson** and **Order Amount**, and Excel decided by default into which areas they'd go. However, you can manually place a database field in any of the four areas in the **PivotTable Field List** by clicking in the field and dragging it into the desired area.

Let's say you're starting the PivotTable again from scratch. Once you've clicked through the **Insert ➤ PivotTable** sequence, you can start to drag on the desired fields instead of resorting to the check boxes. If, for example, you want to lodge the Salesperson field in the **Row Labels** area, you can click, drag, and drop it, as in Figure 8–15.

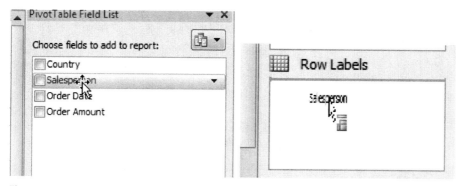

Figure 8–15. *Just click Salesperson, and drag and drop it into the Row Labels area.*

And you can do the same to Order Amount. Again, the reason you want to know about this drag-and-drop technique is that it will let you move any database field to any of the four areas. To remove a field from an area, just click the field, drag it into the worksheet area (or back into the upper area of the **PivotTable Field List**), and release the mouse; the field will disappear from the PivotTable (but not from the source data).

> **TIP:** You can also remove a field from the PivotTable by unchecking the box alongside the field you want to remove. Note that the box becomes checked whenever you place a field in an area, regardless of whether you do so by ticking the box or dragging the field into the area.

Pivoting the Data Sideways Using the Column Labels Area

The **Column Labels** area does exactly the same thing as **Row Labels**, except that it breaks out the data *horizontally*. Thus, this time if you drag **Salesperson** into the **Column Labels** area instead, and leave **Order Amount** in the **Values** area, the PivotTable will look like Figure 8–16.

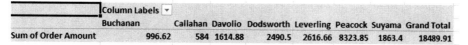

	Column Labels							
	Buchanan	Callahan	Davolio	Dodsworth	Leverling	Peacock	Suyama	Grand Total
Sum of Order Amount	996.62	584	1614.88	2490.5	2616.66	8323.85	1863.4	18489.91

Figure 8–16. *Change of direction: The sales data reading across, instead of down*

Filtering Items Using the Report Filter Area

That takes us to the fourth PivotTable area: **Report Filter**. There's a familiar word in there, of course, and report filters work similarly to the filters you've already learned about, but you need to understand what they do in a PivotTable.

Report filters give a different look to a PivotTable. As with the **Row Labels** and **Column Labels** areas, the **Report Filters** area also breaks out the data in the **Values** area, but lets you isolate the impact of one *item* in the field doing the breaking out. The following short exercise will show you what that means.

1. Drag and drop the Salesperson bar into the Report Filter area. In the PivotTable, you'll see the data shown in Figure 8–17.

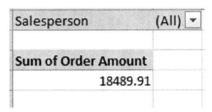

Salesperson	(All) ▼
Sum of Order Amount	
18489.91	

Figure 8–17. *The PivotTable report filter: Just click the drop-down arrow and select a salesperson*

2. Click the drop-down arrow and you'll be presented with a list of the salespersons, as shown in Figure 8–18.

Figure 8–18. *The salespersons: Just click one*

3. What happens next is pretty obvious: click one salesperson name, and click OK. You'll see, for example, the data shown in Figure 8–19.

Salesperson	Callahan ⊤
Sum of Order Amount	
584	

Figure 8–19. *The sales data for Callahan, and only Callahan. Note the filter symbol alongside Callahan's name.*

As with the standard table filters discussed in Chapter 7, we've singled out one salesperson for his or her sales totals. Want to see the totals for another salesperson? Just click the drop-down arrow again and click someone else.

You can also filter two or more salespersons at the same time:

1. Click the filter drop-down arrow.

2. Tick the **Select Multiple Items** check box.

3. Click the salespersons you want. Thus, if you click both Callahan and Levering, you'll filter their combined sales totals, as in Figure 8–20.

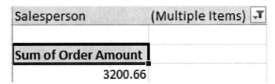

Salesperson	(Multiple Items) ⊤
Sum of Order Amount	
3200.66	

Figure 8–20. *Double duty: Filtering two salespersons' data*

Good to know, but you'll probably find this option slightly uninformative, because it doesn't allow you to see the name of the salespersons you're filtering. Microsoft is aware of this issue, and has supplied an alternative to this approach that you'll learn about later: using the Slicer.

Creating a Report Worksheet for Each Item in a Filter

There's another report filter feature you may want to check out, too: the **Show Report Filter Pages** option. Let's see what this does:

1. Drag the Salesperson field into the filter area without selecting any particular salesperson, so that you see (All), as shown previously in Figure 8–17.

2. Click the **PivotTables Tools Options** tab, and then click the **Options** drop-down arrow. You'll see the options shown in Figure 8–21.

Figure 8–21. *The Show Report Filter Pages... option*

3. Click **Show Report Filter Pages...**, and then click **OK** when you see the **Show Report Filter Pages** dialog box. That click will trigger a rapid-fire production of new worksheets, each named after and bearing a filtered report for each salesperson (see Figure 8–22).

Figure 8–22. *All accounted for: Each salesperson is assigned a separate worksheet, each containing a report filter for that person*

4. Click any worksheet tab and check it out (see Figure 8–23).

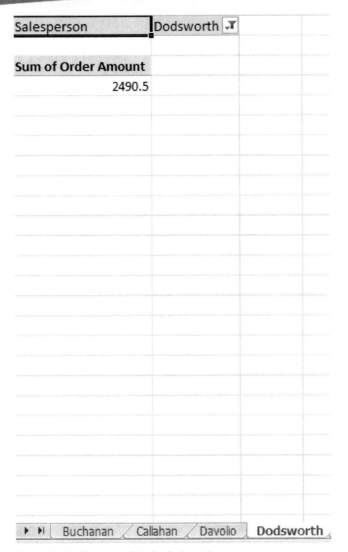

Salesperson	Dodsworth
Sum of Order Amount	
2490.5	

Buchanan / Callahan / Davolio / **Dodsworth**

Figure 8–23. *The report filter for Dodsworth*

This is an impressive option, but truly you could get away with one filter, and simply click any particular salesperson when you need to. But if you need to break out each salesperson's data in separate sheets, the Report Filter Pages command is a worthwhile one.

Counting Records: A Way to Break Out Text Data

Recall our introductory PivotTable example—that hypothetical dinner in which, among other things, we wanted to tally the number of guests assigned to their tables. So how would we go about constructing a PivotTable for this? Well, we want to break out the number of guests by their table numbers, so the Table Number field will be posted in the

Row Labels area. But what field is going to go into the **Values** area? The database in Figure 8–1 consists of exactly two fields: Guest and Table. And believe it not, even though the Guest field comprises text—that is, the names of the guests—we can still drag it into the **Values** area, because Excel will go ahead and perform the only mathematical operation it can on text; it will *count* the guests by their table numbers.

And that's how it works. If you drag a text-based field into the **Values** area, its contents will be counted, and broken out by whatever field populates the **Row Labels** area. Thus, with the dinner example, the guests will be counted by their table assignment—that is, how many have been assigned to Table 1, Table 2, and so on.

But let's try to illustrate this point with our salesperson data. Suppose we now want to determine not how much money each salesperson has earned, but how many sales each one has recorded. This exercise will demonstrate two important aspects of PivotTables: your ability to place a text-based field into the **Values** area, and the fact that you can apply the same field to a PivotTable twice.

First, make sure that the Salesperson field is positioned as usual in the Row Labels area. Nothing new there; but now, we're going to also drag and drop Salesperson into the **Values** area, demonstrating that you can use the same field twice in a PivotTable. Once you maneuver Salesperson into the **Values** area, you'll see the data shown in Figure 8–24.

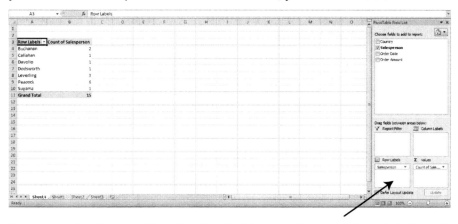

Figure 8–24. *Counting, not adding, sales. Note the Salesperson bars populating both the Row Labels and Values areas.*

The Salesperson bar in the **Values** area is recorded as Count of Salesperson, again because Excel has no choice but to count text data (it can't be added or averaged). In effect, what we've done is count the number of times each salesperson's name appears in the database—which is another way of stating how many sales each one has executed. And again, this will work the same way even if each salesperson has made hundreds or even thousands of sales.

Grouping Related Items Using Two Fields

Up to now we've traveled the basic route to designing a PivotTable, in which one field in the Row Labels area breaks out the data in a field in the Values area. But you can also place *two* fields in the Row Labels area, to carry out a kind of double-breakout.

The PivotTable in Figure 8–25 illustrates what that means.

Row Labels ▼	Count of Salesperson
⊟ **UK**	**4**
Buchanan	2
Dodsworth	1
Suyama	1
⊟ **USA**	**11**
Callahan	1
Davolio	1
Leverling	3
Peacock	6
Grand Total	**15**

Figure 8–25. *National pride: Sales, broken out both by country and salesperson*

Here, the sales data is broken out by two fields, first by country and then by salesperson. We can see that 4 sales were conducted in the United Kingdom and 11 in the United States. Within the United Kingdom, it's Buchanan, Dodsworth, and Suyama who've compiled the sales, while Callahan, Davolio, Leverling, and Peacock have done their sales work in the States.

This double-breakout enhances the viewer's understanding of the sales activity, by introducing Country into the analysis and indicating which salespersons worked in which country.

How is this done? Simple; you just drag and drop Country into the **Row Labels** area, too (see Figure 8–26).

Figure 8–26. *Table for two: Two fields occupy the Row Labels area*

When you drag Country into **Row Labels**, you need to carefully to position it above Salesperson. If you don't, and Salesperson winds up above Country, the PivotTable will look like Figure 8–27.

Row Labels ▼	Sum of Order Amount
⊟ **Buchanan**	**996.62**
UK	996.62
⊟ **Callahan**	**584**
USA	584
⊟ **Davolio**	**1614.88**
USA	1614.88
⊟ **Dodsworth**	**2490.5**
UK	2490.5
⊟ **Leverling**	**2616.66**
USA	2616.66
⊟ **Peacock**	**8323.85**
USA	8323.85
⊟ **Suyama**	**1863.4**
UK	1863.4
Grand Total	**18489.91**

Figure 8–27. *Another look at the same data*

Here the data is broken out first by salesperson and then by country, reversing the order of the initial breakout. This view might be particularly informative if a salesperson worked in both countries, because you'd see the sales data for both UK and USA under the salesperson's name. In any case, you can easily drag one field above the other in the

Row Labels area if you need to, and then just release your mouse when the fields have been properly positioned.

There's another point about breaking out the data by two fields. Note that each salesperson's total—which is a subtotal of all the sales, of course—appears alongside his or her name in bold text. If you want the subtotals to appear at the bottom of each salesperson's group instead, you can click the PivotTable Tools Design tab, and then click Subtotals ➤ Show all Subtotals at Bottom of Group, as in Figure 8–28.

Figure 8–28. *It all adds up: PivotTable subtotal options*

First, let's return Country to a position above Salesperson in the Row Labels area, because subtotaling by country will illustrate the point more clearly (there's more to subtotal this way; because each salesperson works in but one country, there's nothing to subtotal if you group by Salesperson). Then click Show All Subtotals at Bottom of Group, and the PivotTable will be redesigned to take on the appearance shown in Figure 8–29.

Row Labels	Sum of Order Amount
⊟ UK	
Buchanan	996.62
Dodsworth	2490.50
Suyama	1863.40
Walters	1543.73
UK Total	**6894.25**
⊟ USA	
Callahan	584.00
Davolio	1614.88
Leverling	2616.66
Peacock	8323.85
USA Total	**13139.39**
Grand Total	**20033.64**

Figure 8–29. *Another new look to the same data: Subtotals at the bottom of each salesperson group*

Using the Row and Column Value Areas to Group Items

There's still another approach to engineering a two-field breakout of the data. If you click and drag on the Country bar and drop it into the **Column Labels** area, you get what's shown in Figure 8–30.

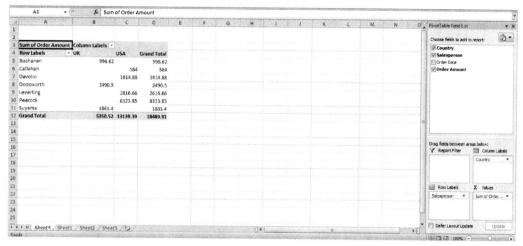

Figure 8–30. *The fields, pivoted: Again, the data is exactly the same, but organized differently*

We've orchestrated still another look to the data—kind of a matrix, in which the two fields intersect in the Values area. Note the field positions in the **Drag field between areas below** section—one in **Row Labels**, the other in **Column Labels**.

Changing the Calculation

By default, PivotTables will add, or sum, numerical fields in the **Value** area. But you may want the table to calculate a different kind of result—say, an average or a maximum. Changing to the kind of calculation you need is easy.

The following example will show you the amount of the average sale each salesperson has made:

1. First, remove the Country field from the **Column Labels** area if you've dragged it there. Remember, you can remove the field by clicking its bar in the **Drag field between areas below** area and dragging into the worksheet; release your mouse and the field will disappear. This will leave you with your original, basic PivotTable result, in which sales are broken out by salesperson.

> **TIP:** You can also remove a field by clicking the bar itself and clicking **Remove Field** on the menu that appears.

2. Then click inside the Values area in the actual PivotTable—not the **Values** area in the **PivotTable Field List**—and if necessary click the PivotTables Tools contextual tab, and then **Options ➤ Summarize Values By.** You'll see the options shown in Figure 8–31.

Figure 8–31. *Where to change the mathematical operation for your PivotTable data*

3. Click **Average**, and you'll see the data shown in Figure 8–32.

Row Labels ▼	Average of Order Amount
Buchanan	498.31
Callahan	584
Davolio	1614.88
Dodsworth	2490.5
Leverling	872.22
Peacock	1387.308333
Suyama	1863.4
Grand Total	**1232.660667**

Figure 8–32. *Average sale size, by salesperson*

That's it—though you probably won't like all those nasty decimal points swelling the numbers. But that's a formatting issue, and we're going to discuss that later in the chapter.

> **TIP:** You can select different mathematical operations by either right-clicking in the Values area in the PivotTable itself and clicking **Value Field Settings** on the context menu, or clicking the **Options** tab and then clicking **Field Settings** in the **Active** button group. Either way, you'll be brought to a **Value Field Settings** dialog box, from which you can choose the operation you want. You can also get to the same destination by right-clicking in that PivotTable value area and selecting **Summarize Values By.**

Grouping PivotTable Data: Organizing Your Time(s)

Earlier in this chapter, Figure 8–6 showed the salesperson data broken out by time—more specifically, the months in which the various sales were conducted. Yet the Salesperson database says nothing about months as a unit of time; each record only notates the precise day on which a sale was completed. But Excel lets you group time data into time units of your choosing, a most useful capability that can give you a big picture of financial activity over time, particularly when you're working with many records.

To illustrate, let's devise a PivotTable for the Salesperson database in which we break out sales (Order Amount) by Order Date, a field we've yet to use.

1. First, remove the Salesperson field from the **Row Labels** area. Then drag Order Date into the **Row Labels** area, and you'll see something like Figure 8–33.

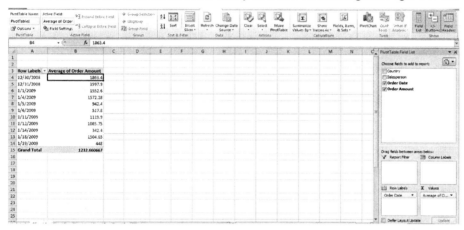

Figure 8–33. *Sales data, organized by date of transaction*

NOTE: Before we continue, remember that data placed in the **Row (or Column) Labels** area is listed uniquely. Figure 8–33 lists 11 dates even though our database has 15 records because some of the sales were carried out on the same date—and hence that date is listed only once.

2. In any case, say we want to break out the sales activity by month. Click anywhere among the dates, then click the **PivotTable Totals Options** tab, and then click **Group Selection** in the **Group** button group (see Figure 8–34).

Figure 8–34. *The Group Selection option*

3. After clicking **Group Selection**, you'll see the dialog shown in Figure 8–35.

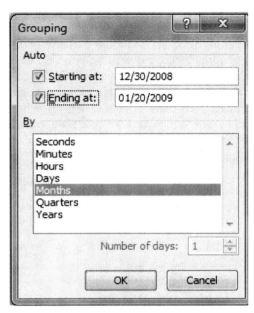

Figure 8–35. *The Grouping dialog box: Organizing your date data into the units of time you want*

4. Then click **Years** (**Months** will remain selected as well). If you don't click **Years**, all the January sales figures, for example, will be totaled together—and that might include Januarys in different years (and the same would of course apply to all the other months). Click **OK**, and you'll see the display shown in Figure 8–36.

Row Labels ▼	Average of Order Amount
⊟ 2008	
Dec	2730.65
⊟ 2009	
Jan	1002.200769
Grand Total	**1232.660667**

Figure 8–36. *Getting it all together: The data organized by months and years*

Now the sales data is grouped, and we can easily tell how sales have proceeded by month. Again, while our database is small, grouping will work with any collection of dates, no matter how large. To ungroup the data and return it to its original row label appearance, just click within the date data and click **Ungroup** in the **Group** button group.

Refreshing the PivotTable: Changing the Data

So far our PivotTables have worked with the same 15-record database throughout, but in the real world, of course, you may need to enter additional records and/or make changes to existing ones, while at the same time seeing to it that your PivotTable results reflect those changes. How does that happen?

Well, the first thing to understand is that, unlike Excel formulas, PivotTables do not perform automatic recalculation. That is, if you change data in your database, the PivotTable will not immediately incorporate the changes and update existing results. You'll have to refresh the PivotTable instead, by clicking the **Refresh** button on the **Options** tab.

To see this, click back into the Salesperson database and change Davolio's sales amount to $2,000. Then click anywhere in the PivotTable and click the **Refresh** button. You'll see the new data, as shown in Figure 8–37.

Row Labels ▾	Average of Order Amount
Buchanan	498.31
Callahan	584.00
Davolio	2000.00
Dodsworth	2490.50
Leverling	872.22
Peacock	1479.31
Suyama	1863.40
Grand Total	**1295.14**

Figure 8–37. *Davolio's sales total has now changed from the original $1614.88.*

If you've modified an *existing* record—that is, one already in the database—all you need to do is click **Refresh**. But if you've added a completely new record, clicking the **Refresh** button won't update the PivotTable. The next section discusses what to do in this case.

Adding New Records to a PivotTable

The easiest way out of this little dilemma is to convert the database into a table. New table records *are* automatically processed by PivotTables, and clicking **Refresh** will then update your results. Let's try it.

1. First, click anywhere in the database, click the **Insert** tab and choose **Table** from the **Tables** button group, and then click **OK**.

2. Then add a new record containing the information shown in Figure 8–38.

UK	Walters	05/04/2009	$1,543.73

Figure 8–38. *New recruit: Walters joins the sales force*

3. Click **Refresh**. Walters' data will be automatically incorporated into the PivotTable, as shown in Figure 8–39.

Row Labels ▾	Average of Order Amount
Buchanan	498.31
Callahan	584.00
Davolio	1614.88
Dodsworth	2490.50
Leverling	872.22
Peacock	1387.31
Suyama	1863.40
Walters	1543.73
Grand Total	**1252.10**

Figure 8–39. *The current PivotTable. Note that Walters' record is included, and sorted, too.*

NOTE: The Data Source button identifies the current range of data being processed by the PivotTable, and you can see that Table1 now appears as the source table, thus incorporating Walters' record.

Now you can enter as many new records as you like into the Salesperson database, and whenever you click **Refresh** those new records will appear in the PivotTable.

NOTE: If your PivotTable shows **Sum of Order Amount** instead of the **Average Amount** as shown in Figure 8–39, it doesn't matter. Adding and refreshing PivotTable data works no matter what mathematical operation you've selected.

Viewing Which Records Are Filtered: Using the Slicer

Recall that when we filtered multiple items, I noted that filtering more than two salespersons at the same time doesn't let you know exactly who's been filtered (see Figure 8–40).

Salesperson	(Multiple Items) ⊤
Average of Order Amount	
1165.06	

Figure 8–40. *Anyone's guess: Which salespersons have been filtered?*

As mentioned, Microsoft recognized this problem, and introduced the Slicer feature in Excel 2010 as a way to solve it. The Slicer is a kind of free-floating filter that enables you to see exactly which records have been selected.

For example, in Figure 8–40 I've filtered the sales data for Buchanan and Peacock. With the Slicer, you'll be able to see what's shown in Figure 8–41.

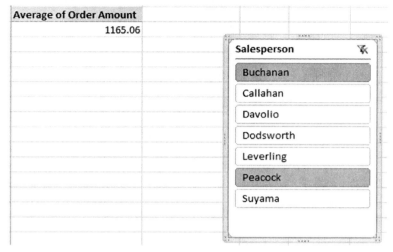

Figure 8–41. *Filter, no longer out of kilter: With the Slicer you can see exactly who's been filtered*

Note that the Slicer isn't exactly *in* the PivotTable, and if you click it the **PivotTable Tools** contextual tab won't appear on the screen. You can drag the Slicer anywhere on the worksheet, and even change its color and style.

How the Slicer Works

Before I demonstrate how to use the Slicer, make sure that the Order Amount data is placed in the Values area of your PivotTable, and place Salesperson in the **Report Filter** area (for this exercise, it doesn't matter if you've added Walters' data or not).

1. Click anywhere in the PivotTable. Then click the **PivotTable Tools Options** tab, and click the **Insert Slicer** button in the **Sort & Filter** button group. You'll see the options shown in Figure 8–42.

Figure 8–42. *Slice of life, PivotTable style. Note that all the database fields are listed.*

2. Click **Salesperson**, and then click **OK**. The Slicer will appear, with all the salespersons listed and colored blue, as in Figure 8–43.

Figure 8–43. *Don't worry if you don't have Walters listed.*

3. This is the equivalent of the (All) indicator shown in the report filter—that is, all the salespersons are currently selected. But if you click any one salesperson's name, only his or her data will appear in the **Value** field. If you click one salesperson, hold down the Ctrl key, and click a second name (see Figure 8–44), the data for both will be totaled in the **Value** field.

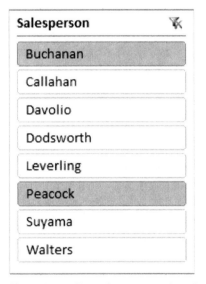

Figure 8–44. *Two salespersons selected with the Slicer. Their combined sales data will appear in the Values area.*

This is the Slicer solution to that report filter multiple-items problem—it allows you to clearly see which salespersons have been filtered. If you want to deselect a salesperson, hold the Ctrl down again and click that salesperson's name.

Note that our PivotTable now has the Order Amount data in the Values area, the Salesperson field in the **Report Filter** area, and the Slicer in place (see Figure 8–45).

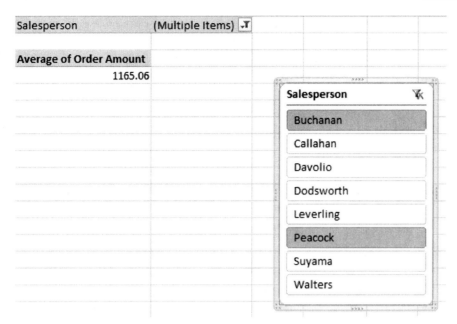

Figure 8–45. *The Salesperson field in two places: The Report Filter area and the Slicer*

And that's a bit redundant, because now the salespersons are being filtered in two places. As a consequence, you can drag Salespersons off the PivotTable, leaving you with what's shown in Figure 8–46.

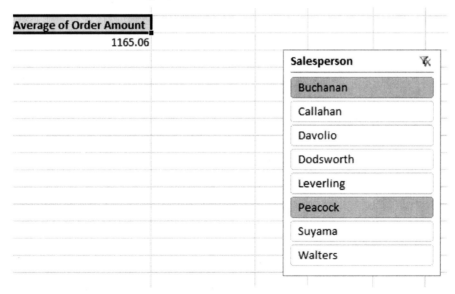

Figure 8–46. *There's no need to use the Report Filter area now, because the Slicer is doing the same job.*

And now you can see exactly who's being filtered.

The **Clear Filter** button—that funnel image accompanied by an X in the upper right of the filter—will turn off the current filter when you click it, but that doesn't mean that it will remove the filter from the PivotTable. It means that it will no longer single out or filter any particular salesperson, but rather combine all the salesperson data in the Value area (see Figure 8–47).

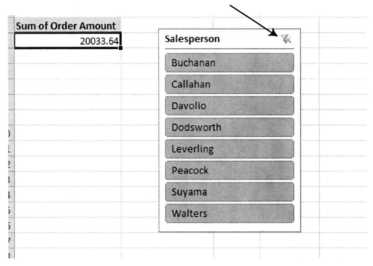

Figure 8–47. The Clear Filter button has been clicked, combining all the salesperson data in the Value area result.

Restyling the Slicer

You can also restyle the Slicer by clicking the Slicer title (i.e., the upper area that reads "Salesperson"—see the arrow in Figure 8–47), and calling up the **Slicer Tools** contextual tab. Click the **Options** tab, followed by the **Slicer Styles** drop-down arrow, and click a style (see Figure 8–48).

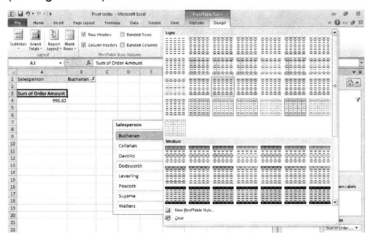

Figure 8–48. Selecting Slicer styles

To remove a Slicer, click in the Slicer title area so that the Slicer is surrounded by a gray border (see Figure 8–49). Then just press the Delete key.

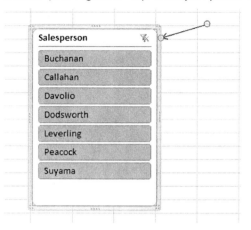

Figure 8–49. *Click the Slicer area to trigger that gray border and press Delete.*

NOTE: You can also resize the Slicer by clicking a dotted area on that gray border and dragging in the desired direction, just as you would resize a chart.

Formatting the PivotTable

Excel offers many options for formatting PivotTables. Perhaps most importantly, you can easily reformat the values in the Value area, which, after all, contains data you need to know. Now, about all those decimal points.

As usual with Excel, there are several ways to access the commands that will enable you to change the appearance of PivotTable values. I'll describe two.

1. First, right-click anywhere in the Values area in the actual PivotTable, and click **Value Field Settings** on the context menu. You'll see the dialog shown in Figure 8–50.

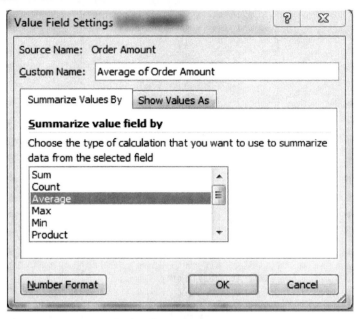

Figure 8–50. *Note the Number Format button.*

2. Just click the **Number Format** button, and you'll be brought to a familiar dialog box (see Figure 8–51).

Figure 8–51. *Déjà vu: The good old Format Cells dialog box*

3. You've seen this collection of options in Chapter 5. We want the values to display just two decimal points, so click **Number** in **Category** list shown in Figure 8–51, and type **2** in the **Decimal Places** field you'll see in the next dialog box (see Figure 8–52). Then click **OK** twice.

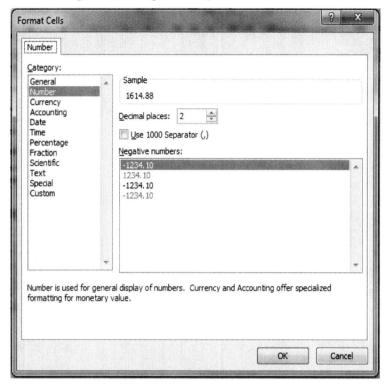

Figure 8–52. *The number formatting options; you've seen it all before*

NOTE: What's different about formatting PivotTable values is that, unlike a standard range, you *don't* select every cell in the Values area before you select the formatting options; all you do is right-click in the area and execute the commands, and all the values will be reformatted. It's an all-or-nothing procedure here.

Styling Your Report

You can also draw upon a large collection of PivotTable styles that resemble the styles available in Excel tables. To view these, just click the **PivotTable Tools Design** tab, select **PivotTable Styles**, and click the **More** drop-down arrow (the lowest of the arrows you'll see). You'll be presented with the options shown in Figure 8–53.

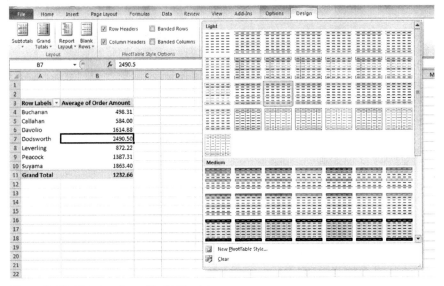

Figure 8–53. *Stylish options: PivotTable styles*

And as with their table cousins, these styles will display themselves in preview mode when you simply place your mouse over them before clicking. You can also introduce row and column banding in the PivotTable just as you can in Excel tables by clicking in the **PivotTable Style Options** button group just to the left of **PivotTable Styles**.

> **NOTE:** Remember, in order to access the **PivotTable** button group options, you must click in the PivotTable first.

Changing PivotTable Headers

Note that Figure 8–53 sports a "Row Labels" header above the Salesperson field, and you might opt for something a bit more specific. If so, all you have to do is click in that header cell directly in the PivotTable, type whatever replacement header you wish, and press Enter. You can do the same to the Values header as well; just note that in the Values case your customized header will also appear in the **Values** area in the **PivotTable Field List**.

> **NOTE:** Changing PivotTable field headers *won't* change the corresponding headers in the database source you've used to produce the PivotTable.

Layout Options

The PivotTable warehouse of design options stocks three principal layouts:

- Compact (the default, shown in Figure 8–54)

Row Labels	Average of Order Amount
UK	**1337.63**
Buchanan	498.31
Dodsworth	2490.50
Suyama	1863.40
USA	**1194.49**
Callahan	584.00
Davolio	1614.88
Leverling	872.22
Peacock	1387.31
Grand Total	**1232.66**

Figure 8–54. *The Compact PivotTable layout option*

- Outline (see Figure 8–55)

Country	Salesperson	Average of Order Amount
UK		**1337.63**
	Buchanan	498.31
	Dodsworth	2490.50
	Suyama	1863.40
USA		**1194.49**
	Callahan	584.00
	Davolio	1614.88
	Leverling	872.22
	Peacock	1387.31
Grand Total		**1232.66**

Figure 8–55. *The Outline PivotTable layout option*

- Tabular (see Figure 8–56)

Country	Salesperson	Average of Order Amount
UK	Buchanan	498.31
	Dodsworth	2490.50
	Suyama	1863.40
UK Total		**1337.63**
USA	Callahan	584.00
	Davolio	1614.88
	Leverling	872.22
	Peacock	1387.31
USA Total		**1194.49**
Grand Total		**1232.66**

Figure 8–56. *The Tabular PivotTable layout option*

These can be easy to confuse, and exactly what distinguishes them becomes clearer when you break out the data by two fields. There are a few differences that separate the three layouts, however:

- The Compact layout tucks the Salespersons data beneath the Country field in the same columns, whereas the other two layouts assign Salesperson a separate column.

- The Outline and Tabular layouts title the columns with the actual names of the fields being broken out, unlike Compact, which can't do that—because it presents two fields in one column.

- The Tabular layout presents the UK and USA subtotals beneath the data, while the other two align the subtotals with the Country titles.

You access the various layout options by clicking the **PivotTable Tools Design** tab, and clicking the **Report Layout** button in the **Layout** button group, as shown in Figure 8–57.

Figure 8–57. *PivotTable layout options*

And what about those minus signs stationed to the left of the country names in all the layouts? When clicked, those buttons conceal, or *collapse*, the salesperson data beneath the country (see Figure 8–58).

Row Labels ▾	Average of Order Amount
⊞ UK	1337.63
⊟ USA	1194.49
Callahan	584.00
Davolio	1614.88
Leverling	872.22
Peacock	1387.31
Grand Total	**1232.66**

Figure 8–58. *Now you see it, now you don't: UK salespersons hidden, or collapsed, beneath the UK category*

Note that the minus has reverted to a plus sign alongside the UK in the figure. Click it now and the UK salesperson records return to view. This plus/minus option gives you a way to streamline the PivotTable's appearance by temporarily obscuring the detail data under a global category—in our case, Country. (Of course, you could achieve a similar effect by simply removing the Salesperson field from the PivotTable.)

In addition, you can collapse and expand the *entire* PivotTable by clicking the **Expand Entire Field/Collapse Entire Field** buttons in the **Options ➤ Active Field** button group (see Figure 8–59).

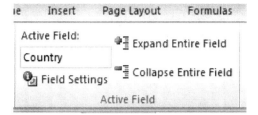

Figure 8–59. *The Expand and Collapse Entire Field buttons*

Clicking the **Collapse Entire Field** button, for example, would be equivalent to clicking the minus signs alongside UK and USA simultaneously, yielding the results shown in Figure 8–60.

Row Labels ▾	Average of Order Amount
⊞ UK	1337.63
⊞ USA	1194.49
Grand Total	1232.66

Figure 8–60. *The entire Salesperson field has been collapsed, impacting both countries.*

Clicking **Expand Entire Field** now would restore all the salesperson names to view.

Creating Charts from PivotTables Using PivotCharts

Just as you can summarize database data with a chart, you can chart PivotTable results too. The principles behind pivot charting are very similar, but not identical, to the techniques we've already discussed for charting database data.

Let's say we want to turn our basic PivotTable—in which sales data is broken out by salesperson totals—into a chart (see Figure 8–61).

Row Labels ▾	Sum of Order Amount
Buchanan	996.62
Callahan	584.00
Davolio	1614.88
Dodsworth	2490.50
Leverling	2616.66
Peacock	8323.85
Suyama	1863.40
Walters	1543.73
Grand Total	20033.64

Figure 8–61. *Back where we started: Sales figures broken out by salesperson. If your data still shows averages instead of sums, it won't affect the chart-making process.*

1. If necessary, restore your PivotTable to the appearance shown in Figure 8–61, in which Salesperson occupies the Row Labels area and Order Amount is in the Values area.

2. Then click anywhere in the PivotTable, click the **PivotTable Tools Options** tab, and choose **PivotChart** from the **Tools** button group. You'll see the familiar dialog box shown in Figure 8–62.

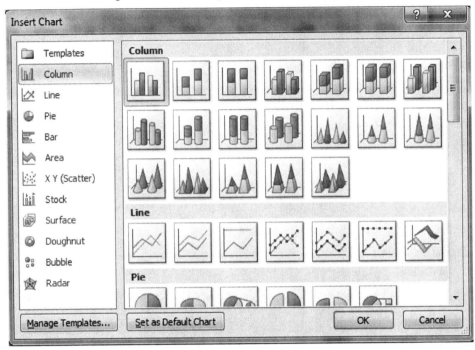

Figure 8–62. *The Insert Chart dialog box, again*

3. Note that you've already seen this box in Chapter 6. Go ahead and click OK to Excel's default selection, that redoubtable Column chart, and you'll see the data presented as in Figure 8–63.

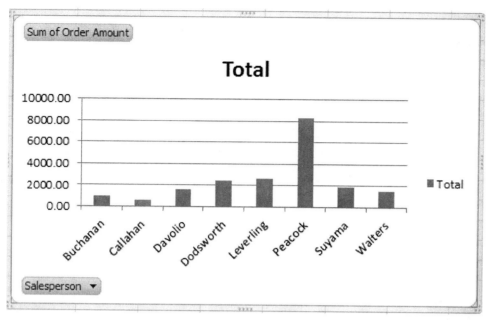

Figure 8–63. *A PivotChart. Note the difference from a standard Excel chart: the appearance of what are called field buttons.*

It isn't a thing of beauty yet, but the chart has captured the PivotTable data. The chart takes the salesperson names (the data in the Row Label), applies them to the horizontal (category) axis, and draws its vertical (value) axis from the sales figures.

> **NOTE:** When you click in a PivotChart, the Row Values area in the **PivotTable Field List** is named **Axis Fields (Categories)**. Click back in the PivotTable, and the Row Values label is restored.

And once the PivotChart makes its appearance in the worksheet, the means for modifying and reformatting it are nearly identical to the options described in Chapter 6. When you click in the chart, a **PivotChart Tools** contextual tab is ushered onto the screen, offering some familiar selections (see Figure 8–64).

Figure 8–64. *PivotChart options available via the PivotChart Tools contextual tab: The Design, Layout, Format, and Analyze tabs*

Filtering Data in the Chart with Field Buttons

Click the PivotChart tabs and you'll recognize nearly all the button groups, because you've seen them on the **Chart Tools** contextual tab, too. There is, however, a fourth tab— **Analyze**—that contains buttons you won't see associated with standard Excel charts (see Figure 8–65).

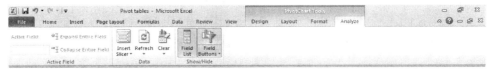

Figure 8–65. *The contents of the PivotChart Tools Analyze tab*

> **NOTE:** Clicking the **Clear** drop-down arrow on the **Analyze** tab will reveal a **Clear All** option, which when clicked will remove both the PivotChart and the PivotTable but leave the underlying grids for the two objects. It's a way allowing you to start all over again by selecting a new set of fields for the PivotTable, which in turn immediately generate a PivotChart. The **Clear** button is also available in the **PivotTable Tools Action** button group.

But PivotCharts themselves reveal an element that is nowhere to be found in conventional charts: *field buttons*. These represent the PivotTable fields that contribute the source data to the chart, and when they're clicked they enable you to make various changes to the chart.

For example, clicking the arrow on the **Salesperson** button on the chart triggers the menu shown in Figure 8–66.

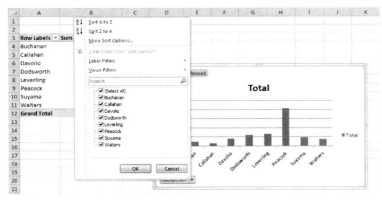

Figure 8–66. *Ticking any check box will remove that salesperson's name—and column—from the chart.*

To illustrate, if you click **Peacock** and then **OK**, Peacock's column bar will be banished from the chart (see Figure 8–67).

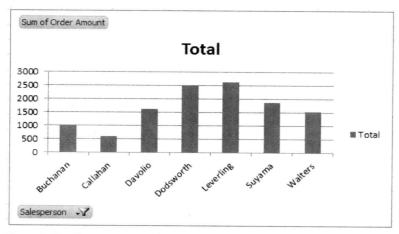

Figure 8–67. *The salespersons, minus Peacock. Note the filter symbol that now appears on the Salesperson field button, indicating that a name has been filtered out of the chart.*

Peacock has flown the coop, and as a result, the value axis, which had established a maximum of 10,000 in order to be able to record Peacock's high sales total, has been reset to 3,000, now that Leverling is the leading salesperson. But more importantly, take a look now at the source PivotTable (see Figure 8–68).

Row Labels ⟱	Sum of Order Amount
Buchanan	996.62
Callahan	584
Davolio	1614.88
Dodsworth	2490.5
Leverling	2616.66
Suyama	1863.4
Walters	1543.73
Grand Total	**11709.79**

Figure 8–68. *Peacock's missing here, too.*

What we see is that filtering the data in the PivotChart changes the source PivotTable correspondingly. If you make a change in the data recorded by the chart, you'll also change the PivotTable that gave rise to the chart in the same way. And, needless to say, the reverse is true, too; any data change in the PivotTable changes the PivotChart as well.

And if you don't want to see those field buttons on the chart, right-click any button and select the **Hide All Field Buttons on Chart** option on the resulting menu. You can also delete a particular field button by right-clicking it and selecting **Remove Field** (see Figure 8–69).

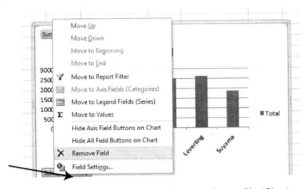

Figure 8–69. *Removing just one field button from a PivotChart*

> **NOTE:** You can also remove individual PivotChart field buttons by clicking the **PivotChart** contextual tab, choosing **Analyze**, and clicking the **Field Buttons** arrow.

If you want to delete the PivotChart, click in its chart area so that you see that gray border surrounding the chart, and press Delete—just as you would with a standard Excel chart.

Creating a PivotTable and PivotChart Together

You can also produce a PivotTable and chart *simultaneously*, by clicking anywhere in the source data (meaning the original database), and then clicking **Insert ➤ Tables ➤ PivotTable ➤ PivotChart**. You'll see what's shown in Figure 8–70.

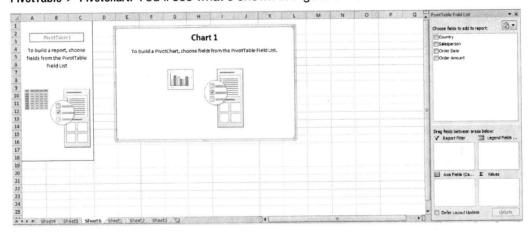

Figure 8–70. *Note that the PivotChart and PivotTable areas appear at the same time.*

Now if you drag Salesperson into what's now called the **Axis Fields (Categories)** area and drag Order Amount into the **Values** area, both the PivotChart *and* PivotTable will materialize onscreen.

Summary

PivotTables are an acquired taste, to be sure, but one worth acquiring, as they can greatly enhance your analyses of spreadsheet data. Understanding basic PivotTable principles will go a long way toward empowering you to fashion them on your own.

Next we'll direct our attention to another analytical enhancement—working with multiple worksheets and how they can work together.

Chapter 9

Managing Your Workbook

Some worksheet tasks require you to step back from those molecule-sized cells that occupy the better part of your attention and take a larger look instead at the entire worksheet—or sometimes, the entire work*book*. You may, for example, decide you need to supplement those default three worksheets with a fourth, or write a formula that reaches over into a second sheet and references a data cell from there. Or you may want to subject several sheets to the same formats for the sake of uniformity, or protect a sheet so that no one will be able to overwrite all the intricate work you've committed to its cells. Well, we're going to address that grab bag of worksheet- and workbook-wide topics right here.

Adding Worksheets to Your Workbook

A worksheet is a big place—over 16 billion cells are at your disposal, offering you way more space than you'll likely ever need to ply your data management tasks. And that's just for starters, because Excel is happy to grant you even more room than that—a lot more room if you need it, in the form of additional worksheets.

Remember that by default Excel supplies the user with three worksheets, each outfitted with that same 16-billion cell allotment; each with the same addresses (i.e., every worksheet has a cell A4, a cell Z235, etc.); each available to receive values, text, formulas, charts—all the data you can conjure. Moreover, you can add even *more* sheets as events warrant—as many sheets as your computer's memory can support, in fact. The question is why you'd want to.

After all, if you can't make do with 16 billion cells, you must be doing something more than a little out of the ordinary—like giving a name to every grain of sand in Coney Island, or assigning tracking numbers to all of Imelda Marcos's shoes. Short of that, the question remains: why would you ever need more than one worksheet?

We'll start with the usual answer to that question: it depends. For a great many spreadsheet tasks, one sheet *will* suffice; but there may be good reasons to assign your data to several sheets.

For example, you may want to compose a collection of complex formulas on one worksheet and present the results on another. That's what *Excel dashboards* do; these are workbooks in which complex number crunching is performed on one sheet, and an assortment of charts built on those numbers is laid out on another worksheet—the one that viewers will see (and as you'll see, worksheets can be completely hidden from view, too, even as the data on them remains usable).

Another reason you might want to deploy more than one worksheet is to place the same kind of data in the same addresses across worksheets. That means something like this: If you're running a small business, you could assign each employee his or her own worksheet and enter the same information for each in the same cell on the respective worksheets—say, every employee name in that sheet's cell A1, the social security number in cell A2, salary in A3, and so on. This approach gives your data entry a uniformity that enables you to easily find equivalent information in the same location across sheets.

Still another reason to use multiple worksheets is a practical one. You may need to enter a large variety of information—say, several different tables—and rather than commit all of these to one worksheet (which would require considerable scrolling up and down the sheet in order to see it all), you could place some tables on another sheet, which you could access more efficiently by just clicking a sheet tab and viewing that data straight away.

But let's now turn to a workbook and introduce a few features of worksheets—in the plural.

Clicking Through the Worksheets

As indicated, Excel starts you off with three worksheets, called Sheet1, Sheet2, and Sheet3 by default, though you can rename any sheet, as you'll see. You'll find tabs representing the sheets in the lower left of your screen, as shown in Figure 9–1.

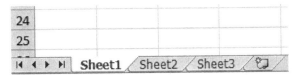

Figure 9–1. *Keeping tabs on your sheets: The three default sheets*

> **TIP:** You can change the three-sheet default allotment for all new workbooks by clicking File ➤ Options and entering a different value in the **Include this many sheets** field.

Click any tab and you'll be taken to that worksheet, which should look just like any other one. As already indicated, all the addresses on the sheets are identical, meaning that their cell references are the same (which raises a question I'll answer in a little while: How exactly does one differentiate between cell S12 on Sheet1 and cell S12 on Sheet2?).

Adding and Moving New Worksheets

To add, or insert, a new sheet into the workbook, you can click the **Insert Worksheet** button (or use its keyboard equivalent, Shift+F11) to the immediate right of Sheet3 (see Figure 9–2).

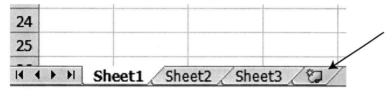

Figure 9–2. *The Insert Worksheet button*

That click will install another sheet to the right of the existing sheets (to be called Sheet4, etc.). If you right-click a sheet tab, however, you can click **Insert** on the resulting context menu (see Figure 9–3).

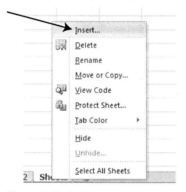

Figure 9–3. *Another way to insert a new sheet*

That click will call up an **Insert** dialog box, in which the **Worksheet** option will be selected by default (see Figure 9–4). Click **OK** to add the new worksheet.

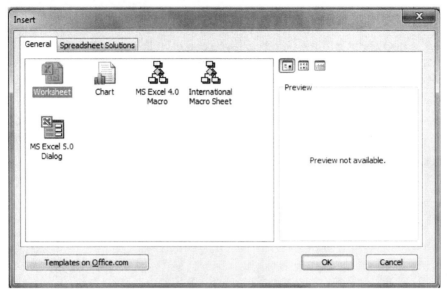

Figure 9–4. *An oldie-but-goodie dialog box: That Excel icon dates back a few versions*

Note that this sequence isn't exactly equivalent to using the **Insert Worksheet** button demonstrated earlier, because here the new worksheet will be inserted to the *left* of whichever worksheet you right-click. Thus, if you right-click and click **Insert** on Sheet3, the new Sheet4 will appear between Sheet2 and Sheet3, even though it'll be numbered out of sequence.

There's even a third way to insert a new sheet, by clicking the **Home ➤ Insert ➤ Insert Sheet** in the **Cells** button group (see Figure 9–5).

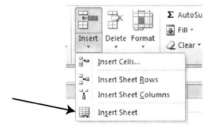

Figure 9–5. *Yet another way to insert a new worksheet*

This too will insert a new sheet to the left of the sheet tab that's been clicked.

But whatever method you choose, don't worry. If you decide a worksheet tab isn't where you want it to be, you can move it by clicking the tab and dragging it to a new position. As you drag, you'll see a page symbol accompanied by a black down arrow, indicating where the sheet will land when you release the mouse. In Figure 9–6, Sheet3 will be moved between Sheet1 and Sheet2.

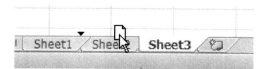

Figure 9–6. *On the move: Sheet3, en route to a new location*

But if you've added many sheets to the workbook, you won't be able to see all the sheet tabs at the same time (see Figure 9–7).

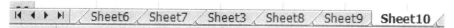

Figure 9–7. *Not all there: You can't see sheets 1 through 5*

By clicking the arrows shown on the left in Figure 9–8, you can reveal additional sheets in either direction.

Figure 9–8. *Exposing hidden sheet tabs by clicking the arrows*

The left-pointing arrow accompanied by the vertical bar will, when clicked, reveal the first sheet tab; the right-pointing arrow with the vertical bar will reveal the last tab in your current complement. But these arrow maneuvers *don't* take you "into" another sheet; they just reveal the sheet tabs. If you're currently working on Sheet10 when you start clicking, you'll stay inside Sheet10.

Deleting Sheets

If you want to delete a sheet, right-click the sheet tab and select the **Delete** option on the context menu. If the sheet has data on it, the prompt in Figure 9–9 will appear.

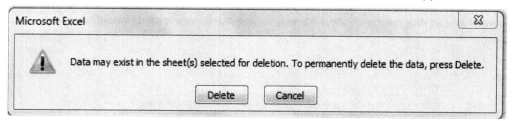

Figure 9–9. *Note this prompt well—if you click Delete, the data on the sheet will be permanently deleted.*

That prompt means business. What it's saying is that if you click **Delete**, the sheet will be dispatched irrevocably to the digital void—that is, you won't be able to undo the deletion. What you'd have to do, then, if you *did* delete the sheet in error, is resort to the ancient plan B—just close the workbook without saving it, and then reopen it. That strategy is messy, because you may lose other changes you may have wanted to save, but at least you'll get your sheet back.

Copying a Sheet

You can also copy a sheet in its entirety by right-clicking that sheet tab, clicking **Move or Copy...**, and clicking **Create a copy** in the resulting dialog box (see Figure 9–10).

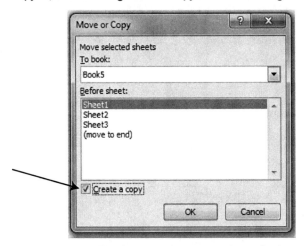

Figure 9–10. *Yes, this dialog box gives you another option for moving a sheet, too.*

Click the sheet *before* which you want the copy to appear, and click **OK**. The copy will then install itself there. If you make a copy of Sheet3, it will be named Sheet3(2). But as you're about to learn, you can rename sheets, too.

Renaming and Recoloring the Worksheet Tabs

You can also rename the worksheet tabs in one of two ways. For one, you can right-click the tab you want to change and click **Rename** in the context menu. The text appears selected in black, and you just type the new name and press Enter (see Figure 9–11).

Figure 9–11. *Once the text is highlighted in black, type a new name and press Enter.*

Alternatively, you can double-click the tab. That will likewise select the tab directly, again turning it black. Then type the new name and press Enter.

> **NOTE:** You can devise multiword names for the tabs, such as 2010 Data. Tab names can be up to 31 characters long.

If you want to recolor a tab, right-click the tab and click **Tab Color**. You'll see the options shown in Figure 9–12.

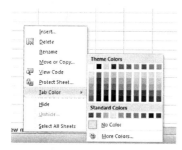

Figure 9–12. *You've heard of tab collars? These are tab colors.*

Just click the color you prefer, and the tab will take on that hue. Keep in mind, though, that when you click the recolored tab, it more or less reverts to its original white color. It's only when you click on a different tab that you'll see the new color you've selected (see Figure 9–13).

Figure 9–13. *Changing tab colors*

Notice that on the left in Figure 9–13, the Sheet3 tab has been clicked, making it appear mostly white. On the right in the figure, Sheet2 has been clicked, which allows Sheet3's color to appear fully.

Hiding Sheets

You can also easily hide a sheet, and there may be good reasons for wanting to do so, though top-secret confidentiality isn't one of them. For example, you may want to hide a sheet containing complex formulas that other viewers don't need to know about. Also, when you hide a sheet, no one—including you—will be able to accidentally overwrite any of the formulas or inflict any other inadvertent damage. To hide a sheet, just right-click its tab and select **Hide**. Presto, the sheet disappears.

When you want to restore the sheet to view, just right-click any available sheet tab and click **Unhide...**, and you'll see the dialog shown in Figure 9–14.

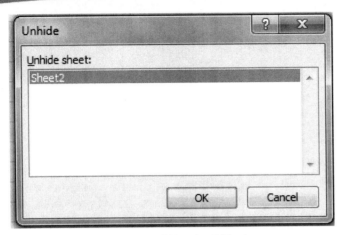

Figure 9–14. *Where to get your hidden sheet(s) back*

Click the name of the sheet you want to reveal (you can hide more than one), click OK, and it will be back in plain sight.

> **NOTE:** The data on hidden sheets can still be used, and its cells can still be referred to in formulas.

Grouping Sheets: Changing Multiple Sheets at the Same Time

Excel makes it easy to *group* several sheets simultaneously, so that changes made to any one sheet will affect the others in the same way; and this option applies both to data entry and formatting.

To get a grasp on what this means, suppose you've designed a workbook, each of whose sheets is devoted to a different employee in a small business. You want every sheet to look the same, with cell A3 containing the caption "Employee Name" in each sheet and A4 displaying the phrase "Social Security Number." Once you group the sheets, all you have to do is enter these captions on just one sheet—and "Employee Name" will appear in every cell A3, and "Social Security Number" in every A4. That's a very efficient way to work, because your business might have a staff of 50 people—and why should you enter the same things 50 times if you can get away with entering them just once?

By the same token, you might want these captions to exhibit a 24-point font size on all the sheets. Again, by grouping the sheets you need only make that change on one sheet, and the change will be automatically extended to all the others.

How to Group Sheets

There are a few ways to group sheets, and they're all pretty easy. If you want to group *all* the sheets in your workbook, just right-click any sheet tab and click **Select All Sheets** (in this context, the word *select* is identical to *group*) on the resulting menu. That's it. Your worksheet title will now be accompanied by the word *[Group]*, too, as shown in Figure 9–15.

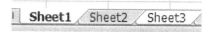

Figure 9–15. *What you'll see alongside your workbook title when you group sheets*

When sheets are selected, their tabs turn white (of course, one sheet will always appear white, because you have to always be "in" at least one sheet), as shown in Figure 9–16.

Figure 9–16. *Before grouping all the sheets (left) and after (right). The boldfaced text represents the active sheet—the one you're currently working with.*

That's the quickest way to group all the sheets in a workbook. If you want to group just *some* sheets, click the first sheet tab you want to group, and then hold down the Ctrl key and click any other sheet(s). In Figure 9–17, Sheet1 and Sheet3 have been selected. Note that Sheet2 displays the default gray color because it hasn't been selected.

Figure 9–17. *Selecting multiple sheets*

If you want to group several *consecutive* sheets, but not all the sheets in your workbook (say, sheets 1 through 5 in an 8-sheet workbook), click the first sheet tab you want to select, and then hold down the Shift key and click the last in the series (in our case Sheet5). All the sheets between 1 and 5 will be selected as well.

One you've carried out the grouping you can start to enter data on the sheet you're currently viewing—and whatever data you entered will appear in the same cells in the other grouped sheets. And the same applies to any formatting changes.

Ungrouping the Sheets

Sooner or later you'll want to ungroup the sheets—because you'll probably need to enter data in a particular sheet that you won't want reproduced in another. For example, once you've entered the "Employee Name" caption in grouped-sheet mode, you'll naturally want to go on and enter specific employee names on specific sheets. But if you don't ungroup the sheets first, the first name you enter will appear on *all* the sheets. The standard way to ungroup sheets is to right-click any grouped sheet and click **Ungroup Sheets** on the resulting menu.

Referring to Cells in Other Worksheets: Using Them in Formulas

Worksheets are, as the name suggests, analogous to pages or sheets in a book. But unlike the hard-copy variety, the information contained on these sheets can be referred to and actively used by other sheets in formulas.

For example, you may want to add the salaries of two or more employees in your company, and that information may be stored in different sheets. How then would you go about adding them in one formula?

The problem is, as already indicated, every sheet has the same bundle of 16 billion addresses; so if each salary is placed in cell its respective cell A3, how is each distinguished from the other and utilized in the same formula besides?

This short exercise will show you how:

1. On a blank spreadsheet, type **23000** in cell A3 on Sheet1, and type **32500** in A3 on Sheet2 (don't worry about formatting here).

2. Now, we want to add these two values—let's say in a formula in D5 on Sheet1. Click in D5 and type **=**, and then, as usual, click cell A3 and type **+**, as shown in Figure 9–18. So far, we haven't done anything new.

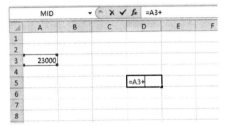

Figure 9–18. Starting to write the formula on Sheet1. First we use cell A3 from Sheet1.

3. Then click the Sheet2 tab and click cell A3 on that sheet, as shown in Figure 9–19.

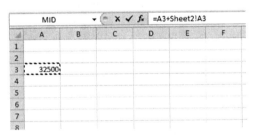

Figure 9–19. Now Sheet2. Note the formula in the formula bar.

4. Then press Enter, or click the check mark by the formula bar. The result, 55500, appears in D5 of Sheet1—where you wanted it to go. The formula reads

    `=A3+Sheet2!A3`

The formula first refers to the value on Sheet1, 23000. We then clicked the other cell whose value we wanted to add, also called A3, but on Sheet2, and that's why we had to click the Sheet2 tab first. In order to distinguish between the two A3s, Excel added the Sheet2! prefix when we clicked that sheet's A3.

That's how Excel works with cells in different sheets—by supplementing cell addresses with the name of the sheet in which the cell is positioned. And if you're asking why the *first* A3 wasn't preceded by the prefix Sheet1! in our formula, good question. It's because Excel assumes by default that any cells referred to in a formula are on the same sheet as the formula. It's only when a cell is located elsewhere that the prefix is needed.

Using Ranges on Other Sheets in Formulas

Your ability to write formulas and functions that call upon cells in other sheets isn't restricted to individual cells. It's easy to work with whole ranges, too.

Say you have a range of values on Sheet2, C11:C15, whose sum you want to calculate on Sheet1 (see Figure 9–20).

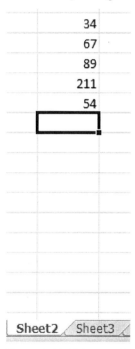

34
67
89
211
54

Sheet2 Sheet3

Figure 9–20. *Values on Sheet2*

1. To start the process, click in the cell on Sheet1 in which you want the answer to appear.

2. Now, because we're working with a range, we could use the SUM function. Let's say you click in cell C12 on Sheet1, where you want the answer to appear. You can then click the **AutoSum** button, and you'll see what's shown in Figure 9–21.

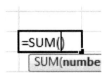

Figure 9–21. *Where's the range between the parentheses?*

3. You won't see any cell references yet, because there are no values in the column above C12, nor are there any in the row to C12's left (values that AutoSum is programmed to look for—but that doesn't bother us, because the values we want to add are on Sheet2 anyway). Next, click the Sheet2 tab and simply drag the range you want, as in Figure 9–22.

Figure 9–22. *Dragging the range on Sheet2. Again, note how the formula bar records this expression.*

4. Then just click **OK** or click the check mark. On Sheet1, you'll see the answer, as shown in Figure 9–23.

Figure 9–23. *The answer, recorded in cell C12 on Sheet1*

Again, the range referenced between SUM's parentheses is on Sheet2, and that Sheet2! prefix is Excel's way of declaring that this range is *not* C11:C15 on Sheet1, in which the function has been written.

Using the View Context Tab to Show and Hide Basic Screen Elements

The Excel worksheet features a number of characteristics that are so basic you probably don't even think about them—namely, the gridlines that demarcate each cell, and the row and column headings that help you identify cell addresses. But if you want, you can remove these elements from the worksheet (though of course you can always return them to the screen when you want).

So why would you want to do this? After all, the cell gridlines and row and column headers help you line up cells visually. The answer to the question, then, is presentational. Once you've completed a worksheet and finished your design work and formula-writing, and you need to show it to others, eliminating the gridlines and headers imparts a cleaner look to your data. Compare the two views shown in Figure 9–24.

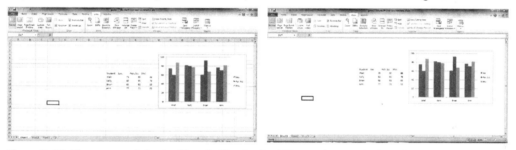

Figure 9–24. *The same worksheet, with and without cell gridlines and row and column headers*

Turning these elements off and back on is easy. Just click the **View** tab, and click **Gridlines** and/or **Headings** in the **Show** button group (see Figure 9–25).

Figure 9–25. *Show and tell: Where to turn gridlines and headings on and off*

Just uncheck the boxes to turn the features off, and check the boxes again to turn the features back on. And as you see, you can even hide the formula bar, too.

NOTE: These options are sheet specific. That means that if you turn off the gridlines on Sheet1, they will still remain visible on the other sheets. Remember also that if your turn the gridlines off, you can still draw borders around selected cells (see Chapter 5).

Showing Formulas in Cells

If you've constructed a workbook with lots of formulas, you may need to inspect the formulas for mistakes, or at least review them to remind yourself exactly how you put the worksheet together. With that in mind, you can tell Excel to show the *formulas* in their cells instead of the results of those formulas.

To show the formulas in a particular worksheet's cells, click **File ➤ Options ➤ Advanced**, and then check the **Show formulas in cells instead of their calculated results** box in the **Display options for this worksheet** area (see Figure 9–26).

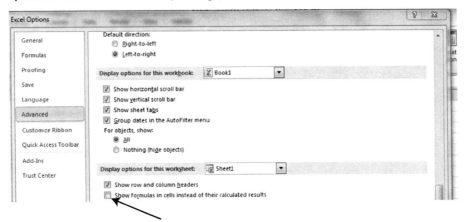

Figure 9–26. *Where to display worksheet formulas in their cells*

Click OK. All your worksheet's formulas will now appear in their cells, something like Figure 9–27.

3
4
5
6
=SUM(H14:H17)

Figure 9–27. *What you'll see in the cell instead of the result*

To turn this visual effect off, return to the **Advanced** area of the **File** tab and uncheck the **Show formulas in cells instead of their calculated results** option.

NOTE: You can also turn the show-formulas option on and off via the keyboard, by pressing Ctrl+` (i.e., the character usually positioned right beneath the Esc key).

Hiding the Ribbon

To take matters even further, if you right-click any tab and click **Minimize the Ribbon** on the ensuing menu, the ribbon will disappear, too (see Figure 9–28). And if you're looking for a keyboard equivalent, try Ctrl-F1.

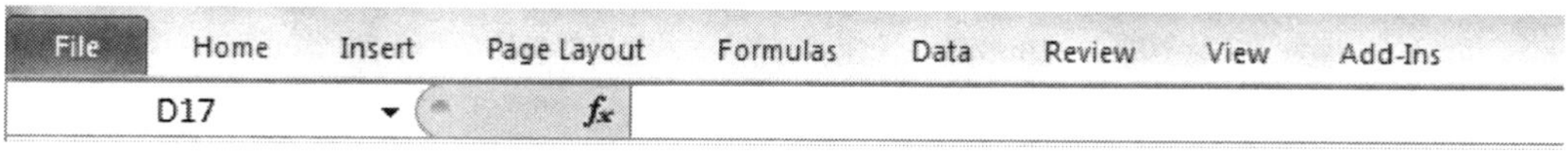

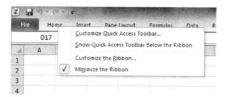

Figure 9–28. The ribbon—nowhere to be found

Needless to say, you can get the ribbon back by right-clicking the context tab heading and deselecting Minimize the Ribbon (see Figure 9–29), or executing Ctrl-F1 a second time.

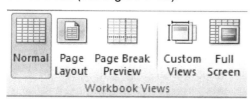

Figure 9–29. Getting your ribbon back

A related option is **Full Screen**, found in the **Workbook Views** button group within the **View** context tab (see Figure 9–30).

![Workbook Views button group showing Normal, Page Layout, Page Break Preview, Custom Views, Full Screen]

Figure 9–30. The Workbook Views button group

Click it and your screen will change to look like Figure 9–31.

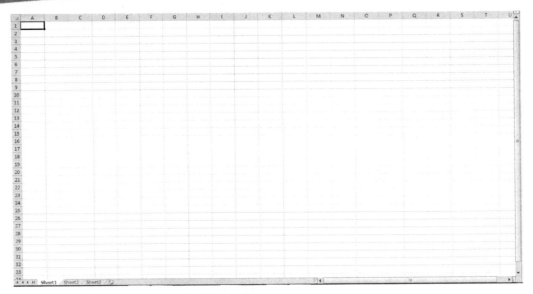

Figure 9–31. *Nothing but screen: The Full Screen view*

To get the normal view back, just press the Esc key, or click the standard **Restore** button in the upper-right corner of the window (the middle of the three buttons you'll see there), or double-click the worksheet's Title Bar – the border at the very uppermost part of the screen bearing the workbook's title..

> **NOTE:** Clicking the **Full Screen** option will introduce this view to *all* the worksheets in a workbook at the same time.

Keeping Important Data in View with the Freeze Panes Option

There may be times when you'll be working with a lengthy worksheet database containing many rows and/or columns, and you want to keep the header row—and/or column—in view.

For example, say you've devised a worksheet that compiles sales data for salespersons by week, across a series of columns—52 to be exact, spanning an entire year (see Figure 9–32).

Figure 9–32. *A weekly sales data worksheet*

The problem—a classic spreadsheet dilemma—is that once you begin scrolling to the right in order to view the later weeks, the first columns disappear (see Figure 9–33).

Figure 9–33. *The salesperson names and weeks 1 through 3 are no longer visible.*

The solution is to click the **Freeze Panes** button in the **Window** button group on the **View** tab (see Figure 9–34).

Figure 9–34. *The Freeze Panes button*

In order to ensure that the salesperson names persist on the screen no matter how far to the right you scroll, click anywhere in the workbook (as long as you can see column A) and click **Freeze Panes ➤ Freeze First Column**. That will draw a black line down the boundary between columns A and B (see Figure 9–35).

	A	B
1		
2		
3		Weeks
4	SALESPERSON	1
5	Jones	
6	Wilson	
7	Daniels	
8		
9		
10		
11		
12		
13		
14		
15		
16		
17		
18		
19		
20		

Figure 9–35. *The black line tells you that the first column (A) will be remain in view even when you scroll to the right.*

Now if you scroll right, you'll see what's shown in Figure 9–36.

SALESPERSON	9	10	11	12	13	14	15
Jones							
Wilson							
Daniels							

Figure 9–36. *Can't stay away: The salesperson names are still there*

And you can do the same for the first row, by clicking **Freeze Top Row**.

> **NOTE:** When you click **Freeze Top Row** or **Freeze First Column**, Excel will freeze the first row or column you can *currently see on screen*. That is, if you choose **Freeze First Column** when column C is the leftmost column on the screen, it will freeze column C, not A. If row 6 is currently the top row you can see, **Freeze First Row** will keep row 6 at the top of the screen.

To turn off a freeze view, click **Freeze Panes ➤ Unfreeze Panes**.

Freezing Rows and Columns at the Same Time

There may be other times when you need to freeze some rows and columns simultaneously. In our case, we might want to always be able to see both the salesperson names and the week numbers as we scroll in either direction—vertically or horizontally. Thus, we'd want to freeze the salesperson name column and the row listing week numbers, something like Figure 9–37.

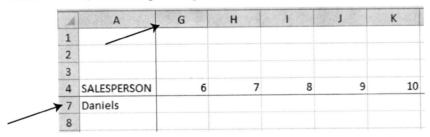

◢	A	G	H	I	J	K
1						
2						
3						
4	SALESPERSON	6	7	8	9	10
7	Daniels					
8						

Figure 9–37. *The first two salesperson names and the first five week numbers have disappeared, because we've scrolled both down and across the worksheet after having clicked Freeze Panes. Note the row header numbers and column header gaps (4 through 7 and A through G).*

To achieve this effect, you need to click the **Freeze Panes** option once you decide exactly which rows and columns you want to freeze. The rule is this: to freeze a column you click in the column immediately to the right of the one you want to freeze, and to freeze a row you click in the row immediately beneath the one you want to freeze. Thus, in this case you'd click in the cell shown in Figure 9–38.

Figure 9–38. *Clicking directly to the right of the column you want to freeze and directly beneath the row you want to freeze*

Once you've gotten a handle on where you want to locate the freeze, click **Freeze Panes ➤ Freeze Panes**. If you've discovered you've clicked in the wrong place, just click the **Unfreeze Panes** option and try again.

NOTE: As mentioned earlier, converting a database to a table will automatically freeze the top table row, which is the header of the table.

Protecting the Worksheet and the Workbook

Once you've put all that work into your workbook, having outfitted it with rows of complex formulas and breathtaking charts, you may get a bit nervous about what might happen next. What if you were to accidentally overwrite—or delete—a formula? True, you might be able to bring it back with an Undo command, but that prospect would depend on exactly when you discovered the mishap. Worse yet, what if your five-year-old nephew began to type some formulas of his own on the sheet?

Have no fear. Excel has anticipated those calamities, by allowing you to *protect* your workbooks and individual worksheets with a set of options that should help you fend off little Timmy's editorial changes and leave your masterpiece intact.

By way of introduction, you need to understand what protecting a sheet does and doesn't do. Protecting a sheet *won't* seal off your sheet with industrial-strength invincibility, foiling the bad guys who want to compromise or steal your data. Not quite, because workbook and worksheet protection is more about warding off mistakes than disarming hackers who have your formulas in their sights. Still, protection can do a pretty good job of, well, protecting your work.

The process of protecting worksheets and workbooks is actually quite easy, but the details get a bit quirky, as you'll see.

Protecting a Worksheet

To start the process of protecting a worksheet (you can try this out on a blank worksheet), just click anywhere in the sheet, click the **Review** tab, and select **Protect Sheet** from the **Changes** button group (see Figure 9–39).

Figure 9–39. *The Changes button group. We want to click Protect Sheet here, not Protect Workbook.*

When you click **Protect Sheet**, you'll see the dialog shown in Figure 9–40.

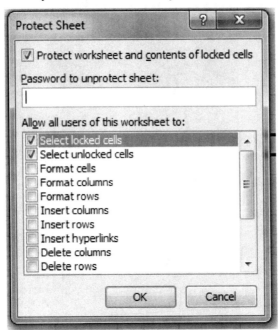

Figure 9–40. *The Protect Sheet dialog box*

Note that some check boxes are selected by default, and typically you'll accept these and simply click OK. The various options displayed in the dialog box give you control over exactly which operations you'll allow a user to perform on various worksheet elements (e.g., whether a user will be allowed to format cells or insert rows even if the worksheet is protected). If you accept all the defaults and click OK, the worksheet won't look any different. But when you try to type anything in any cell, you'll be greeted with the prompt shown in Figure 9–41 even before you can press Enter.

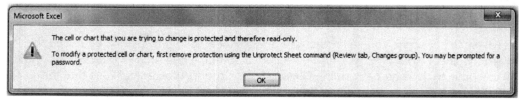

Figure 9–41. *Do not enter: What you'll see when you try to enter data in a cell in a protected worksheet*

You'll be prevented from entering the data, and that's what protecting a worksheet largely entails—blocking any subsequent data entry to a worksheet.

> **NOTE:** This type of protection protects only a single worksheet in the workbook. The other workbooks are unaffected by this action, and would still have to be protected individually.

Again, you should understand the limitations of worksheet protection. Even though users will be prevented from entering data on the protected sheet, no one will be stopped from *copying* the data on that sheet and pasting it into another workbook.

Using a Password: Some Extra Protection

You also can devise an optional password you'll be asked to enter in order to protect the sheet. When you first choose a password, another dialog box will then ask you to retype or confirm it (see Figure 9–42).

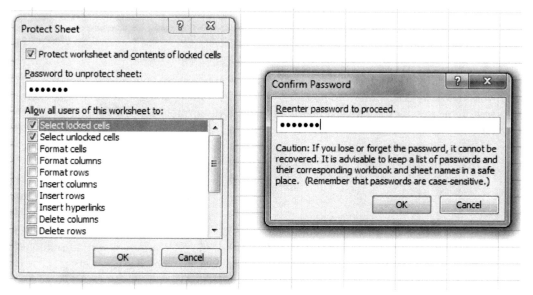

Figure 9–42. *How to enter a sheet protection password*

Unprotecting a Worksheet

Needless to say, once you've protected the worksheet, you may decide you need to return the sheet to its original unprotected state so that it can receive data entries again. All you have to do is go back to the **Changes** button group, where you'll see that the **Protect Sheet** button has toggled to display **Unprotect Sheet** (see Figure 9–43).

Figure 9–43. *Flip side: The Unprotect Sheet button is the same one you clicked to protect the sheet*

Just click **Unprotect Sheet**, and the sheet will be unprotected again—type away.

If you've used a password to protect a sheet and later decide to unprotect it, clicking **Unprotect Sheet** will call up an **Unprotect Sheet** dialog box, prompting you to reenter your password, as shown in Figure 9–44.

Figure 9–44. *The Unprotect Sheet dialog box requests your password if you've selected one.*

Just make sure you've written that password down somewhere, because if you forget it, you won't be able to unprotect the sheet. Remember as well that if you haven't availed yourself of the password possibility, anyone else can unprotect the worksheet—provided of course they know how to do that.

Protecting Some, but Not All, of a Worksheet

In some cases, you may want to be able to enter data in *some* cells in a worksheet, even as the remainder of the cells are blocked or protected. Recall our grading worksheet, in which we calculated point bonus awards that supplemented students' test scores (see Chapter 4). In such a case, you might want to protect the cells containing the bonus formulas while continuing to leave other cells available, in which you could enter additional student test scores.

So how do you protect *some*, but not all, of a worksheet? It's here where some of those workbook protection quirks mentioned earlier come into play.

In order to make some cells available to receive data in a worksheet that's otherwise protected, you need first to select those cells and instruct Excel not to protect them.

> **NOTE:** In order to designate some cells to receive data, the entire sheet has to have been unprotected first.

The following short exercise will demonstrate how this works:

1. Select cells B7:B16.

2. Now click **Home ➤ Format ➤ Format Cells...** in the **Cells** button group, as shown in Figure 9–45.

Figure 9–45. *Starting the individual cell protection process by clicking Format Cells....*

3. After selecting that option, you'll be reintroduced to an old friend, the **Format Cells** dialog box; only this time, you need to click one of its tabs that we haven't visited before: **Protection** (see Figure 9–46).

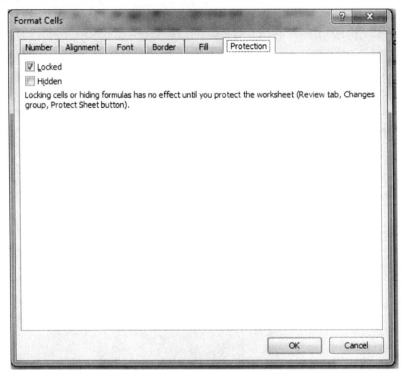

Figure 9–46. *The Protection tab of the Format Cells dialog box*

4.   Note that the **Locked** check box is checked by default. That means simply that if you protect the sheet, all its cells will be protected. But since you've selected B7:B16, uncheck the **Locked** box. Now, once you protect the sheet, cells B7:B16 will still remain unlocked—that is, you'll be able to enter data in only these cells.

And that's how unlocking cells works—first you designate those cells to be unlocked, and only then do you protect the sheet. So now if you activate workbook protection, it will still be possible to enter data in cells B7:B16.

Hiding Formulas

Earlier in this chapter I described how you can reveal your worksheet's formulas in the cells in which they're written. There's also a kind of flip side to this option—you can *hide* worksheet formulas so that they can't be seen at all, not even in the formula bar.

To hide formulas in cells, you have to work prospectively and select those cells *before* you protect the worksheet, just as when unlocking selected cells. The following exercise demonstrates:

1.   Enter these values shown in Figure 9–47 in cells D4:D8 and perform a SUM in cell D9.

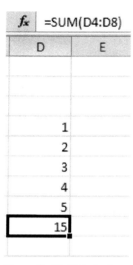

fx =SUM(D4:D8)

D	E
1	
2	
3	
4	
5	
15	

Figure 9–47. *Note the formula bar*

2. Then return to the **Format Cells** dialog box and click the **Protection** tab (see Figure 9–48).

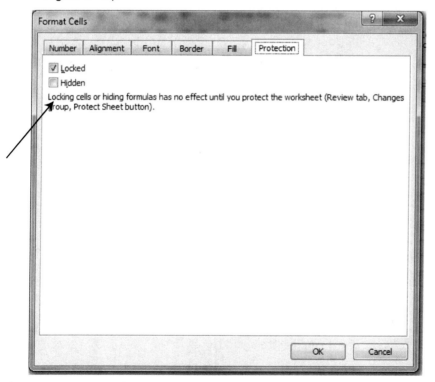

Figure 9–48. *The Format Cells dialog box. Note the caption beneath the Hidden option.*

3. Click Hidden, and then click OK. Then protect the worksheet, and click in cell D9 and observe the formula bar (see Figure 9–49).

fx		
C	**D**	**E**
	1	
	2	
	3	
	4	
	5	
	15	

Figure 9–49. *Drawing a blank: The formula's no longer visible*

The formula is nowhere to be seen, even though it's still safely stored in cell D9. To restore the formula to view, just unprotect the sheet.

NOTE: If you want to render all the worksheet formulas invisible, you need to select all the cells in the worksheet (via Ctrl+A or by clicking the **Select All** button) and select **Format Cells**. Click Hidden on the **Protection** tab, and then protect the sheet.

Protecting a Workbook

You can also protect an entire workbook, which does something completely different from protecting a worksheet.

When you protect a workbook, you protect what Excel calls its *structure*—and that means that when workbook protection is turned on, you won't be able to delete or move a worksheet, or restore a hidden worksheet to view.

Another workbook protection option—a less central one—enables you to protect the window arrangement of worksheets. If, for example, you resize a worksheet window and you need to maintain precisely that worksheet size and position on the screen, protecting the workbook for windows will hold the worksheet right there—and you'll be able neither to move nor resize it (see Figure 9–50).

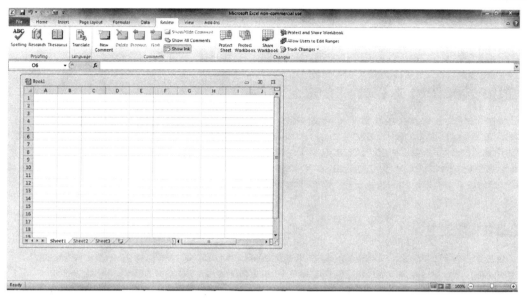

Figure 9–50. *A downsized worksheet*

To protect a workbook, click the **Review** tab, and click **Protect Workbook** in the **Changes** button group (see Figure 9–51).

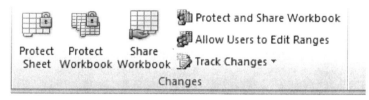

Figure 9–51. *Protecting a workbook*

You'll next see the dialog shown in Figure 9–52.

Figure 9–52. *Note that the dialog box isn't titled Protect Workbook, but that's what it's about to do.*

Note again that you're provided with a password option. Whether you use a password or not, when you click **OK** you won't be able to move, delete, or add any worksheet—but you *will* continue to be able to enter and edit data and formulas.

Unprotecting a Workbook

Unprotecting a workbook is about as easy as it gets. Just click the **Protect Workbook** button a second time. Oddly enough, unlike the **Protect Sheet** button, the **Protect Workbook** button doesn't appear as "Unprotect Workbook" once you've protected the workbook. It just doesn't change. Of course, if you've designated a password, you'll be prompted to supply it before you can unprotect the workbook.

Summary

Every Excel workbook gives its users a massive amount of territory to work with, and knowing how to work with its multisheet character is a valuable asset. Next, we'll explore what you need to know to print your Excel data once you decide to commit all the information you've compiled in a workbook to hard copy.

Chapter 10

Printing Your Worksheets: Hard Copies Made Easy

We hear about the paperless office all the time, but just cast a glance at your office or your desk at home—lots of paper still out there, no?

That's the reality, of course. Sooner or later, you'll be called upon to commit your spreadsheet data to printed form—for distribution at meetings, or for handing in to instructors, or for inclusion in booklets and brochures.

Once you get to it, you'll find printing in Excel to be pretty simple—as it should be. In some ways it's almost self-evident, meaning that with just a bit of exposure to the feature you'll probably be able to figure out a good deal of what you need to know by yourself. And as usual, Excel gives you more than one way to carry out many of the basic printing tasks.

Deciding What You Want to Print

The first consideration in printing the data on your worksheet is how much of it you want to print. Your intention may be simple: to print everything on the sheet, and that makes your job easy. On the other hand, you may want to print just part of the data, but that objective only makes the job slightly harder.

Printing the Entire Worksheet

Let's say that for starters you want to print all the data on one worksheet (not the entire workbook, though). To illustrate, enter the values from Figure 10–1 in cells C9:D13.

1	6
2	7
3	8
4	9
5	10

Figure 10–1. *Fit to print: Ten cells worth of data*

The next step is to access the Print command sequence, either by clicking the **File** command tab and choosing **Print**, or by calling upon the venerable Ctrl+P keyboard shortcut. Either way, you'll be brought to the Backstage (see Figure 10–2).

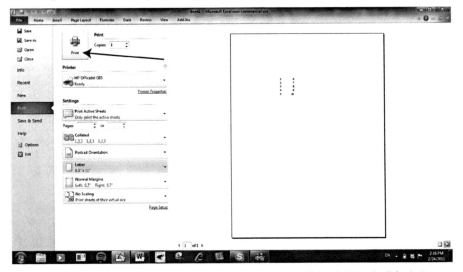

Figure 10–2. *A visit backstage: Your print options (at least most of them). Note the Print button.*

Note the large print review pane to the right. In the simplest-case scenario, all you have to do now is click the large **Print** button and head for your printer to collect your copy.

OK, it isn't always quite that easy, but it usually doesn't get much more challenging than that. To delve into something slightly more complex than printing a worksheet, let's first see how to print a selection.

Printing a Selection

Let's call up that Student Scores workbook, in which all those bonus grades were handed out. The data there was stored in the range J7:L12, and now we want to print the contents of just that range (see Figure 10–3).

Student	Score	Bonus
John	77	81
Bill	91	91
Dorothy	62	62
Sue	59	59
Ed	78	78

Figure 10–3. *Those student scores again, this time to be printed*

First, delete any charts you may have on the sheet. Again, you can activate the Print command, but this time you'll see the screen shown in Figure 10–4.

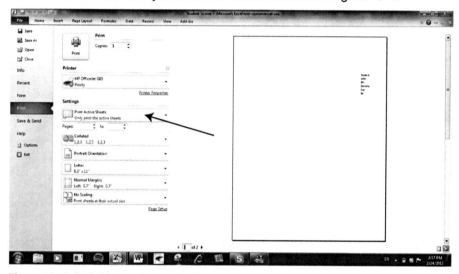

Figure 10–4. *Probably not what you had in mind. There are the names, but where are the grades? Note the Print Active Sheets option.*

Well, that's not terribly satisfactory, is it? All we're seeing are the student names, which aren't accompanied by their grades. Note as well the legend at the bottom of the screen that states 1 of 2, referring to pages; if you click the arrow to the right of the number 2 to travel to that page, you'll see what's shown in Figure 10–5.

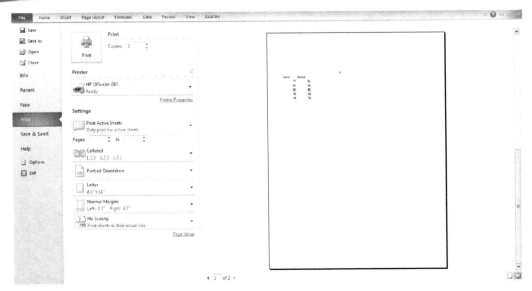

Figure 10–5. *There are the scores, but not where we want them.*

So what's going on? Really, two things:

- When you instruct Excel to print a worksheet, it searches by default for data by proceeding from the beginning of the sheet (i.e., the A column), and will *include* all the blank areas it finds en route to the data until it actually finds the data. It'll thus print this worksheet starting at column A up to and including the area containing the data, starting in the J column.

- The **Print Active Sheets** option will also print *everything* on the sheet, no matter where that data is located.

For sake of the illustration, this means that if you had devised a worksheet whose data starts in the X column, Excel would by default print columns A through W—all of these blank—before reaching the actual data to print, meaning you'd end up with a collection of empty printed pages before the page you wanted to print rolled out. It also means that if you have a small range in A7:B19 that you want to print, and you also happen to have squirreled away a bit of data in cell ZA241, Excel will by default print all the blank columns between B and ZA too, until it finally stops at ZA241.

But all that happens by default, when you simply click the **Print** button without giving any additional thought to what you wanted to see on paper, and leave the **Print Active Sheets** option selected. And that default makes sense if you've started your data entry in the A column and have a confined range of data to print, as is often the case.

But it doesn't make sense in our case, where we'd end up with a two-page printout, with the student names on one page and their grades on another.

Needless to say, there's a way to deal with our little problem—by selecting precisely the range you do want to print and then telling Excel to print only that area. You do that by selecting the range (in our case J7:L12), and then returning to the **Print** dialog and clicking **Print Selection**, thus overruling the default **Print Active Sheets** option (see Figure 10–6).

Figure 10–6. *Printing only want we want to print: Choosing the Print Selection option*

Once you've clicked that option, you'll see what's shown in Figure 10–7.

Figure 10–7. *All the data is on one sheet now, and the print output will only require one page.*

Thus, in order to print some, but not all, of the data on a worksheet, you just select the desired range, activate the Print command, and select the **Print Selection** option. Then just click **Print**.

NOTE: If you've been clicking along with the exercises so far, your print views may not precisely correspond with the screenshots. If that's the case, it's probably due to having a different page size default set up in your system. If you live in the United Kingdom, for example, Excel probably assumes you're working with A4-sized paper, which would yield a different print preview from the ones shown.

Surveying Printing Options: The Print Backstage

Now let's take a closer look at the various options you'll encounter when you enter the Print section of the Backstage (see Figure 10–8; also see the Quick Start Guide for a reminder of what the Backstage is).

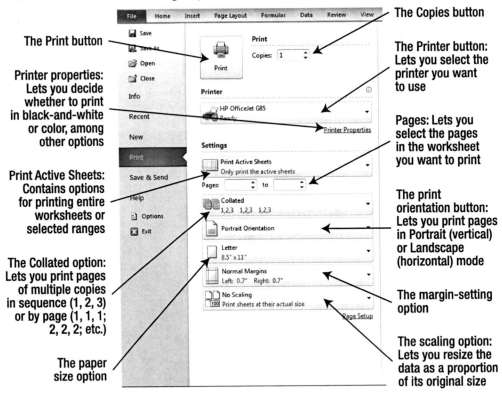

Figure 10–8. *The various Print options in the Backstage*

Again, many of these options are easy to figure out on your own:

■ The Print button actually executes the print when clicked.

■ Copies allows you to set the number of copies you want to print.

■ The **Printer** button lets you select the printer to which you want to print, if you have access to more than device. Clicking the **Printer** drop-down arrow reveals a menu enabling you to click the printer to which you want to direct the print (see Figure 10–9).

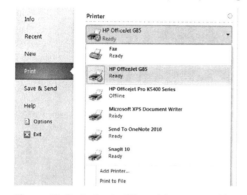

Figure 10–9. *Just select the printer you want to use.*

■ **Print Active Sheets**, as mentioned, is the default option for this command, and offers the selections shown in Figure 10–10. You can elect to print the entire workbook—that is, all its sheets—or just the range you've selected (**Print Selection**). The reference to **Print Active Sheets** (in the plural) means that if you've grouped two or more sheets, their data will be printed.

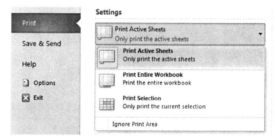

Figure 10–10. *These options allow you to choose what segment of the workbook you want to print.*

■ **Pages** lets you decide which pages on the worksheet you want to print. If you print a large swath of a workbook, the overall print area may be too large to capture on one page, so Excel will need to print additional pages, as in our student grades printout before we selected a specific range to print. When multiple pages are required, the page boundaries are represented in the workbook by dotted lines, which appear once you've viewed the imminent printout in the Backstage (see Figure 10–11).

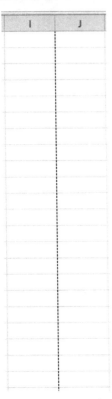

Figure 10–11. *The dotted line indicates where a new page will begin in a printout.*

- The **Collated** option only applies if you're printing at least two copies (see Figure 10–12).

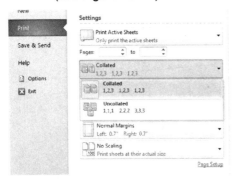

Figure 10–12. *The Collated and Uncollated options*

By default printouts are collated, meaning that if your output will consist of three pages, the pages will appear in sequence (e.g., 1, 2, 3 and 1, 2, 3 again). But if you select **Uncollated**, all the page 1s will print first, followed by all the page 2s, and so on. You might want to use the **Uncollated** option if you need to make some hand-entered corrections on all page 3s, for example.

■ **Orientation** gives you two print options: **Portrait** and **Landscape** (or vertical and horizontal, respectively). Landscape orientation is commonly used for printouts that contain many columns of data and would spill across multiple pages if they were they printed in Portrait mode.

■ The paper size option lets you select the size of paper with which you're working. Obviously, paper size will affect how and where the data gets distributed in a printout (see Figure 10–13).

Figure 10–13. *Sizing up your printouts with the paper size option.*

■ The **Margins** option is easy to overlook, but it's important because Excel printouts have to work with page margins. Excel's default margins (called Normal) stand at .7 inches left and right, and .75 top and bottom (see Figure 10–14).

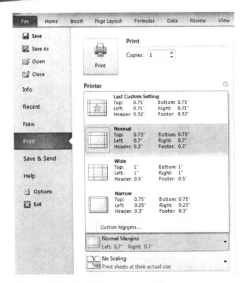

Figure 10–14. *Print margin settings*

You can select any of the recommended settings shown, including the **Custom Margins…** option, which sits at the base of the menu. Clicking that choice presents you with the **Margins** tab in the **Page Setup** dialog box (see Figure 10–15).

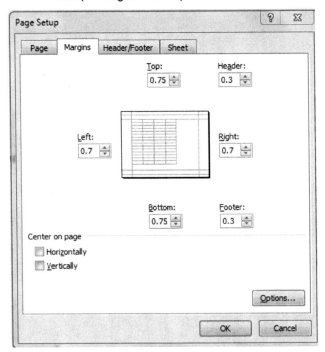

Figure 10–15. *Where you can customize print margins*

Just type the desired margin(s) and click OK.

Note the **Center on page** option. Clicking both **Horizontally** and **Vertically** will position the data you want smack-dab in the middle of the page. Recall that our Student Scores print preview indicated that the scores would be printed in the upper-left corner of the page (see Figure 10–16).

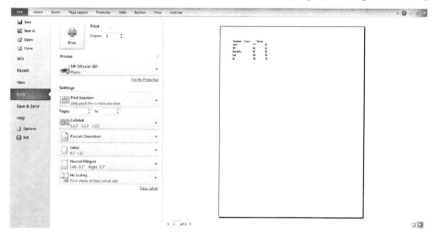

Figure 10–16. *The student scores: Ready to print, but leaving a great deal of white space on the page*

Select both **Center on page** options and the printout will be redesigned, as shown in Figure 10–17.

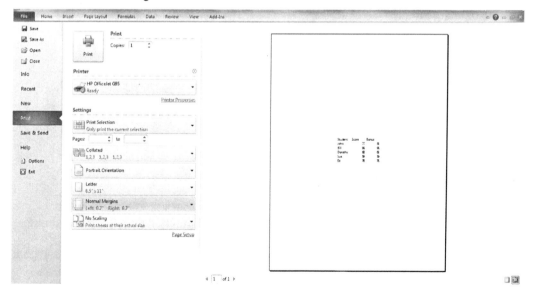

Figure 10–17. *It's still not a museum piece, but the data is now centered both horizontally and vertically.*

■ The scaling options (see Figure 10–18) allow you to modify the size of the data to be printed—not by directly changing the font, but rather by refitting the data on the page so as to tidy the results.

Figure 10–18. *Economy of scale: The print scaling options*

Here's a classic example: you need to print data consisting of many columns, and the print preview reveals that the last column is going to have to be shunted to a second page, because the first page has simply run out of room. And that's messy. By selecting **Fit All Columns on One Page**, Excel will slightly downsize all the data on the printout so that the renegade column will be able to join the other columns on the first—and what is now the only—page.

Setting the Print Area

In addition to the printing capabilities you'll find in the Backstage, there are some additional and important options stored in other areas of the worksheet. You've already seen that by selecting a specific range to print, you can avoid the problem of overprinting (i.e., printing blank areas of the worksheet that you don't need to see in your printed results). But selecting a print range may cause a problem or two on its own, because once you select that range you need to print it right away. If you decide you want to work elsewhere in the sheet before printing, you'll have to click elsewhere to begin your work, which will deselect the range you want to print.

But Excel lets you have it both ways by letting you designate and *save* a print area so you can go on do to work somewhere else before printing.

To see how the **Print Area** option works, select the student grades and click the **Page Layout** contextual tab, and then click **Print Area ➤ Set Print Area** in the **Page Setup** button group (see Figure 10–19).

Figure 10–19. *Setting the print area*

You'll see a dotted-line border surrounding the area you've chosen to print, which will remain in place even if you click somewhere else on the worksheet (see Figure 10–20).

Student	Score	Bonus
John	77	77
Bill	91	91
Dorothy	62	62
Sue	59	59
Ed	78	78

Figure 10–20. *The print area is designated by the dotted-line boundary.*

Now whenever you're ready to print, just return to the Backstage and click that large **Print** button. Just make sure you don't select **Print Selection** at the point of actual printing though, because if you do, any range you happen to have currently selected will be printed instead of the print area you designated. Click **Print Active Sheets** or **Print Entire Workbook** instead. If you save the document, the print area will be saved, too. To clear the print area, click the **Page Layout** contextual tab, and then click **Print Area ➤ Clear Print Area** in the **Page Setup** button group.

NOTE: When you save a print area and close the workbook, and then retrieve the workbook again, the dotted-line print area won't immediately appear. But when you get back into the Backstage the print area will appear in the print preview; and when you leave the Backstage and return to the worksheet, the dotted-line boundary will then reappear. Note as well that if you want to only *temporarily* override the print area, click **Ignore Print Area** in the settings (it's found in the drop-down menu headed by the **Print Active Sheets** option). To return to the original print area you've selected, you'll need to uncheck the box that will now appear alongside **Ignore Print Area**.

Customizing Your Printing

In addition to the **Print Area** button, several other useful print-related options are scattered among Excel's ribbon tabs. The **Page Layout** tab contains a number of buttons that emulate many features available in the Backstage (see Figure 10–21).

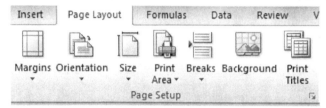

Figure 10–21. The Page Layout tab

Working with Page Breaks

The first three buttons on the **Page Layout** tab—**Margins**, **Orientation**, and **Size**, provide alternative ways to access the same trio of options in the Backstage; their menus are identical to the ones shown earlier (see Figure 10–22).

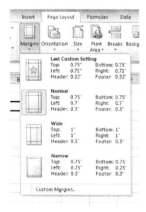

Figure 10–22. *Look familiar? You'll see the same menu when you work with margins in the Backstage.*

But the button to the right of **Print Area** (Breaks; see Figure 10–23) does something different.

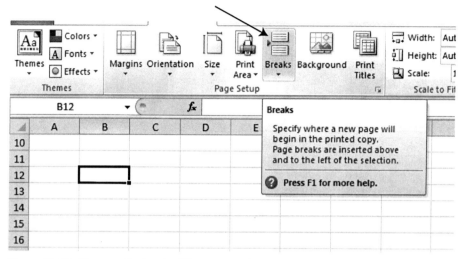

Figure 10–23. *Those are the breaks: Where to establish a page break*

Click the arrow beneath the **Breaks** title and you'll see the options shown in Figure 10–24.

Figure 10–24. *The Insert Page Break option*

What does inserting a page break do to your printout? Well, first consider what Excel does by default. When you execute a printout, Excel prints as much of the data as it can on the first page, until it runs out of space. It then goes on to print additional pages if it needs them. But what the **Insert Page Break** option does is let you produce a second page *earlier* than necessary; that is, before a second page would naturally have to be printed.

For example, recall the PivotTables workbook, spanning the range A1:D17 (we had added one record in the course of our exercise). Open that workbook and survey the data. Because the data encompasses only 17 rows and starts in the A column, we'd only require one page to print it all (see Figure 10–25).

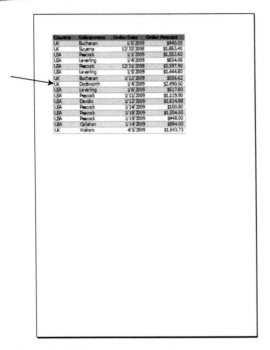

Figure 10–25. *Only one page required*

But let's say that you needed a new, second page, starting with Dodsworth's sales record. If that's what you want, click in cell A9—where Dodsworth's record starts, and click the **Insert Page Break** command. You'll see the data shown in Figure 10–26.

Country	Salesperson	Order Date	Order Amount	
UK	Buchanan	1/5/2009	$440.00	
UK	Suyama	12/30/2008	$1,863.40	
USA	Peacock	1/1/2009	$1,552.60	
USA	Leverling	1/4/2009	$654.06	
USA	Peacock	12/31/2008	$3,597.90	
USA	Leverling	1/5/2009	$1,444.80	
UK	Buchanan	1/12/2009	$556.62	
UK	Dodsworth	1/4/2009	$2,490.50	
USA	Leverling	1/6/2009	$517.80	
USA	Peacock	1/11/2009	$1,119.90	
USA	Davolio	1/12/2009	$1,614.88	
USA	Peacock	1/14/2009	$100.80	
USA	Peacock	1/18/2009	$1,504.65	
USA	Peacock	1/19/2009	$448.00	
USA	Callahan	1/14/2009	$584.00	
UK	Walters	4/5/2009	$1,543.73	

Figure 10–26. *Note the dotted line, which signifies where the second page will start.*

Now your printout will result in two pages. If you decide to reconsider this two-page motif, you can remove the page break by clicking the worksheet where you've instituted the break (in row 9, on Dodsworth's record), and clicking **Remove Page Break**—the option which appears right beneath **Insert Page Break** on the **Breaks** button. Doing so will return you to the original one-page printout.

> **NOTE:** The Reset All Page Breaks option under the **Breaks** button allows you to remove multiple page breaks at one time, if you've introduced more than one break to the printout.

Previewing the Page Break: Getting a Bird's-Eye View of the Printout

If the data you want to print contains many records and will likely result in a multipage print, or if you've inserted your own page breaks as illustrated previously, you may want to get a global idea of how the printout will look in its entirety. Realizing that the normal worksheet view may not be able to display all the data at one time without you having to scroll down and/or across repeatedly, Excel offers a *page break preview*, which presents the printout-to-be in a curiously miniaturized form (see Figure 10–27).

	A	B	C	D	E
1	Count	Salespers	Order Dat	Order Amou	
2	UK	Buchanan	1/5/2009	$440.00	
3	UK	Suyama	12/30/2008	$1,863.40	
4	USA	Peacock	1/1/2009	$1,552.60	
5	USA	Leverling	1/4/2009	$654.06	
6	USA	Peacock	12/31/2008	$3,597.90	
7	USA	Leverling	1/5/2009	$1,444.80	
8	UK	Buchanan	1/12/2009	$556.62	
9	UK	Dodsworth	1/4/2009	$2,490.50	
10	USA	Leverling	1/6/2009	$517.80	
11	USA	Peacock	1/11/2009	$1,119.90	
12	USA	Davolio	1/12/2009	$1,614.88	
13	USA	Peacock	1/14/2009	$100.80	
14	USA	Peacock	1/18/2009	$1,504.65	
15	USA	Peacock	1/19/2009	$448.00	
16	USA	Callahan	1/14/2009	$584.00	
17	UK	Walters	4/5/2009	$1,543.73	
18					

Figure 10–27. *The page break preview: The two-page salesperson printout, with the page break inserted by Dodsworth's name*

Note the watermark-like Page 1 and Page 2 indicators, superimposed on the data. The page break preview does two things:

- It shrinks the print preview so you can see all, or at least considerably more, of the data on one screen.

- It lets you move the current position of the page break.

To illustrate, in the PivotTables workbook, click the **View** contextual tab, and then click **Page Break Preview** in the **Workbook Views** button group (make sure the page break by Dodsworth's name is in place) (see Figure 10–28).

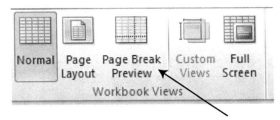

Figure 10–28. *The Workbook Views button group*

TIP: You can also access the page break preview by clicking the **Page Break Preview** button on the status bar (see Figure 10–29).

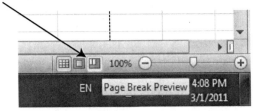

Figure 10–29. *Another Page Break Preview button*

After clicking **Page Break Preview**, click **OK** on the introductory dialog box, and you'll see the preview shown in Figure 10–30.

	A	B	C	D
1	Count▼	Salespers▼	Order Da▼	Order Amou▼
2	UK	Buchanan	1/5/2009	$440.00
3	UK	Suyama	12/30/2008	$1,863.40
4	USA	Peacock	1/1/2009	$1,552.60
5	USA	Leverling	1/4/2009	$654.06
6	USA	Peacock	12/31/2008	$3,597.90
7	USA	Leverling	1/5/2009	$1,444.80
8	UK	Buchanan	1/12/2009	$556.62
9	UK	Dodsworth	1/4/2009	$2,490.50
10	USA	Leverling	1/6/2009	$517.80
11	USA	Peacock	1/11/2009	$1,119.90
12	USA	Davolio	1/12/2009	$1,614.88
13	USA	Peacock	1/14/2009	$100.80
14	USA	Peacock	1/18/2009	$1,504.65
15	USA	Peacock	1/19/2009	$448.00
16	USA	Callahan	1/14/2009	$584.00
17	UK	Walters	4/5/2009	$1,543.73

Figure 10–30. *Getting the big picture with the page break preview*

Again, because the view of the data is scaled down, you'll still be able to see many if not all of the records in a large set of data in one glance.

In addition, note the solid blue line demarcating Page 1 and Page 2. You can click and drag that line if you want to readjust the point at which the second page begins.

To illustrate, say you want to move the page break to a position above Peacock's record in row 11. Click the blue line and drag it down two rows, as shown in Figure 10–31.

	A	B	C	D
1	Count	Salespers	Order Da	Order Amou
2	UK	Buchanan	1/5/2009	$440.00
3	UK	Suyama	12/30/2008	$1,863.40
4	USA	Peacock	1/1/2009	$1,552.60
5	USA	Leverling	1/4/2009	$654.06
6	USA	Peacock	12/31/2008	$3,597.90
7	USA	Leverling	1/5/2009	$1,444.80
8	UK	Buchanan	1/12/2009	$556.62
9	UK	Dodsworth	1/4/2009	$2,490.50
10	USA	Leverling	1/6/2009	$517.80
11	USA	Peacock	1/11/2009	$1,119.90
12	USA	Davolio	1/12/2009	$1,614.88
13	USA	Peacock	1/14/2009	$100.80
14	USA	Peacock	1/18/2009	$1,504.65
15	USA	Peacock	1/19/2009	$448.00
16	USA	Callahan	1/14/2009	$584.00
17	UK	Walters	4/5/2009	$1,543.73

Figure 10–31. You can click when you see the double-sided arrow, and then drag.

Then release the mouse. You'll see the display shown in Figure 10–32.

	A	B	C	D
1	Count	Salespers	Order Da	Order Amou
2	UK	Buchanan	1/5/2009	$440.00
3	UK	Suyama	12/30/2008	$1,863.40
4	USA	Peacock	1/1/2009	$1,552.60
5	USA	Leverling	1/4/2009	$654.06
6	USA	Peacock	12/31/2008	$3,597.90
7	USA	Leverling	1/5/2009	$1,444.80
8	UK	Buchanan	1/12/2009	$556.62
9	UK	Dodsworth	1/4/2009	$2,490.50
10	USA	Leverling	1/6/2009	$517.80
11	USA	Peacock	1/11/2009	$1,119.90
12	USA	Davolio	1/12/2009	$1,614.88
13	USA	Peacock	1/14/2009	$100.80
14	USA	Peacock	1/18/2009	$1,504.65
15	USA	Peacock	1/19/2009	$448.00
16	USA	Callahan	1/14/2009	$584.00
17	UK	Walters	4/5/2009	$1,543.73

Figure 10-32. The newly designated page break

Note, by the way, that if you have a lengthy collection of records and you examine it in the page break preview, you'll see dotted lines instead (see Figure 10–33).

47	USA	Davolio	3/3/2009	$848.70
48	USA	Peacock	2/25/2009	$1,887.60
49	USA	Fuller	3/2/2009	$121.60
50	UK	Suyama	3/3/2009	$1,050.60
51	UK	Buchanan	3/2/2009	$1,420.00
52	UK	Suyama	3/3/2009	$2,645.00
53	USA	Peacock	3/5/2009	$349.50
54	USA	Fuller	3/10/2009	$608.00
55	USA	Callahan	3/9/2009	$755.00
56	USA	Peacock	3/31/2009	$2,708.80
57	UK	King	3/10/2009	$1,117.80
58	USA	Davolio	3/9/2009	$954.40
59	USA	Callahan	3/31/2009	$3,741.30
60	USA	Davolio	3/15/2009	$498.50
61	USA	Fuller	3/17/2009	$424.00
62	UK	King	3/16/2009	$88.80
63	USA	Leverling	4/14/2009	$1,762.00
64	USA	Callahan	3/19/2009	$336.00
65	USA	Davolio	3/18/2009	$268.80
66	USA	Fuller	3/25/2009	$1,614.80
67	USA	Fuller	3/26/2009	$182.40
68	USA	Davolio	3/26/2009	$2,094.30
69	USA	Peacock	3/25/2009	$516.80
70	USA	Davolio	3/30/2009	$2,835.00
71	UK	Suyama	4/1/2009	$288.00
72	USA	Callahan	3/26/2009	$240.40
73	UK	King	4/2/2009	$1,191.20
74	UK	Buchanan	4/3/2009	$516.00
75	USA	Leverling	4/2/2009	$144.00
76	UK	King	4/14/2009	$112.00
77	USA	Peacock	4/5/2009	$164.40
78	UK	Dodsworth	4/1/2009	$5,275.71
79	USA	Davolio	4/5/2009	$1,497.00
80	USA	Peacock	4/5/2009	$982.00

Figure 10–33. *An excerpt of a larger set of records as portrayed by the page break preview*

The dotted line here represents a natural page break—that is, the point where the page simply runs out of room and has to continue the data on a next page.

When you've completed your visit to the page break preview, you can restore the basic default view of the worksheet by clicking the **View** contextual tab, and then clicking the **Normal** button in the **Workbook Views** button group.

NOTE: You can continue to enter data even while you're in the page break preview.

Printing Titles

Returning to the **Page Setup** group, you'll find another button that deserves your attention: **Print Titles** (see Figure 10–34).

Figure 10–34. *The Print Titles button*

Print Titles offers one way to resolve another one of those classic spreadsheet issues—one already discussed in a slightly different context. If you print a long set of records topped by a header row, that header row will print, naturally, but it'll only appear on page 1. And if you need to print a page 2, 3, and so on, these pages *won't* display the header—at least not by default.

But **Print Titles** offers a kind of a Freeze Panes command for printing (see Chapter 9). Just as Freeze Panes keeps designated rows or columns on the screen even as you scroll away from them, **Print Titles** allows you to print header rows (or columns) on every page of a multipage printout, reminding you which data is stored under which heading.

To illustrate, printing this worksheet with 800 rows of data will display the header row on page 1 only, at least at the outset (see Figure 10–35).

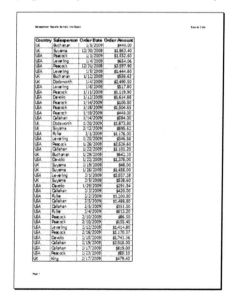

Figure 10–35. *Pages 1 and 2 of a lengthy printout: The header row appears only on the first page*

As a result, you may not be able to easily tell on page 2 which data is associated with which heading.

And that's where **Print Titles** comes in.

1. To try it, go back to the PivotTables workbook and make sure you've kept that page break in the row right above row 11. In the Backstage print preview, you'll see two pages (see Figure 10–36).

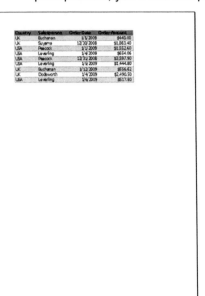
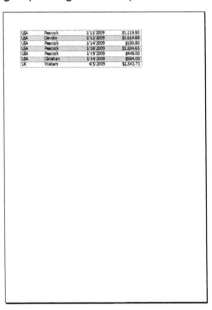

Figure 10–36. *Again, the header row only displays in page 1.*

2. Click the **Page Layout** contextual tab, and then click **Print Titles** in the **Page Setup** button group. You'll see the dialog shown in Figure 10–37.

Figure 10–37. *The Sheet tab of the Page Setup dialog box*

3. In the Rows to repeat at top field, just click anywhere in row 1 on the worksheet. You'll see what's shown in Figure 10–38.

Figure 10–38. Row 1 will now print at the top of every page.

4. Click OK, and return to the Backstage print review and look at the two pages (see Figure 10–39).

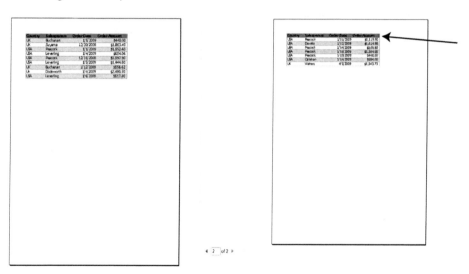

Figure 10–39. Now page 2 also exhibits the header row.

Now every page will display the header row, no matter how many pages are required by the printout.

Adding Headers and Footers

There's still another way to engineer your printout so that the same text appears at the top (or the bottom) of every page: by adding a header and/or footer. As with Word, headers and footers feature recurring text on every printed page, such as the name of the designer of the spreadsheet, the current page number, the date on which the worksheet was printed, or really anything you want to see there.

Now, introducing headers and footers into a printout may trigger a question: Doesn't the Print Titles feature just discussed do the same thing that headers do—namely, repeat some selected text across the top of every page?

The answer is, sort of. It's true that the Print Titles select-a-row selection and page headers both emblazon the tops of printed pages with text, but there's a difference: the Print Titles option grabs its data from rows on the actual worksheet, while header and footer data is entered in a separate area external to the worksheet, so it won't be found in any cells. Thus, you'll never see header data in A1. If you *do* want to see the data in row 1 at the top of each page, use Print Titles.

Adding Headers and Footers in the Page Layout View

As usual, there are a couple of ways to compose a header or footer. One is to enter it in the Page Layout view, which offers another way of viewing a worksheet; it's accessible via the **Workbook Views** button group (see Figure 10–40).

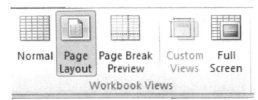

Figure 10–40. *Where to find the Page Layout button.*

Click that button while in the PivotTables worksheet and you'll see the screen shown in Figure 10–41.

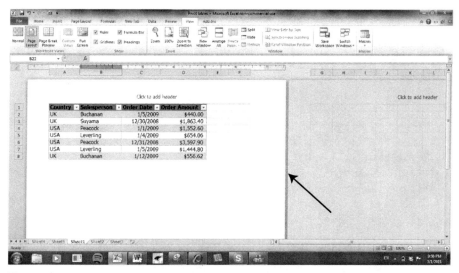

Figure 10–41. *How the salesperson data looks in the Page Layout view. This is page 1.*

The Page Layout view attempts to portray your data exactly as it will print. Note the narrow space representing the physical edge of the page (by the arrow), and the ruler atop the page, indicating the dimensions of each column.

You can enter headers and footers in this view. Note the "Click to add header" area; resting your mouse there reveals three subsections: a left, center, and right area, each of which turns blue when your mouse is poised atop it (see Figure 10–42).

Country	Salesperson	Order Date	Order Amount
UK	Buchanan	1/5/2009	$440.00
UK	Suyama	12/30/2008	$1,863.40
USA	Peacock	1/1/2009	$1,552.60
USA	Leverling	1/4/2009	$654.06
USA	Peacock	12/31/2008	$3,597.90
USA	Leverling	1/5/2009	$1,444.80
UK	Buchanan	1/12/2009	$556.62

Figure 10–42. *Click where you see the blue tint and simply start to type; the header will appear there.*

Click in any or all of the three blue areas and type whatever text you want. You can also scroll to the bottom of the page to the "Click to add footer" caption, which works the same way (see Figure 10–43).

Country	Salesperson	Order Date	Order Amount	
UK	Buchanan	1/5/2009	$440.00	
UK	Suyama	12/30/2008	$1,863.40	
USA	Peacock	1/1/2009	$1,552.60	
USA	Leverling	1/4/2009	$654.06	
USA	Peacock	12/31/2008	$3,597.90	
USA	Leverling	1/5/2009	$1,444.80	
UK	Buchanan	1/12/2009	$556.62	

A Katz — Sales data — Acme Widgets

Figure 10–43. Three headers, one each positioned in the left, center, and right header areas

Once you've typed in your text, each header will appear at the top of every printed page.

NOTE: Remember, you can always return to the standard, default view of the worksheet by clicking the **Normal** button in the **Worksheet Views** button group, or the **Normal** button in the status bar (alongside the **Page Layout** button).

Adding Headers and Footers Using the Page Setup Dialog Box

You can take another route to adding headers and/or footers via the **Page Setup** dialog box, which you can access directly by clicking the Page Setup dialog box launcher (see Figure 10–44).

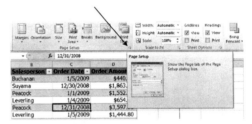

Figure 10–44. Clicking the dialog launcher button brings you to the Page Setup dialog box.

Once you've clicked to activate the dialog box, click its **Header/Footer** tab. You'll see the screen shown in Figure 10–45.

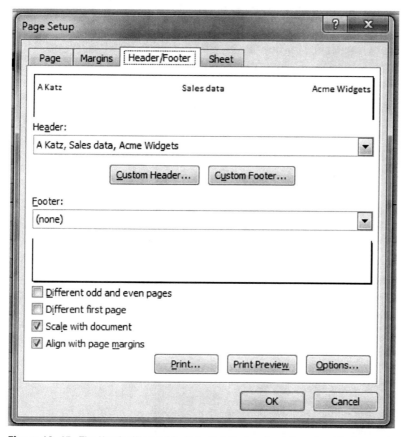

Figure 10–45. *The Header/Footer tab. Note that the header data entered in the previous exericise is visible.*

The header information entered previously is still visible, but if you click the arrow by the header field, you'll see some additional, built-in header options (see Figure 10–46).

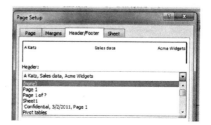

Figure 10–46. *Built-in header options. You'll see the same choices if you click the arrow in the Footer field.*

Among other things, these selections will record the page number in the header, or a Page 1 of *x* option, which notes the current page number relative to the total page printout count. For example, the header on page 1 of a three-page printout would read Page 1 of 3. Other built-in options provide the user's name and the date on which the print was executed in the header/footer.

Adding Custom Headers and Footers

You can access even more header/footer options by clicking the **Custom Header** and **Custom Footer** buttons (see Figure 10–47), though most of these really just offer equivalents to the options already discussed.

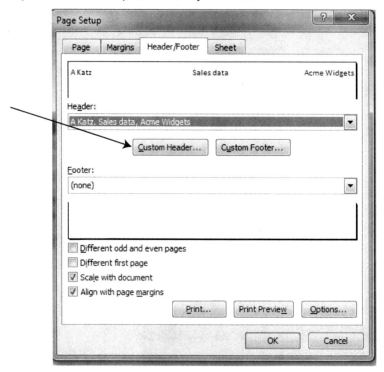

Figure 10–47. *Where you can access additional header and footer options*

Click **Custom Header** and you'll see the dialog shown in Figure 10–48.

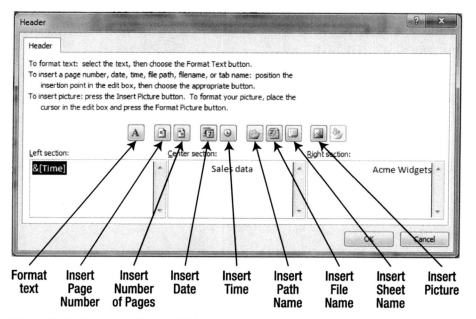

Format Insert Insert Insert Insert Insert Insert Insert Insert
text   Page   Number Date   Time   Path   File   Sheet   Picture
        Number of Pages   Name   Name   Name

Figure 10–48. *The Custom Header dialog box*

Here you can see three *edit boxes*, or sections, which correspond to the three header areas (that turn blue) in the Page Layout view. Note the existing header data lurking behind all those button descriptions, too. This text can be deleted in word-processing fashion: just select the relevant header and press the Delete key.

You can click in any one of the edit boxes and type any header data you wish, and you can click any of the buttons above the edit boxes to access additional options. The following list reviews what these buttons do (from left to right):

- **Format Text**: Clicking this button will call up Excel's standard **Font** dialog box, enabling you format header text.

- **Insert Page Number**: This button posts a page number on each printed page.

- **Insert Number of Pages**: This places the total number of pages in a printout in each page's header/footer. Thus, in a three-page printout, a 3 will be displayed on each page.

- **Insert Date**: This records the date on which the printout was executed. This means of course that the header/footer will change according to the date on which you print.

- **Insert Time**: This displays the time when the printout was issued.

  When you click one of these buttons in the desired section, a strange-looking code is installed in that area. For example, if you click the **Insert Date** button in the right edit box, you'll see what's shown in Figure 10–49.

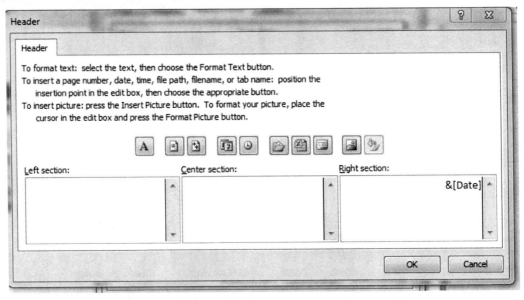

Figure 10–49. *Inserting today's date in the header, whatever today's date happens to be*

Click OK and you'll be returned to the **Header/Footer** tab, where you'll see the date previewed (see Figure 10–50).

Figure 10–50. *The date displayed on the Header/Footer tab*

Click **OK** again and the date header will be incorporated into the printout.

- **Insert File Path**: This lists both the workbook name and the folder(s) in which the workbook has been saved (e.g., C:\Users\Abbott\Documents\PivotTables). This option is widely used in the corporate world, because it informs viewers of the workbook where it is stored in a network.

- **Insert File Name**: This just prints the name of the workbook (e.g., PivotTables).

- **Insert Sheet Name**: This prints the name of the *worksheet* whose data is being printed (e.g., Sheet1, or any customized name).

- **Insert Picture**: A rather exotic option, this lets you position a photo or clip art in the header/footer, such as a company logo. The dimmed button to its right is **Format Picture**, which contains options enabling you to modify that picture.

Printing the Gridlines and Headings

Another pair of options you'll find in the print repertoire let you print both the gridlines that border every cell in the worksheet and the row and column headings themselves—the actual numbers and letters that identify cells by their addresses.

Both are easy to do, and the options are alongside one another in the **Sheet Options** button group on the **Page Layout** contextual tab (see Figure 10–51).

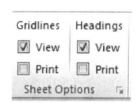

Figure 10–51. *The Print Gridlines and Headings options*

Checking the **Print** box of the **Gridlines** option will print the lines around every cell selected for printing. This option is *not* identical to drawing lines around cells with the Borders command in the **Font** button group. That latter option allows you to select exactly those cells around which you want to see borders. Print Gridlines, however, will automatically print gridlines around *all* the cells in your printout.

Thus, if you select the range to print shown in Figure 10–52 and click the **Print box of the Gridlines button**, the results will look like Figure 10–53.

| 1 |
| 2 |
| 3 |

Figure 10–52. *Six cells selected for printing*

Figure 10–53. *The gridlines around each cell will print. No borders have been drawn around the cells.*

If you click the **Print Headings** (that's *Headings*, not Headers) option, you'll see something like Figure 10–54, for example.

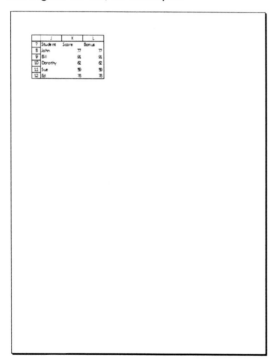

Figure 10–54. *Printing row and column headings*

You might want to print headings when you want viewers of the printout to see exactly which cells contain particular data.

Summary

As stated at the outset of the chapter, printing is generally a simple task: select the range you want to print and print exactly that selection, or set the print area and print. The embellishments—printing titles at the top of your pages or headers and/or footers— are simple too.

Now that you've learned how to convert your data to hard-copy form, we're going to return to Excel's native electronic environment and talk about macros, which provide a surprisingly easy way to automate tasks you'd just as soon have someone else do. And that someone else is Excel

Chapter 11

Automating Your Work with Macros

In the course of your work with Excel you may find yourself having to carry out the same data entry tasks repeatedly, such as entering your company's name and address at the top of many of your spreadsheets. Rather than having to perform that recurring (and irritating) chore over and over again, you can compose a *macro* instead to enter that information.

A macro is a little program saved to your spreadsheet, one that automatically executes a set of Excel commands at your instruction and thus spares *you* the need to execute them. At the click of a mouse or the tap of a keyboard shortcut, the commands play themselves out—and do so far more swiftly than you could type or click them.

For example, you may have put together a custom list (see Chapter 2) of your business clients, and if you're doing well, the list may be lengthy. A macro can copy that list into your workbook in a flash, without asking you to drag that fill handle down 50 rows worth of names. Or perhaps you want to be able to apply a set of formatting changes to a range. A macro can handle that assignment pronto, too.

The Two Kinds of Macros

A macro can be constructed in one of two ways. One is to put it together by deploying the Visual Basic for Applications (VBA) programming language built into Excel, a method that can let you build highly complex sequences of commands, including actions you can't execute through Excel's standard complement of buttons. But breathe easy— we're not going to turn you into a VBA honcho here (though you'll be happy to know that the Apress catalog lists several books on just this subject if you want to learn more about it).

The other approach—which is whole lot easier—is to activate the *macro-recording* process, and then simply execute the commands you want the macro to play back, just as you would under normal data entry conditions. Once you're done you can save the macro and play it back whenever you wish. Let's see how that works.

Composing a Macro

In order to see what macros have to offer, let's return to the example with which we introduced the chapter. Your company often identifies its workbooks by posting its name and address somewhere near the top of Sheet 1, something like what's shown in Figure 11–1.

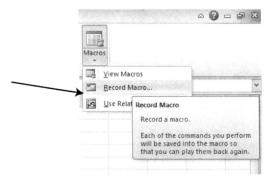

Figure 11–1. *It pays to advertise: Your company logo*

Again, this set of information appears at the top of many of your spreadsheets, and you're getting slightly fed up with having to type it all those times.

That's where the macro comes in, and here's how it works:

1. Click the **View** tab, choose **Macros**, and then click the **Macros** drop-down arrow, as in Figure 11–2.

Figure 11–2. *Click that arrow to reveal the Macros drop-down menu.*

2. Click **Record Macro...**, and you'll see the dialog shown in Figure 11–3.

Figure 11–3. *The Record Macro dialog*

3. Type a name for the macro in the **Macro name** field. A multiword name must be linked by an underscore (e.g., Company_Logo), but in the interests of simplicity, we'll call our macro Logo. We'll discuss the optional **Shortcut key** and **Store macro in** fields a bit later, but note here that you can enter a summary of what the macro does in the **Description** field (though this is optional).

4. Then click **OK**. Note the small blue rectangle that appears in the lower-left corner of the worksheet, an indicator that you've entered macro-recording mode; this is the button you'll click to *stop* recording. Hover your mouse over the button and you'll see the message shown in Figure 11–4.

Figure 11–4. *In the studio: The macro recording is in progress*

5. Then simply click in cell A1 (you should click your mouse in A1 even if you're in it already, for technical reasons) and type the logo in cells A1:A3, as you would normally. I've used Arial Black 14-point font here, but you can choose your own formatting. If you've mistyped a word, just correct it and keep going.

6. When you've completed typing the logo, click that blue macro button. That stops the recording and saves what you've done. The macro is now available to use.

7. Save the workbook under the name "Macro lesson." Here you need to save the workbook as an Excel Macro-Enabled Workbook, which I'll explain next.

About Saving a Workbook with a Macro

Normally, saving an Excel workbook is a pretty straightforward thing: you activate the Save command (typically by either clicking the **Save** button on the Quick Access toolbar or pressing Ctrl+S), call up the familiar **Save As** window, assign a name to the workbook, and decide where you want to save it (see Figure 11–5).

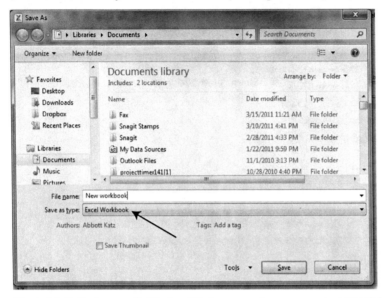

Figure 11–5. *You've seen it all before: What you see when you save a workbook for the first time. Note the default Excel Workbook selection by "Save as type."*

But when you begin to save a workbook containing a macro, something else happens.

1. Start the save process, and when you click **Save**, you'll see the message shown in Figure 11–6.

Figure 11–6. *You'll see this message when you try to save a workbook containing a macro.*

2. The reference to "VB project" points to the macro(s) in the workbooks, which are automatically written in VBA, as discussed. If you want to save the workbooks with any macros, click **No**. You'll be brought back to the **Save As** window.

3. When you get there, click the **Save As type** drop-down arrow and click **Excel Macro-Enabled Workbook**, as in Figure 11–7.

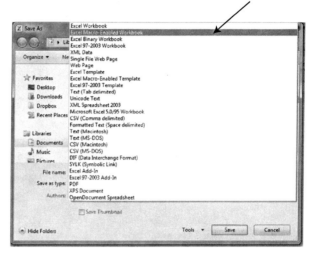

Figure 11–7. *Where to save a workbook in which a macro is stored*

4. Then click **Save**.

Playing Back the Macro

Now let's see how the macro works.

1. First, because our macro is going to enter the company logo in cells A1:A3, delete the logo we've just typed there.

2. Then click **View**, and click the **Macros** button (or click the down arrow and select **View Macros**, as shown in Figure 11–8, but that's a bit long-winded).

Figure 11–8. *The View Macros option*

3. You'll next see the **Macro** dialog. Click **Run**, as shown in Figure 11–9. The macro should execute immediately and very swiftly—a lot quicker than you could enter the logo manually, in fact.

Figure 11–9. *There's the logo macro.*

What We've Done

That's basically it. Let's quickly review the process:

1. Enter macro-recording mode.

2. Execute the commands on the worksheet you want the macro to capture.

3. Stop recording (you'll want to remember this step, because if you neglect to click the stop-recording button, all your subsequent spreadsheet actions will be recorded to the macro, too).

When you're ready to play the macro back, open the **Macro** dialog box shown previously in Figure 11–9, click the name of the macro you want to execute (because you can record multiple macros on the same worksheet), and click **Run**.

Relative References in a Macro

The macro we've just designed transports the cell pointer to A1, where it then begins the process of automatically entering the logo. And by default the macro will *always* travel to cell A1, and then start to do its thing.

Well, *of course* it will, you'll likely reply; isn't that exactly where we want the macro to start? Yes it is—and what that means in turn is that no matter where the cell pointer happens to be positioned *before* you trigger the macro, it will start back in cell A1 just the same. If you've landed the cell pointer in cell ZA458102—or any other cell in the worksheet for that matter—and you then run the macro, the logo will nevertheless return to cells A1:A3. And that's usually just what you want.

But sometimes you want a macro to start up in a cell that *depends* on where the cell pointer is *currently* situated. Consider this follow-up example: because your worksheets exhibit various layouts, there may be times when you want to place your logo in different areas on the worksheet—that is, different ranges. As a result, you'll want a macro that will let you click in the first cell in which you want the logo to appear and have it enter the logo starting right with that cell, rather than automatically making its way back to cell A1. If you click in cell G3, you'll want the macro to inscribe the logo in G3:G5. Zoom over to R13 instead, and the macro will deliver the logo to R13:R15—in other words, in whatever cell you've started the process.

In order to give your macro this sort of flexibility, you need to work with the Use Relative References feature (shown in Figure 11–10).

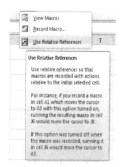

Figure 11–10. *Where to find the Use Relative References option*

Take a close look at the caption accompanying the **Use Relative References** selection. What it's telling you is that this macro option maneuvers the cell pointer (called the *cursor* in the caption) to cells *relative* to wherever you've started the macro. Thus, if you record a relative-reference macro in A1 and then click in A3, when you play it back the macro will always move two cells to the right of *whatever* cell you've started in.

Thus, in our case, where we want to be able to post our logo in whichever cell we've clicked, we need to use the **Use Relative References** option. Let's try it.

1. First, click in any cell on the worksheet—again, any cell, because the macro we're about to record will execute starting in any cell in which we click, because of relative referencing.

2. Then activate Use Relative References by clicking **View**, clicking the **Macros** drop-down arrow, and choosing **Use Relative References**.

3. Then enter macro-recording mode precisely as before, by clicking **View** ➤ **Macros** (drop-down arrow) ➤ **Record Macro**.

4. Name the macro (say, Logo2) in the resulting **Record Macro** dialog box, click **OK**, and type the logo information as per our first macro.

5. Click the stop-recording button, and you're done.

Playing back the macro is identical to our earlier macro example, with one difference: before running this macro, we need to click precisely in the cell in which we want the first line of the logo—Gidget's Widgets—to appear. That's because while our first macro was programmed to start its logo-writing activity in cell A1—no matter where the cell pointer happened to be at the macro's outset—here, the Use Relative References feature instructs the macro *not* to travel to a specific cell (A1), but rather to begin wherever the cell pointer happens to find itself.

Thus, if you're currently in cell L3 and click **View ➤ Macros ➤ View Macros**, click the macro name (Logo2), and click **Run**, the logo will appear in cells L3:L5. Click in a different cell (say, B12), run the macro again, and the Gidget's Widgets logo will install itself in B12:B14.

Saving a Macro to the Personal Macro Workbook

Whenever you record a macro, it automatically makes itself available to any other *open* workbooks, to be used there as well. Thus, if you're working with the "Macro lesson" workbook, and you open a second workbook and click **View ➤ Macros ➤ View Macros** there, you'll see the dialog shown in Figure 11–11.

Figure 11–11. *The macros from the open "Macro lesson" workbook are usable in any other open workbook.*

You can click **Run** and activate either of the macros shown in the figure, even as you're working in a different workbook.

But what if you want a macro to always be available to *every* workbook, without having to actually open any other workbook in particular? You can make that happen by recording macros and saving them to what's called the *Personal Macro Workbook*, a hidden workbook that opens whenever you access Excel. Any macro stored there can be called upon by any other workbook that's currently open. It works like this:

1. When you begin to record a macro, click the down arrow by **Store macro in**. You'll see the options shown in Figure 11-12.

Figure 11-12. *How to store a macro in the Personal Macro Workbook*

2. Click **Personal Macro Workbook** and **OK**, and then record the macro as usual.

You don't even have to save the actual workbook in which you've devised the macro, because the macro is being saved to the Personal Macro Workbook (but if you're prompted to save the Personal Macro Workbook itself, you should).

Now whenever you open any workbook and click **View ➤ Macros ➤ View Macros**, you'll immediately be presented with the macros saved to the Personal Macro Workbook (see Figure 11-13).

Figure 11-13. *All that's left to do is click Run.*

Deleting a Macro

If you want to delete a macro, just return to the **Macro** dialog box, click the macro you want to remove, and click **Delete** (see Figure 11–14).

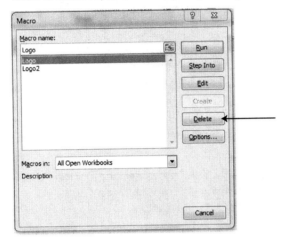

Figure 11–14. *Where to delete a macro*

Once you click **Delete**, a cautionary prompt appears (see Figure 11–15), something that often happens when you're about to delete an important Excel object. Click **Yes** if you're sure you want to delete the macro. But click **No** here, because we want do something else with the Logo macro—namely, edit it.

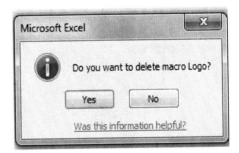

Figure 11–15. *The prompt for deleting a macro*

Editing a Macro by Tweaking It in VBA

What if your macro contains a mistake, or you just want to change it? What if, for example, you really wanted the Gidget's Widgets logo to exhibit 10-point text instead of its current 14-point size?

The simplest way to modify the macro would be record it over again and delete the original. That might work if your macros are likely to be brief, but that scenario is still a bit bothersome—and once a macro gets a bit lengthier, the prospect of a do-over is less appealing still, in part because in the process of rerecording the macro you might very well make another mistake.

Is there an alternative? Yes—you can edit the macro in VBA.

Now, as mentioned, I'm not going to teach you the VBA language here; rather, we're just going to take a look at it and explore some easy ways to tweak it in order to edit a macro.

VBA: Written Behind the Scenes

It's far from obvious, but whenever you record a macro of the sort demonstrated here, its commands are also transcribed simultaneously in the VBA language, on a separate worksheet that's usually hidden. But once you reveal that worksheet, you'll see the Logo and Logo2 macros as they appear in VBA translation, so to speak, giving you the chance to actually rewrite the script and affect the ways in which the macros play out.

Exposing the VBA Worksheet

Revealing that hidden VBA worksheet is easy. Just click **View** ➤ **Macros** (down arrow) ➤ **View Macros**, and in the **Macro** dialog click **Logo**, and then click **Edit** (see Figure 11–16).

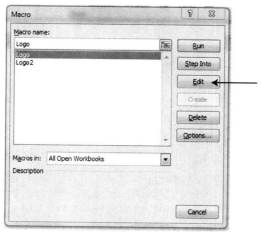

Figure 11–16. *Clicking Edit will take you to the worksheet's Visual Basic window.*

When you do, you'll see the macro as shown in Figure 11–17 (the window here has been maximized in the figure).

Figure 11–17. *The Logo macro in VBA*

Now that may look pretty scary at first glance, but take a closer look. Many of the VBA entries will start to make more sense when you study the terms they use. Note, for example, the reference to "Gidget's Widgets" (see the first arrow in the figure) beneath the line that reads Range ("A1").Select. That means that the macro selects cell A1 and proceeds to enter "Gidget's Widgets" there.

Now look at the line that reads as follows (see the bottom arrow in Figure 11–17):

.Size = 14

You'll probably, and correctly, interpret that bit of programming code as an instruction to change the font size of the logo to 14 points, as our macro specified. But what that *also* means is that you can simply click the number 14, delete it, and type, say, 10 instead. That editing change will downsize the logo text to 10 points the next time you run the macro. And if you delete Widgets and replace it with Gadgets, the next time you run the macro you'll see "Gidget's Gadgets" in cell A1. Try it.

> **NOTE:** Keep in mind that after you make such changes, you can close that VBA window; the rest of the workbook displaying your logo will nevertheless remain open, and you can try the macro again and continue to work on that worksheet.

Once you study how the VBA code operates, you'll be able to make small changes like these pretty easily. And it beats having to record the whole macro over again.

Activating a Macro with a Keyboard Shortcut

Until now we've been triggering our macros with a series of mouse clicks, an ever-so-slightly tedious routine that can be streamlined by designating a keyboard shortcut to do the job instead. You can assign a shortcut key to a macro either during the macro design process or retroactively. Let's look at these options.

First, recall that when you compose a macro, you're brought to the **Record Macro** dialog box, shown in Figure 11–18. Notice the **Shortcut key** option, which enables you to designate a key that teams with the Ctrl key. Pressing that combination will start the macro.

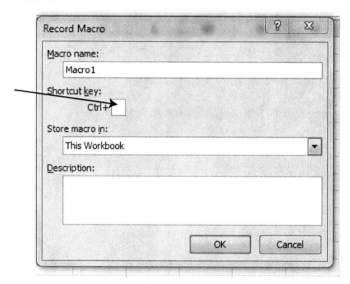

Figure 11–18. *The Shortcut key option: A speedy way to initiate a macro*

You can assign a shortcut key to a macro that you've already created as well. Here's how:

1. Click **View ➤ Macros** (you needn't click the arrow), and click the name of the macro to which you want to assign the shortcut key. You'll see the dialog shown in Figure 11–19.

Figure 11–19. *Click the name of the macro to which you want to assign the shortcut key.*

2. Click Options, and you'll be brought to the dialog shown in Figure 11–20.

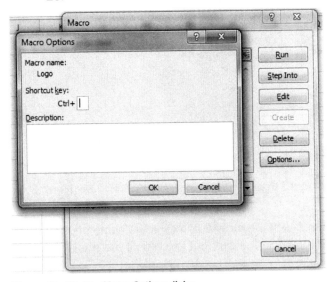

Figure 11–20. *The Macro Options dialog*

3. Just enter your key selection, and click OK.

4. You then have to click the close button on the remaining **Macro** dialog box (that X in the upper right-hand corner), because oddly enough, there's no **Close** or **OK** button available in it.

> **NOTE:** You can select any keyboard key as the shortcut key—even one that's already been assigned to an existing Excel action (e.g., C, which in combination with Ctrl serves as the standard Copy shortcut key). But don't worry—if you assign such a key to the macro, the macro will only play its shortcut role in that particular workbook. Ctrl+C will continue to work as Copy on other workbooks. Ctrl+E and Ctrl+J are unassigned, and thus available without having to "borrow" from an existing shortcut. You can also supplement a shortcut with the Shift key—for example, you can assign Ctrl+Shift+W to a macro.

A Note on Macro Security

You often hear about Internet viruses that infiltrate your computer from a variety of sources. Files containing macros are often prime suspects as virus bearers, so Excel allows you to decide what kind of defense you want mount against these potentially unwanted intruders.

Excel's anti-macro-virus defense system is headquartered in what's called the *Trust Center*, which you can visit by clicking **File ➤ Options ➤ Trust Center**. Once you get there, click the **Trust Center Settings…** button and then **Macro Settings**. You'll see the options shown in Figure 11–21.

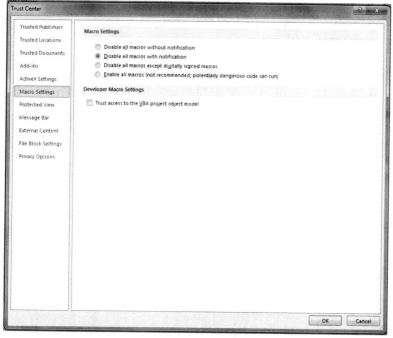

Figure 11–21. *Where to modify macro acceptance settings*

The figure shows Excel's default setting, which will open a downloaded workbook after disabling its macros. When this happens, you'll see the prompt shown in Figure 11-22.

Figure 11-22. *By default the macros are disabled.*

By clicking **Enable Content**, you'll be able to activate the macros, however. But if you select the **Disable all macros without notification** option in the Trust Center, no macros in downloaded workbooks can be turned on. Needless to say, if you're only working with your own macros, or with workbooks sent your way from the proverbial trusted sources, you'll probably want to opt for the disable-with-notification setting, or even enable all macros.

Summary

A macro is a great way to speed a routine Excel task. Just record and save it, and the commands you've executed will be played back at your request—and in *all* your workbooks, if you save the macro to the Personal Macro Workbook. Remember the role relative references play in the macro-recording process too, and your data entry activities will be simplified significantly.

Also, don't be too wary about the VBA editing option. Remember that your recorded macros are automatically rendered into VBA, and by perusing that code you'll begin to recognize the opportunities it affords to let you make small but important adjustments to the macros you've already recorded.

Index

G

CPSIA information can be obtained at www.ICGtesting.com
Printed in the USA
236276LV00009B/2/P